THE eCoaching CONTINUUM
FOR EDUCATORS

THE eCoaching CONTINUUM
FOR EDUCATORS

USING TECHNOLOGY TO ENRICH PROFESSIONAL DEVELOPMENT AND IMPROVE STUDENT OUTCOMES

Alexandria, Virginia USA

1703 N. Beauregard St. • Alexandria, VA 22311-1714 USA
Phone: 800-933-2723 or 703-578-9600 • Fax: 703-575-5400
Website: www.ascd.org • E-mail: member@ascd.org
Author guidelines: www.ascd.org/write

Ronn Nozoe, *Interim CEO and Executive Director;* Stefani Roth, *Publisher;* Genny Ostertag, *Director, Content Acquisitions;* Allison Scott, *Acquisitions Editor;* Julie Houtz, *Director, Book Editing & Production;* Joy Scott Ressler, *Editor;* Judi Connelly, *Senior Art Director;* Jose Coll, *Graphic Designer;* Circle Graphics, *Typesetter;* Kelly Marshall, *Interim Manager, Production Services;* Trinay Blake, *E-Publishing Specialist;* Tristan Coffelt, *Production Specialist.*

All web links in this book are correct as of the publication date below but may have become inactive or otherwise modified since that time. If you notice a deactivated or changed link, please e-mail books@ascd.org with the words "Link Update" in the subject line. In your message, please specify the web link, the book title, and the page number on which the link appears.

PAPERBACK ISBN: 978-1-4166-2788-3   ASCD product #117048   n9/19
PDF E-BOOK ISBN: 978-1-4166-2789-0

Quantity discounts are available: e-mail programteam@ascd.org or call 800-933-2723, ext. 5773, or 703-575-5773. For desk copies, go to www.ascd.org/deskcopy.

Library of Congress Cataloging-in-Publication Data

Names: Rock, Marcia L., author.
Title: The eCoaching continuum for educators: using technology to enrich professional development
   and improve student outcomes / Marcia L. Rock.
Description: Alexandria, VA: ACSD, [2019] | Includes bibliographical references and index.
Identifiers: LCCN 2019009799 (print) | LCCN 2019981473 (ebook) | ISBN 9781416627883 (paperback) |
   ISBN 9781416627890 (pdf)
Subjects: LCSH: Teachers—Training of. | Educational technology. | School improvement programs. |
   Special education teachers—Training of. | Motivation in education.
Classification: LCC LB1707.R64 2019 (print) | LCC LB1707 (ebook) | DDC 370.71/1—dc23
LC record available at https://lccn.loc.gov/2019009799
LC ebook record available at https://lccn.loc.gov/2019981473

27 26 25 24 23 22 21 20 19   1 2 3 4 5 6 7 8 9 10 11 12

THE eCoaching CONTINUUM FOR EDUCATORS

USING TECHNOLOGY TO ENRICH PROFESSIONAL DEVELOPMENT AND IMPROVE STUDENT OUTCOMES

MARCIA ROCK

Acknowledgments

Developing the blueprint for the eCoaching continuum has been a professional and a personal pursuit that spans the course of more than a decade. Long before Skype was a household name, my son and I spent many an evening hour trialing online video conferencing platforms and experimenting with codecs for online video capture—he from our home and me in my campus office. When my daughter, then a toddler, was ill, I would eCoach from home. At the time, which was also long before the current onslaught of cybersecurity issues, she thought I could see everyone and everything through the computer—prophetic in many ways! Needless to say, my family, including my husband, Chris, son, Mason, and daughter, Olivia, have contributed to this work in many unique and varied ways. Words fall short in expressing my gratitude to them and my love for them.

My special thanks also go to contributing authors Morgan V. Blanton, Aftynne E. Cheek, Paula Crawford, Kara B. Holden, Jennie Jones, and Melissa Sullivan-Walker—all of whom supported not only the development but also the implementation of the eCoaching continuum with preservice and inservice teachers.

My deep appreciation extends to the Alabama Angels, Dr. Donna Ploessl, Dr. Pam Howard, and Sharron Maughn, who contributed to the development and trialing of this work. They, along with Alabama native Beth Thead, are among the trailblazers of the eCoaching continuum and the technologies that support it. All were with me from the beginning.

Input and feedback from scholars, frontline practitioners, and K–12 students have also informed the content included in this book. Though for differing reasons, including protecting privacy and confidentiality, I will refrain from listing them individually, I wish to acknowledge all those who have contributed to and carried out the eCoaching continuum—across the United States and around the globe. They remain among the pioneers—those who also think there must be a better way to prepare, develop, and support 21st century teachers. To them and for them, I remain truly thankful.

I am also grateful to the consultants, regional coaches, and local school district personnel affiliated with the North Carolina Department of Public Instruction's

Exceptional Children Division's State Improvement Grant. All have joined in efforts to transform static, ineffective professional development into dynamic eCoaching on a continuum with positive impact. They, too, have advanced this work in a variety of important ways for those whom it matters the most—teachers and K–12 students.

Last, but certainly not least, I offer thanks to ASCD's Stefani Roth, Allison Scott, and Joy Scott Ressler, and to Amy Marks, for their expert guidance and editing acumen. And, I applaud ASCD's pioneering professional development authors—Bruce Joyce and Beverly Showers. I am also grateful to my academic mentors, Drs. Naomi Zigmond and Robert Gable, for their support, guidance, feedback, and encouragement over the years. All inspired and made this work, *The eCoaching Continuum for Educators*, possible. Thank you.

Introduction

Connected Coaching: Making Sense of Professional Development on a Continuum

At its best, the future of staff development will be one of integrity, equity, innovation, and interdependence. Otherwise, domination, dependency, and divisiveness are all that beckon. The choices are vital—and critical, committed, courageous staff developers must strive to make the right ones. —Andy Hargreaves (2007, p. 38)

How many times have you sat through a training or a workshop, rolled your eyes, folded your arms across your chest, heaved a heavy sigh, checked e-mail on your mobile phone, and muttered silently to yourself, "This is a complete waste of my time. There has to be a better way"? If so, this book is for you and your colleagues, many of whom have experienced and thought the same.

A Better Way: What We Know About Good Professional Development

Recognizing the need to reverse the time lost in ineffective professional development, in what follows I describe what's known about effective professional development and how to put it into practice in a way that maximizes teacher and student growth. In other words, not all is doom and gloom. There is good news about professional development that can help us make sense of how to go about it effectively and efficiently.

Evidence of Effectiveness

Although estimates vary regarding the amount of time needed for effective professional development, we can turn to the literature for some guidance. In 2007, Yoon and colleagues reported that when teachers participated in a minimum of 49 hours of high-quality professional development over the course of a year, their students evidenced achievement gains of up to 21 percentile points. By comparison, Guskey and Yoon (2009) concluded that positive effects were achieved through 30 or more contact hours of professional development.

When it comes to the features of effective professional development, there is also some variation. Joyce and Showers (2002) found that when professional development included support for implementation, 95 percent of new knowledge transferred to classroom practice. Generally, support for implementation consists of coaching and collaboration (Gulamhussein, 2013). More specifically, Fixsen, Naoom, Blasé, Friedman, and Wallace (2005) pointed out that the results of Joyce and Showers's meta-analysis confirmed that "effective training workshops consisted of presenting information (knowledge), providing demonstrations (live or taped) of the important aspects of the practice or program, and assuring opportunities to practice key skills in the training setting (behavioral rehearsal)" (p. 41). More recently, drawing on extant literature, Desimone (2009) identified five features of effective professional development, which included content focus (studying subject matter), active learning (observing, reviewing, discussing), coherence (demonstrating consistency with knowledge, beliefs, policies, and reforms), duration (engaging in 20 or more hours of contact time spread over a semester), and collective participation (interacting and conversing with colleagues).

Evidence of Benefit

Not surprisingly, more encouraging outcomes are achieved through professional development characterized by comprehensive, sustained, and intensive approaches, such as those described by Desimone (2009) and Joyce and Showers (2002). For example, researchers have found preliminary evidence suggesting effective professional development is a key factor in school improvement (Borko & Putnam, 1996; Darling-Hammond, 1993), effective policy and practice (Desimone, Smith, & Frisvold, 2007), and student achievement (Desimone, Smith, Hayes, & Frisvold, 2005; Yoon, Duncan, Lee, Scarloss, & Shapley, 2007).

Recognizing Persistent and Unresolved Challenges

The good news mentioned previously provides a common understanding of what good professional development looks like. Developing shared knowledge about effective professional development is, no doubt, the first step in creating a pathway for lasting change. Still, in clearing the path for others, we must also recognize the many pitfalls plaguing contemporary professional development. Doing so helps us resist the traps inherent in "sit and get" professional development, which, although ineffective and often unwelcome, has become the default, in part because it has been the way we have always done it.

Continuing education, more commonly referred to as staff development or professional development, plays a vital role in improving one's performance across the career span. Although definitions of professional development have varied over time, it is currently defined as "a comprehensive, sustained, and intensive approach to improving teachers' and principals' effectiveness in raising student achievement" (Educational Testing Service, 2011, p. 36). In today's schools, professional development occurs informally through hallway discussions between teachers, which are commonplace, often taking place on the fly, or formally via day or weeklong training sessions or workshops, which are also popular but are typically scheduled in advance (Desimone, 2009). Unfortunately, most present-day professional development approaches, whether formal or informal, fall short in reflecting the spirit and the letter of the definition. The stark reality is that contemporary approaches are, more often than not, characterized by stand and deliver, random acts that are costly, piecemeal, fragmented, and ineffective (Desimone, 2009; Gulamhussein, 2013; Hargreaves, 2007), often resulting in the brief scenario offered at the beginning of this Introduction. More than two decades ago, Sykes (1996) declared professional development "the most serious unsolved problem for policy and practice in American education today" (p. 465). Sadly, little has changed since then.

Evidence of Fragmentation

Despite the need for professional development that is "comprehensive, sustained, and intensive," the vast majority of teachers (i.e., 90 percent) take part in traditional, stand-alone workshops annually (Wei, Darling-Hammond, Andree, Richardson, & Orphanos, 2009). Birman, Desimone, Porter, and Garet (2000) also reported that only slightly over half of the teachers in their study participated in professional development activities that emphasized content. Even more concerning, however, was their finding that fewer than 20 percent of their teacher participants, and as few as 5 percent, were coached or observed.

Evidence of Ineffectiveness

Given the absence of comprehensive, sustained, and intensive approaches to contemporary professional development, there is reason to suspect that not much of the content transfers to classroom practice. In fact, Joyce and Showers (2002) confirmed that traditional approaches to professional development that did not include support for classroom application, such as coaching or observation, yielded less than 10 percent transfer of the newly learned knowledge and skill. More recently, Yoon and colleagues (2007) reported that when teachers participated in professional development programs lasting between 5 and 14 hours, there was no statistically significant effect on their students' achievement. And through extensive analysis of data secured through school administrative records in Florida, Harris and Sass (2011) concluded that professional development did not result in increased student achievement.

Evidence of Cost

And then there are cost considerations. Birman and colleagues (2000) estimated the cost of effective professional development at $512 per teacher— a figure that was twice what the typical district spent on it for each teacher in 2000. In a 2007 update, Birman and colleagues reported the federal government spent approximately $1.5 billion in professional development for teachers. Unfortunately, despite federal, state, and local investments in professional development, the return on investment has yielded little benefit, particularly in terms of lasting changes in teacher practice or improvements in student outcomes.

A Blueprint for Effective Professional Development: The Coaching Continuum

Drawing on Joyce and Showers's seminal article published in *Educational Leadership* in 1982, titled "The Coaching of Teaching," I offer a blueprint for professional development true to the definition. By that I mean professional development that reflects a "comprehensive, sustained, and intensive approach to improving teachers' and principals' effectiveness in raising student achievement," which I call the coaching continuum.

Why bother with a continuum? First and foremost, the coaching continuum reflects an authentic, job-embedded approach to professional development. Croft, Coggshall, Dolan, Powers, and Killion (2010) defined job-embedded professional development (JEPD) as "teacher learning that is grounded in day-to-day teaching practice and is designed to enhance teachers' content-specific instructional practices with the intent of improving student learning" (p. 2). As the name implies, the coaching continuum is *not* based on random acts or piecemeal approaches to professional development. Instead, the coaching continuum is formed by connecting and coordinating a series of components identified by Joyce and Showers (1982) more than 30 years ago—the study of theory and practice, the observation of theory and practice, one-on-one coaching, and group coaching—all of which are carried out within the context of everyday teaching and learning. The coaching continuum is illustrated in Figure I.1.

Study Theory and Practice

The first component in the coaching continuum involves the study of theory and practice. Education professionals study theory and practice intentionally and systematically to build their knowledge of specific content or particular pedagogy. In short, one cannot use what one does not know. Before engaging in the study of theory and practice, teachers and other school professionals should ask themselves the following guiding questions:

- What theory and practice should we study?
- How do we know we have identified the most important theory and practice for study?
- What do we need to know about the theory and practice before carrying it out in the classroom?
- How will we go about studying the theory and practice?
- How will we demonstrate understanding of our newly acquired knowledge about the theory and practice?

School professionals should base their responses to the first and second questions on data obtained, in part, through needs assessment at the district, building, grade, or teacher or classroom level. For example, after reviewing goals included in a school improvement plan, teachers and other school professionals might choose to study questioning as a means to enhance student engagement and to improve K–12 student learning.

When answering the third and fourth questions, teachers and other school professionals should consider principles of instructional design (Dick, Carey, & Carey, 2005) and adult learning theory (Knowles, 1984). Continuing with the questioning example, for instance, differing case-based examples should be included because they provide context, which is essential not only to building one's knowledge but also to fostering transfer (Bransford, Brown, & Cocking, 2000; Brown, Roediger, & McDaniel, 2014). How much time should teachers and other school professionals spend studying the theory and practice they wish to improve? Joyce and Showers (1982) recommended 20–30 hours and suggested adding more time when studying complex topics. With this rule of thumb in mind, teachers and other school professionals might schedule regular times for book study using ASCD's *Questioning for Classroom Discussion* (Walsh & Sattes, 2015).

FIGURE I.1   THE COACHING CONTINUUM

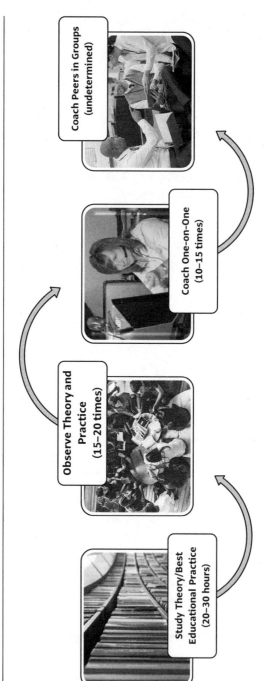

Coach Peers in Groups
(undetermined)

Coach One-on-One
(10–15 times)

Observe Theory and
Practice
(15–20 times)

Study Theory/Best
Educational Practice
(20–30 hours)

Adapted from Joyce and Showers, 1982.

Responding to the fifth question requires that teachers and other school professionals determine how they will assess their understanding of the newly learned content. For instance, they could opt for oral or written quizzes (Brown et al., 2014). Remember, at this point, the focus is on building one's new knowledge. Consequently, assessment of understanding should align with knowledge rather than performance. Concerned about authenticity with this kind of assessment? No worries. Performance-based assessments of competence are included in the one-on-one and peer coaching components of the continuum.

Observe Theory and Practice

The second component of the coaching continuum centers on observation. Observation aids the transfer of new knowledge to classroom practice. Consider the questioning example. In conjunction with a study of *Questioning for Classroom Discussion* (Walsh & Sattes, 2015), observation of a variety of professionals using questioning effectively in different classrooms strengthens teachers' newly formed knowledge of effective questioning and improves the likelihood they will use it. How often does observation need to take place? Joyce and Showers (1982) recommended 15–20 times, which does not necessarily equate to 15–20 hours. Observations can be carried out effectively and efficiently using small increments of time (e.g., 10–15 minutes). Although it is natural to skip this component in the coaching continuum because of time constraints, overcoming this temptation is vital. Without models of effective classroom practice, teachers and other school professionals are unlikely to succeed in applying what they have learned through the study of theory and practice.

Coach One-on-One

The third component in the coaching continuum is one-on-one coaching. The goal in this component is to aid in the transfer of newly learned knowledge by providing teachers and other school professionals with opportunities to deliberately practice its use with feedback. Returning to the questioning example, teachers would receive coaching on their use of questioning during classroom instruction. Joyce and Showers's (2002) seminal research on coaching confirms its value in the continuum. They found that traditional techniques, such as demonstration and practice, had an effect size of 0.0 on transfer of new knowledge. However, when coaching was added, the effect size increased to 1.42. More recently, Knight (2007) reported that teachers who received coaching were four times more likely to carry out newly learned skills than those who did not. Joyce and Showers estimated that 10–15 one-on-one coaching sessions are needed. As is the case with observations, coaching sessions can be carried out using small increments of time effectively. For instance, a 20- to 30-minute coaching session can be at least as effective as a 60- to 90-minute session.

Coach in Groups

The fourth component in the coaching continuum is group coaching. The purpose of group coaching is to create infrastructure and build capacity that promotes accountability and fosters sustainability. In this way, group coaching brings educators together to identify problems of professional practice and to solve them collaboratively (https://www.ccl.org/leadership-solutions/coaching-services/). Two common approaches to group coaching are critical friends groups (CFGs; Bambino, 2002) and grand rounds (City, 2011), also referred to as instructional rounds. Both use established protocols that require some training prior to implementation. In terms of the questioning example, teachers would observe and coach one another on problems of practice specific to questioning, using CFGs or instructional rounds protocols. Although Joyce and Showers (1982) did not specify how much time is needed for group coaching, CFGs and instructional rounds are most effective when scheduled regularly and carried out consistently (e.g., weekly, biweekly, monthly).

Figure I.2 presents an example of how teachers and other school professionals would use the coaching continuum not only to improve teachers' questioning tactics in the classroom but also to enhance their students' engagement and learning.

The four components of the coaching continuum mentioned also reflect the five features of effective professional development described by Desimone

Figure I.2

The Coaching Continuum–Questioning Example

Coaching Continuum			
Study Theory and Practice (20–30 hours)	Observe Theory and Practice (15–20 times)	Coach One-on-One (10–15 times)	Coach Peers in Groups (undetermined)
Engage in book study of effective questioning tactics, using ASCD's *Questioning for Classroom Discussion* (Walsh & Sattes, 2015).	Take turns demonstrating and observing effective questioning for classroom discussion.	External Coaching: Provide one-on-one coaching in the classroom, during instruction, to foster a teacher's use of effective questioning. Self-Coaching: Record teacher questioning while teaching using tally marks or audio/video recording.	Use traditional face-to-face protocols to conduct critical friends groups or instructional grand rounds with peers to investigate problems of practice specific to questioning for classroom discussion.

(2009)—content focus, active learning, coherence, duration, and collective participation. A focus on content is found in the study of theory and practice, while active learning is embedded in all four components. Coherence and duration are reflected across the continuum, especially when connections between the components are structured intentionally and carried out over time. Collective participation, by contrast, is typically considered a hallmark of group coaching.

Support for Professional Development as a Continuum

If we are to engage in professional development that is economical, connected, and effective, then we must begin to think differently about it. Instead of viewing professional development as stand-alone random acts, it must be viewed as a series of connected, coordinated components on a continuum. Although numerous books are available on the topic of professional development, the content included generally reflects the former, not the latter. That is, the content is often dedicated to piecemeal tactics, such as coaching, professional learning communities (PLCs), or personalized learning networks (PLNs), which is, without question, well intended. Unfortunately, these approaches only add fuel to the proverbial fire in professional development. For example, coaching without in-depth study of theory and practice inadvertently promotes teacher dependence on the coach. Similarly, the absence of group or peer coaching paves the way for changes in practice that are not sustainable over time. And when teachers focus exclusively on the study of theory and practice, through book study, for instance, the outcome yields insufficient transfer to classroom practice.

Recognizing that some readers will be critical of and skeptical about the amount of time needed for the coaching continuum, I offer the following considerations. First, the continuum should be carried out, to the greatest extent possible, as an "add-in" approach, not an "add-on" appendage. By that I mean the four components should be embedded in the day-to-day work of teaching and learning through regularly scheduled opportunities for studying, observing, and coaching that are built into the instructional day, not added on at the end. Stay tuned for more about how to do this in the chapters that follow. Second, the amount of time recommended for each component of the continuum is based on estimates, rather than hard science, and should be monitored and adjusted according to the results. Third, differentiation is also possible, which can save time. For example, a pre-test could be made available prior to the study of theory and practice. If a teacher passes the pre-test, then she has demonstrated requisite knowledge and can spend her time more effectively and efficiently participating in the transfer components of the continuum (e.g., one-on-one coaching, group coaching). Taken together, these considerations should ease most feasibility concerns.

Support for a Technology-Enabled Professional Development Continuum

No doubt, technology can be a blessing or a curse. This truism applies to every facet of our 21st century lives; professional development is no exception. Choosing to focus on the former, while giving a realistic nod to the latter, I offer six compelling reasons why technology should serve as the foundation for the coaching continuum.

First, we live and work in the digital age, wherein technology use is aimed at increasing human efficiency and effectiveness. Our approaches to professional development should reflect that. Moreover, there is emerging evidence that we may be able to leverage technology-enabled professional development to work smarter and better. For instance, Allen, Pianta, Gregory, Mikami, and Lun (2011) conducted a randomized control trial of web-based coaching (i.e., My Teaching Partner–Secondary) aimed at improving teacher-student interactions in the classroom with 78 secondary school teachers and 2,237 students. They reported achievement test score gains equivalent to the 50th–59th percentile. Also, they found the improvements appeared to be mediated by changes in teacher-student interaction, which were targeted through the web-based professional development. Moreover, based on the results of a recent literature review, Blitz (2013) reported that teachers who participated in online PLCs outperformed those who participated in face-to-face PLCs in self-reflection and use of effective instruction. Why teachers engaged in online PLCs outperformed those who participated in face-to-face delivery seems to be attributed, in part, to the flexibility afforded by online learning. For instance, based on facilitator interview data, Harlen and Doubler (2004) concluded that "real-time boundaries" did not exist in the online PLC environment (p. 1263). As such, there was more time and space for mediated learning. In their words, "Before responding, the facilitator had time to assess the learning, consider, and plan carefully the best way to further the learning" (p. 1263).

Second, each professional development component included in the continuum can be technology enabled in many varied and unique ways. The options range from low to high tech, while the costs reflect various price points. For example, when studying theory and practice, teachers and school professionals can use Twitter chats, free of charge, to engage in professional dialogue with others from around the globe, regarding the specific topic at hand (e.g., #questioningfor classroomdiscussion). Observing one another using questioning tactics during classroom discussion may be achieved using FaceTime through iPads or Skype via a desktop computer, both of which can be downloaded at no cost. Bluetooth earpieces for discreet, live, one-on-one, in-ear coaching (also referred to as bug-in-ear [BIE] coaching) of questioning during classroom discussion may be purchased for under $100, and online videoconferencing for group coaching of the same with peers may also be carried out at no expense using Google Hangouts or ooVoo. These are only a few examples. Information included in the chapters that follow, as well as in the Appendix, offers more detailed discussion of technology options.

Third, many school districts in the United States face unprecedented fiscal constraints. Using technology to support the coaching continuum only makes sense, especially when it comes to saving time and money. For example, e-books for studying theory and practice can be downloaded immediately for less money. Also, teachers and other school professionals can observe the study of theory and practice by viewing video clips for free online via the Teaching Channel without leaving their classrooms. In terms of one-on-one coaching, the time and money a coach spends traveling from one school to another may be reduced considerably through online visits. Finally, group coaching with peers to explore problems of practice may be carried out using webcams and Google Hangouts, which also eliminates coverage and release-time costs.

Fourth, several of the low- and high-tech options used to support the coaching continuum offer teachers and other school professionals access to "just-in-time support." In other words, teachers and other school professionals can use the technology to access on-demand professional development that supports and connects the components. For instance, a teacher might choose to Skype his coach during a particularly problematic lesson wherein questioning during classroom instruction is not going as planned. This authentic, real-time coaching through a hot spot may prove invaluable in overcoming thorny transfer problems that often erupt unexpectedly, but rarely, during scheduled coaching sessions.

Fifth, technology allows each component in the continuum to be personalized and customized to meet the needs of teachers, administrators, and other professional development team members. Today's frontline education professionals harbor a wide array of technology know-how and skill. Some are Luddites; others are digital natives. The remainder are somewhere in between. The technology that teachers and other school professionals choose to support and connect the continuum components can be geared to their comfort level. For instance, during one-on-one coaching, more tech-savvy teachers may opt for live, in-ear coaching using Bluetooth and online videoconferencing. Others with less technology know-how may decide to begin by using an iPad or a webcam to capture a lesson electronically and then debrief on it later with their coach.

Sixth, technology-enabled coaching on a continuum promotes self-coaching. As mentioned previously, even when traditional professional development includes coaching, it is typically time, labor, and cost prohibitive—often exceeding the resources and capabilities of many school districts. Harnessing the power of technology overcomes these obstacles, strategically and systematically, by transferring teachers' and other school professionals' reliance on external coaching to self-coaching, which is the goal of professional development. For example, applications (i.e., apps) for mobile devices, such as TeachFX (https://teachfx.com), allow teachers and other school professionals to collect data and receive automated feedback on selected teaching and learning goals. Consider, again, questioning. Rather than relying continuously on an external coach, by downloading and using the TeachFX app, teachers and other school professionals can capture real-time classroom data on teacher questioning and student response *and* receive immediate feedback on both through automated visualizations (i.e., charts, graphs, percentages). They can then use these data, in part, to determine what further study is needed, when additional observations are in order, why additional one-on-one, real-time coaching is requested, and how group coaching can further build individual and collective capacity—all of which are centered on questioning and student engagement.

The eCoaching Continuum

Based on the same four components described previously in the coaching continuum section, I refer to the technology-enabled variation as the eCoaching continuum. The difference is that in the eCoaching continuum, the design and delivery of each component is enhanced through technology. That said, the eCoaching continuum is flexible and can also be designed and carried out using a hybrid approach. Examples of these two options, based again on questioning, are presented in Figures I.3 and I.4.

Distinguishing Features of the eCoaching Continuum

Although the eCoaching continuum is based on components described more than three decades ago by Joyce and Showers (1982), there are important features that distinguish the 21st century variation from its predecessor.

Teaching and learning focused. I expand the focus of coaching to encompass teaching *and* learning. This means that when professional development is approached through the eCoaching continuum, the aim is not only to support the ongoing development of teachers' classroom practices but also to enhance the educational outcomes achieved by their K–12 students. By contrast, Joyce and

Figure I.3

The eCoaching Continuum–Questioning Example (Fully Technology Enabled)

eCoaching Continuum			
Study Theory and Practice (20–30 hours)	Observe Theory and Practice (15–20 times)	Coach One-on-One (10–15 times)	Coach Peers in Groups (undetermined)
Engage in e-book study of effective questioning tactics, using ASCD's electronic version of *Questioning for Classroom Discussion* (Walsh & Sattes, 2015) and Download study guide for *Questioning for Classroom Discussion* from the ASCD website (http://www.ascd.org/publications/books/115012/chapters/An-ASCD-Study-Guide-for-Questioning-for-Classroom-Discussion@-Purposeful-Speaking,-Engaged-Listening,-Deep-Thinking.aspx).	Use Teaching Channel QR codes provided in Walsh and Sattes (2015) to view videos illustrating effective questioning and classroom discussion.	External Coach: Use online videoconferencing to conduct critical friends groups or instructional grand rounds with colleagues to investigate problems of practice specific to questioning for classroom discussion. Self-Coach: Use mobile apps, such as TeachFX, to capture and display automated feedback on teacher questioning and student responding.	Use online videoconferencing and Bluetooth technologies to provide discreet, one-on-one coaching during classroom instruction to foster a teacher's use of questioning for classroom instruction.

Showers (1982) focused primarily on the former. Broadening the focus to include student learning supports ongoing emphasis on continuous educational improvement and accountability.

Technology enabled. I enhance the power and the connectedness of the original four components through technology. Recent advances and innovations in desktop and mobile technologies provide opportunities for designing and delivering deeper professional development with more teachers. We are now able to remotely study theory and practice, observe theory and practice, engage in one-on-one coaching, and participate in group coaching with peers in ways that were not possible previously. Leveraging 21st century technologies enables frontline practitioners to carry out and to connect the components of the continuum with greater flexibility, effectiveness, and efficiency.

Data informed. In shifting the focus of the continuum from teaching to teaching and learning, I bring teacher and student data, assessment, and evaluation to the forefront. Historically, teacher assessment and evaluation have been conducted separately from professional development. Because of an increased emphasis on

Figure I.4

The eCoaching Continuum–Questioning Example (Hybrid Variation)

eCoaching Continuum with Some Technology-Enabled Features			
Study Theory and Practice (20–30 hours)	Observe Theory and Practice (15–20 times)	Coach One-on-One (10–15 times)	Coach Peers in Groups (undetermined)
Engage in book study of effective questioning tactics, using ASCD's *Questioning for Classroom Discussion* (Walsh & Sattes, 2015) and Download study guide for *Questioning for Classroom Discussion* from the ASCD website (http://www.ascd.org/publications/books/115012/chapters/An-ASCD-Study-Guide-for-Questioning-for-Classroom-Discussion@-Purposeful-Speaking,-Engaged-Listening,-Deep-Thinking.aspx).	Electronically capture, upload, and share video files demonstrating effective questioning during classroom discussion or Take turns demonstrating and observing effective questioning for classroom discussion.	*External Coach:* Electronically capture and upload video files illustrating the use of a teacher's questioning tactics during classroom discussion, then debrief face-to-face with a coach at a later date. *Self-Coach:* Use mobile apps, such as Teach*FX*, to capture and display automated feedback on teacher questioning and student response and either share with the external coach during a traditional face-to-face coaching session or share with peers during group coaching to update professional development goals related to teacher questioning.	Electronically capture and upload videos illustrating problems of practice to a secure cloud-based storage platform, then debrief face-to-face with colleagues using critical friends groups or instructional grand rounds protocols to solve issues related to questioning for classroom discussion.

continuous educational improvement and accountability, the role of teacher assessment and evaluation in professional development must be reconsidered. Using the eCoaching continuum, we can craft and carry out formative and summative assessments, based not only on knowledge but also on performance, that can be used to inform teacher assessment and evaluation of impact in authentic and meaningful ways.

Research based. I base the blueprint for the eCoaching continuum on the science of learning and professional development. Joyce and Showers proposed the four components of professional development in 1982. Since then, we have learned a great deal. The eCoaching continuum reflects that. For example, taken together and viewed interdependently, the time teachers and other school professionals spend immersed in the four components of the eCoaching continuum constitute the recommended 30–49 hours noted previously.

Theoretically grounded. I establish the theoretical foundation for the eCoaching continuum on connectivism, a relatively recent epistemological and ontological perspective on teaching and learning. Connectivism is one of the most widely accepted learning theories for the digital age (Siemens, 2004). In many ways, connectivism is the integration of behaviorism, cognitivism, and constructivism. This too is reflected in the eCoaching continuum, with cognitivism undergirding the study and observation components, behaviorism supporting the one-on-one coaching component, and constructivism guiding the group coaching component. Thus, connectivism supports teaching (knowledge, modeling, and demonstration) and learning (deliberate practice, feedback, dialogue, and reflection) within and across each component of the eCoaching continuum.

Cultivating a Culture Where eCoaching on a Continuum Can Take Root

"Culture eats strategy for breakfast." This quotation is most often credited to leadership guru Peter Drucker. No doubt, successfully shifting professional development from piecemeal, random acts to a seamless, technology-enabled continuum requires mention of instructional culture. Cultivating an instructional climate in which the eCoaching continuum can take root requires leadership, and it requires that teachers and other school professionals take part in establishing a strong, supportive culture comprising equal parts growth mindset (Dweck, 2007) and grit (Duckworth, 2016). To do just that, teachers and other school professionals must share a common vision of instructional excellence, embrace high expectations for teaching and learning, and commit to ongoing instructional improvement. Some evidence confirms that cultivating a strong instructional culture pays off not only in retaining teachers but also in improving student performance. Consider, for instance, Greenhouse Schools, which across the United States emphasize a strong instructional culture and share five characteristics: a high hiring bar, a focus on student learning, authentic instructional leadership, effective professional development, and support for teacher performance. "Compared to schools with weak instructional cultures, the average student proficiency rates at Greenhouse Schools were 21 percentage points higher in math and 14 percentage points higher in reading" (The New Teacher Project's Greenhouse Report, 2012, p. 1).

Adopting eCoaching on a Continuum Through Flexible Use

The eCoaching continuum can be used effectively for professional development by teams or by individuals. For example, members of a PLC may decide that adopting the eCoaching continuum would strengthen their approach to professional development. Similarly, members of grade-level or content-area teams may decide the same. Individual teachers may also use the eCoaching continuum when crafting their professional development plan for the school year.

Regardless of whether teams or individuals adopt the continuum, one approach to carrying it out is for the district, building, or grade-level coach to facilitate and coordinate each component. In this way, the coach serves as the glue that adheres the four components together, which, in turn, form the continuum. The coach works with the team or individual teachers, ensuring the four components included in the continuum are provided and connected. Doing so ensures the professional development reflects the comprehensive, intensive alternative that is needed and prevents the fragmented, piecemeal tactics of the past from taking root. The most effective way to support coaches, teams, and individuals in carrying out the eCoaching continuum, however, is through district-level support and adoption.

Using This Book Effectively

In this book, I, along with contributors, describe how to engage in professional development based on a series of four connected technology-enabled components that form the eCoaching continuum. The aims are twofold: to bring professional development out of the industrial age and into the digital age, while also improving the effectiveness of professional development by using a continuum, rather than a piecemeal approach. That said, this is not just another "how to" book. The content, while clearly practical, is also intended to inspire and empower education professionals. In short, in writing this book, we kept in mind teams and individuals who are interested in taking on and participating in more worthwhile, substantive, and effective professional development pursuits.

This book is organized into six chapters. Chapters 1 through 4 describe each component of the eCoaching continuum in detail. We offer the reader practical explanations and examples for developing each technology-enabled component, including the study of theory and practice, the observation of theory and practice, one-on-one coaching, and group coaching. Chapters 5 and 6 detail not only how to carry out the eCoaching continuum approach within a team context, but also how to capture the impact on schools, teachers, and students. As the framework requires a shift from current piecemeal practices, Chapter 5 describes team composition and member responsibilities. Chapter 6 explains how to collect, use, and interpret formative and summative teacher and K–12 student data as an inquiry-based approach for making informed decisions about teaching *and* learning. We provide illustrations throughout to strengthen understanding and enhance application.

Readers might be surprised by their familiarity with components included in the eCoaching continuum, such as group coaching (critical friends groups or grand rounds). This is actually desirable, because the content builds on prior knowledge and extends past experiences, positioning readers to carry out the content effectively and efficiently. Readers will likely find the contribution this book makes is in describing how the four components are put together and carried out through a variety of low- and high-tech options at differing price points. Readers, too, may find the flexibility of the model appealing and somewhat surprising. The eCoaching continuum is not a rigid, prescriptive approach. Instead, it is designed like a blueprint that can be customized to meet individual teacher or team needs. As long as the four components of the continuum remain intact, the content can be crafted within and across it to meet professional development needs at the classroom (as teacher self-directed professional development), grade, building, or district level. Readers should find case examples especially useful in aiding transfer. And readers can extend the eCoaching continuum to support ongoing development of coaches. To do so, coaches would use the four components to study coaching and the eCoaching continuum, observe one another while engaged in the practice of it, receive one-on-one coaching while coaching, and participate in group coaching with peers (i.e., other coaches) to dialogue and solve problems of practice specific to carrying out the eCoaching continuum.

What Adopting the eCoaching Continuum Will Accomplish

I began this Introduction with a quote by Andy Hargreaves. We seem to be at a crossroads in professional development. The choice is clear. Continue with antiquated, ineffective approaches or embrace promising alternatives. If we are to achieve the improvements in teaching and learning that can be realized through effective professional development alternatives, such as the eCoaching continuum, then we must challenge and support one another in taking on their use. In short, adopting the eCoaching continuum enables teachers, principals, and other school professionals to engage in deeper, more meaningful, connected professional development that transfers to classroom practice, sticks over time, and improves outcomes for K–12 students. Yet, because shifts in professional practice, no matter how welcome or needed, are shorter lived than not, there is more to consider.

In a 2011 *New Yorker* article entitled "Cowboys and Pit Crews," widely acclaimed and well-respected Harvard surgeon and scholar Atul Gawande grappled with this very issue—albeit in medicine rather than education. Clearly, medicine and education are different and unique disciplines. Still, many parallels warrant consideration: increasing professional engagement, improving working conditions, and alleviating personnel shortages, to name a few.

Essentially, Gawande (2011) asserted "the reality is that medicine's complexity has exceeded our individual capabilities as doctors." Given that we work and live in the digital age, coupled with the rapid advancements that have also occurred in education and related fields, his insight regarding complexities exceeding individual capabilities warrants consideration. Like medical doctors, professional development providers are often hired as cowboys or cowgirls—riding in to save the district and to arm frontline practitioners with new knowledge. But, as Gawande put it, "that's not what we need." Instead, we need pit crews—teams comprising dedicated, trained professionals who share a common goal—improving teaching and learning for all. The eCoaching continuum does just that.

Because I have pioneered the development of this work, personally conducting more than 800 one-on-one, real-time, in-ear coaching sessions, I am often asked what has been the most surprising or rewarding aspect of it. Over the years, one response consistently comes to mind—it was an unanticipated outcome. Using online, in-ear technology during classroom instruction, I was eCoaching an in-service teacher who taught secondary students with emotional and behavioral disorders at an alternative school. At the beginning of the lesson, she explained to the students why she was wearing the Bluetooth earpiece. One of the students, an African American male who was academically disengaged and on the verge of dropping out due to a history of chronic school failure, sat up, leaned forward, and began asking the teacher a series of questions. He was intrigued by the notion that I was supporting and eCoaching his teacher from afar, so much so that for the first time in a very long time, he was able to see the value of education—proclaiming aloud for all to hear that he just might stay in high school and go on to college. That, to me, is perhaps the most poignant illustration of the power of eCoaching and among the most compelling reasons for adopting the continuum; I hope that you agree.

1

Technology-Enabled Study
Laying the Foundation for Practical, Powerful, and Impactful Professional Development

Marcia Rock and Melissa Sullivan-Walker

Too many professional development initiatives are done to teachers—not for or with them. —Andy Hargreaves (n.d.)

How can teachers and other school professionals use technology effectively and efficiently to develop and refine content knowledge and pedagogical know-how?

Understanding the Purpose of Using Technology to Build Content Knowledge and Pedagogical Know-How

Dedicated to lifelong learning throughout their early, middle, and late careers, effective teachers and school professionals value the role professional development plays in deepening and expanding their content knowledge and pedagogical know-how. Also, they understand that meaningful professional development requires ongoing in-depth study of specific content (what to teach) or pedagogy (how to teach). As noted in the Introduction, Joyce and Showers (1982) referred to this aspect of professional development as the study of theory and best practice and recommended that teachers and other school professionals dedicate 20–30 hours to it. More recently, as also described in the Introduction, Desimone (2009) identified content focus (studying subject matter) as one of the five features of effective professional development, recommending that teachers and other school professionals engage in 20 or more hours of contact time. We consider the study of theory and practice as foundational and as the first of four components in the coaching continuum.

Traditionally, teachers and administrators have studied theory and practice through passive professional learning activities, such as workshops and conference presentations. In recent years, however, more interactive approaches to study, such as book studies and professional learning communities, have increased in popularity. Many of these approaches to study, whether passive or interactive, are costly, inconvenient, and inefficient. By contrast, in the digital age, teachers and other school professionals have many varied and unique technology options at their fingertips that can be leveraged to study specific content or a pedagogical practice in ways that maximize interaction, effectiveness, and efficiency. Accordingly, the primary purpose of using technology to study a theory or practice of interest is to build teachers' and other school professionals' specific content knowledge or particular pedagogical skill more effectively at a lower cost with greater convenience. When considering technology options and materials to support the study of specific content or a pedagogical practice, teachers and other school professionals should seek technologies that decrease time constraints and alleviate stressors rather than those that compound them.

As is the case when teachers and administrators study theory and best practice (Joyce & Showers, 1982) without technology, the technology-enabled variation provides opportunities for them to become immersed in critical study and intentional dialogue—both of which are essential to knowledge building. Simply put, the goal remains the same—to bolster professional learning. Yet, because teachers and other school professionals possess differing knowledge and skills, they will likely require differentiated study. Technology-enabled study is especially well suited to differentiation, because teachers and other school professionals can customize the content or pedagogy to meet their unique learning needs. For instance, the purposes for in-depth study include reviewing previously learned content or pedagogy, updating current knowledge or pedagogy, learning new content or pedagogy, clarifying knowledge or pedagogy to correct inaccuracies or misconceptions, improving fidelity to a particular pedagogical practice, reducing discomfort with specific content or pedagogy, or enhancing specific content knowledge or pedagogy. Figure 1.1 provides examples of traditional and technology-enabled study as well as the purposes they share.

One primary distinction that occurs when teachers and other school professionals use technology to study theory and best practice is that the constraints of traditional face-to-face or brick-and-mortar approaches no longer limit them. Opting for technology-enabled study offers teachers and other school professionals a number of advantages. For example, study through online modules or massive

Figure 1.1

Examples of Traditional Study Versus Technology-Enabled Study and the Shared Purposes of Both

Traditional Study	Shared Purposes	Technology–Enabled Study
• Workshops • Conference presentations • Book study • Face-to-face PLCs or PLNs • Face-to-face peer presentations • Face-to-face courses	• Review previously learned content or pedagogy • Update current content knowledge or pedagogy • Learn new content or pedagogy • Clarify knowledge or pedagogy to correct inaccuracies or misconceptions • Improve fidelity of a particular pedagogy • Enhance specific content knowledge or pedagogy	• Questioning the author or expert via online videoconferencing technology • Virtual conferences or webinars • E-books • Online or blended PLCs or PLNs • Interactive digital presentations by peers • Online or blended courses and modules, including MOOCs

open online courses (MOOCs) typically offers more flexibility and convenience than do face-to-face workshops, professional conferences, or courses. Technology-enabled study, via e-books, Twitter chats, private or public Facebook pages, and interactive online videoconferencing, also offers teachers and other school professionals greater access to a broader array of experts, frontline practitioners, and resources that can all be tailored to meet team members' or individuals' unique professional development needs. For example, a teacher who possesses in-depth content knowledge and pedagogical know-how could facilitate a Twitter chat on a specific topic of study, providing examples of effective classroom application, highlighting important ideas, or answering questions. One who does not have this knowledge and know-how could participate in the chat by posing questions, requesting clarification, or asking for illustrations of classroom application.

When teachers and other school professionals leverage technology to support the study of theory and best practice, they need to use it to acquire and extend content knowledge and pedagogical practice, and they also need to consider how doing so increases opportunities for making sense of the topic at hand (e.g., content they are reading in an e-book or learning through an online course). Taking time to consider how technology could be used to support communication and interaction with one another as they are studying specific content or a pedagogical practice is time well spent. For example, teachers and other school professionals could consider gathering synchronously and regularly for purposeful discussion regarding the topic of study via online videoconferencing. Why is doing so important? Increased opportunities to dialogue and interact with colleagues about the topic of study (i.e., theory or best practice) may improve teachers' learning, which can be facilitated through discussion with peers (Bandura, 1977; Vygotsky 1962, 1978).

Determining the Focus of Technology-Enabled Study of Theory and Practice

As is the case when determining the focus or topic for the study of theory and practice without technology, when deciding on the topic for the technology-enabled variation, teachers and school professionals should consider several key factors to ensure that the content reflects their professional development needs and their K–12 students' learning and behavioral needs. To aid in determining the focus or topic of study, five guiding questions were identified in the Introduction. When teachers and other school professionals use the questions proactively and modify them as needed during the course of study, they go a long way toward establishing a solid foundation for the coaching or eCoaching continuum. As noted in the Introduction, when teachers and other school professionals engage in coaching or eCoaching without the study of specific content or a pedagogical practice, they are more likely to become dependent on the coach or the eCoach. Before engaging in the study of theory and practice, teachers and other school professionals should consider the following questions to help them identify a topic of study:

- What theory and practice should we study?
- How do we know we have identified the most important theory and practice for study?
- What do we need to know about the theory and practice before carrying it out in the classroom?
- How will we go about studying the theory and practice?
- How will we demonstrate understanding of our newly acquired knowledge about the theory and practice?

As teachers and school professionals endeavor to answer the first and second questions, we recommend that they consider several relevant factors: joint selection, theory of change, availability and credibility, and instructional design integrity.

Joint Selection

Too often, building or district administrators determine the topic for professional development with little input from teachers or other school professionals

(Carpenter, 2016; Diaz-Maggioli, 2004). When deciding on the topic for technology-enabled study of specific content or a pedagogical practice, we recommend avoiding a "top-down" approach for decision making and opting instead for a combined "bottom-up, top-down" approach. In other words, identifying topics for study should be a shared endeavor. How so? Joining together, teachers and other school professionals, including administrators and eCoaches, should review student-specific performance data to determine where the greatest needs are evident. Members of grade-level teams or content-area teams or individual professionals can review district, school, grade, classroom, or teacher data (see Figure 1.2).

Reviewing these data and plans should help teachers and other school professionals to jointly and more accurately identify high-priority target knowledge or pedagogical skills for in-depth study. Traditionally, this is accomplished through a series of one-to-one meetings or team meetings. Using a technology-enabled approach, teachers and other school professionals, including the eCoach and administrators, could do so via Box (https://chrome.google.com/webstore/detail/box/ejnkaeblpdcamcioiiabclakabcbjmbl?hl=en), a Google app that allows participants to share documents securely from any computer or mobile device. For example, based on a goal included in the school improvement plan, indicating that 100 percent of students will achieve proficiency in literacy, teachers and other school professionals might choose to study questioning as a means to enhance K–12 student learning during literacy instruction. Why study questioning to improve students' proficiency in literacy? In an Institute of Education Sciences (IES)–sponsored

Figure 1.2

Sources to Consider for Joint Topic Selection

District, School, Grade, or Classroom	Teacher
• Student self-report data (e.g., interviews, surveys) • Student work sample data • Student report card data • Student end-of-year decision data (i.e., promotion, retention, referral to multitiered systems of support [MTSS] team, referral for special services eligibility) • Student achievement data • Student attendance data • Student discipline data • Student demographic data • Parent/family engagement data • Community engagement data • District or School Improvement Plan	• Annual performance review data • Observation data • Survey or interview data • Coaching data • Walk-through data • Professional Development Plan

study conducted in general education, researchers investigated mediation—what explained the relationship between what teachers did during reading instruction (independent variable) and their students' reading performance (dependent variable)—within a school-based coaching context (Matsumura, Garnier, & Spybrook, 2013). They found that the quality of classroom text discussions mediated students' reading achievement.

Also, because of the increasing diversity of the school-age population in the United States, it is vital that teachers and other school professionals, including administrators and eCoaches, consider how the topics selected for technology-enabled study address issues related to cultural responsiveness. For instance, in the example we provided, teachers and other school professionals would study both effective questioning and how to craft culturally responsive questions to better meet the needs of their diverse students—especially those who are not achieving proficiency in literacy.

Theory of Change

The topic selected for study should also be grounded in a theory of change or a logic model. Teachers and other school professionals, including administrators and eCoaches, should consider how studying the topic (i.e., content or pedagogy) will lead to improvements in teachers' classroom practices as well as in their K–12 students' learning and behavior. Simply put, theory-of-change or logic-model planning comprises a series of *if . . . then* statements that, when carried out within the context of technology-enabled study, lead to the desired outcomes. For example, Dash, de Kramer, O'Dwyer, Masters, and Russell (2012) used a theory of change to improve teachers' content knowledge in math through online professional development. The theory of change that guided the online professional development was that if teachers' content knowledge in fractions, algebraic thinking, and measurement improved, then their instructional practices would too, which would result in increased math achievement by their K–12 students. Figure 1.3 provides an example of a completed logic model or theory of change for the topics for study specific to effective, culturally responsive questioning. As can be seen through these examples, logic-model/theory-of-change planning ensures that teachers and other school professionals have selected a topic of study with a clear link to classroom practice and improved K–12 student outcomes. Although in this chapter we've shared an abbreviated description for developing logic models/theories of change, teachers and other school professionals can access an extensive guide to developing logic models/theories of change online, courtesy of the W.K.

Figure 1.3

Questioning Example–Logic-Model or Theory-of-Change Planning Related to Topic Selection

Planned Study Technology-Enabled Study Planning		Intended Results Technology-Enabled Study Results		
Resources/ Inputs	Activities	Outputs	Outcomes	Impact
• Teachers' and other school professionals' learning goals • Teachers' and other school professionals' schedules • E-books • PDF informational documents • Interactive online videoconferencing platform (e.g., Skype, Google Hangouts, Zoom) • PDF study guides • Reputable websites • Twitter handle and hashtags • District technology support • Criteria for earning digital badges	• Create a timeline for tech-enabled study • Design a blueprint for technology-enabled study • Engage in technology-enabled study in accordance with timeline and blueprint, modifying and adjusting as needed	• Study guides completed • E-book discussions, including "question the author/expert" electronically archived • Effective, culturally responsive questioning and procedures for creating and sustaining a positive, consistent, organized learning environment included in lesson plans for literacy • Digital badges earned • Time and money saved	• Heightened interest and "buy-in" in technology-enabled study of content and pedagogy • Improved pedagogy (questioning) knowledge • Positive impact on planning for effective, culturally relevant questioning tactics during literacy instruction • Enhanced learning climate conducive to supporting student success • Heightened satisfaction with technology-enabled professional learning	• Continued interest and "buy-in" in technology-enabled study of content and pedagogy • Continued improvement of pedagogy (questioning) knowledge • Continued impact on planning for effective, culturally relevant questioning tactics during literacy instruction • Continued enhancement of learning climate conducive to supporting student success • Continued satisfaction with technology-enabled professional learning

Source: W. K. Kellogg Foundation Logic Model Development Guide. Retrieved from https://www.wkkf.org/resource-directory/resource/2006/02/wk-kellogg-foundation-logic-model-development-guide. Adapted.

Kellogg Foundation (https://www.wkkf.org/resource-directory/resource/2006/02/wk-kellogg-foundation-logic-model-development-guide). The logic-model/theory-of-change planning will be revisited in the chapters ahead.

When answering the third and fourth guiding questions, teachers and school professionals should consider two primary factors: the availability and credibility of technology-enabled options and materials to support the desired study as well as the design integrity of the instructional plan for technology-enabled study as evidenced by principles of effective instruction (Bransford et al., 2000; Brown et al., 2014; Dick et al., 2005) and multimedia design (Mayer, 2001) reflected in the approach.

Availability and Credibility

First and foremost, teachers and other school professionals should identify what technology-enabled options and materials are available specific to the content or pedagogical practice chosen for study. For example, what e-books, online courses, MOOCs, webinars, websites, electronic repositories, and so forth are available? While searching online and inventorying the availability of various technology options on a given topic of study, teachers and other school professionals should track the results and archive them electronically. Using a shared Google Doc (https://www.google.com/docs/about/) may facilitate this process. Doing so allows new teachers and school professionals to access the material and get up to speed on the topic at their convenience. It also allows those teachers and other school professionals who have completed technology-enabled study on a specific topic to review and update the material at any time.

If technology-enabled options are scant on a given topic of study, then teachers and other school professionals need to decide whether to engage in traditional study, to create their own materials, to use a blended approach, or to contract with universities or other professional organizations, such as ASCD, to develop materials. If technology-enabled options and materials are not readily available and must be developed internally or externally, the time frame and the budget for study may be adversely impacted.

Recognizing that educational professionals work in an unprecedented era of educational accountability, it is especially important that teachers and other school professionals evaluate the credibility of the information presented in technology-enabled materials. In other words, it is vital for teachers and other school professionals, including eCoaches and administrators, to ensure that the content and pedagogical information presented in technology-enabled materials comes from reputable sources and reflects evidence-based practice or practice-based evidence. For example, because the content on many professional development websites is not monitored or peer reviewed by experts, the information might not be reputable or credible. To avoid wasting valuable teaching and learning time, don't place too much stock in one instructional strategy shared by one teacher or one source. Consult free online resources, such as practice guides, intervention reports, single study reviews, and quick reviews available through the IES What Works Clearinghouse (https://ies.ed.gov/ncee/wwc/), to ensure the recommended content or pedagogical practice is valid, reliable, and effective.

Instructional Design Integrity

Availability and credibility aside, teachers and other school professionals should also consider how the technology-enabled options and materials could best be put together to support in-depth study of content or pedagogy in ways that incorporate basic principles of effective instruction and multimedia design. Why bother? Doing so makes technology-enabled study stick. Cognitive psychologists (Brown et al., 2014) caution, "People are generally going about learning the wrong way" (p. ix). Reversing this troubling trend in professional development involves dedicating some time to ensuring that technology-enabled study includes rich opportunities to

- Stimulate background knowledge;
- Gain meaning over time;
- Study specific content or pedagogy in depth;
- Prompt critical thinking;
- Practice retrieving important ideas;
- Elaborate on new knowledge;
- Generate examples and nonexamples of new knowledge;
- Reflect on new knowledge;
- Collaborate with colleagues to discuss and apply new knowledge;
- Produce mnemonic devices relevant to new knowledge; and
- Practice interleaving, which means studying one topic while learning another.

Because technology-enabled study typically includes more than one option or type of material, each option or type of material would *not* likely reflect all of the aforementioned. Instead, teachers and school professionals should consider how, when combined, they do so. For example, during technology-enabled study of content or pedagogy, surfing a few relevant websites first could stimulate background knowledge. Then, engaging in an e-book study with embedded case examples could offer opportunities for in-depth study, collaboration, elaboration, critical thinking, and reflection. Finally, demonstrating newly acquired knowledge via online quizzes or interactive web-based presentations by colleagues could offer opportunities for retrieval practice, generation, and mnemonic devices. In this way, the instructional integrity stems from the combined use of technology-enabled options and materials that support the specific content or pedagogical practice selected for study.

When considering the technology-enabled options and materials available to support study, teachers and other school professionals should evaluate each to determine how Mayer's (2001) 12 multimedia design principles are incorporated. Doing so helps new knowledge stick and helps alleviate the frustration, anxiety, and tension that often result when too many unnecessary bells and whistles are embedded in technology. Figure 1.4 includes a checklist for evaluating technology-enabled options and materials according to Mayer's (2001) multimedia design principles.

Recall that responding to the fifth guiding question requires that teachers and other school professionals determine how they will assess their understanding of

Figure 1.4

Checklist for Mayer's 12 Multimedia Design Principles

Reviewer(s):				
Technology-Enabled Study Topic(s):				
Technology-Enabled Option or Material Reviewed (Including URL):				
Mayer's (2001) Principle	**Look for multimedia options and materials . . .**	**Yes**	**No**	
Coherence	Without unnecessary words, pictures, or sound			
Signaling	That include cues that highlight important material			
Redundancy	That include graphics and narration rather than graphics, narration, and on-screen text			
Spatial Contiguity	With corresponding words and graphics in close proximity to each other			
Temporal Contiguity	With words and graphics presented together			
Segmenting	That offer self-paced segments			
Pretraining	That introduce important vocabulary, background knowledge, and essential concepts prior to the information			
Modality	That include graphics and narrations rather than animation and text			
Multimedia	That include graphics and text rather than solely text			
Personalization	With text presented in a conversational style			
Voice	With narration characterized by a human voice			
Image	Without the narrator's image			
Advantages:				
Disadvantages:				
Overall Recommendation:				

Source: From *Multimedia Learning*, by R. E. Mayer, 2001, New York: Cambridge University Press. Copyright 2001 by Cambridge University Press. Adapted with permission.

the newly learned content or pedagogical practice. Why? Like it or not, deeper, more durable learning comes from retrieval practice, which comes, in part, from some form of external or self-assessment (Brown et al., 2014). For instance, during an e-book study, teachers and other school professionals could opt for oral or written quizzes, using Google Docs (https://www.google.com/docs /about/), Qualtrics (https://www.qualtrics.com/), or SurveyMonkey (https://www .surveymonkey.com/). Remember, too, at this point, the focus is on building or refining one's knowledge; the stakes should be low, not high. During technology-enabled study, teachers and other school professionals could demonstrate understanding by designing and delivering interactive presentations with peers/colleagues using Pear Deck (https://www.peardeck.com/), Nearpod (https:// nearpod.com/) or Classkick (https://classkick.com/); creating electronic professional portfolios, using Weebly (https://www.weebly.com/) or Blogger (https://www .blogger.com/features); or earning digital badges or microcredentials through ASCD or Digital Promise (http://digitalpromise.org/initiative/educator-micro-credentials/). Regardless, as noted in the Introduction, assessment of understanding should align with knowledge rather than performance. That does not mean we are abandoning performance-based assessment. Performance-based assessment will be addressed in upcoming chapters, including those pertaining to one-on-one coaching and group coaching.

Considering the Technology Options for Studying Theory and Best Practice

Several technology options aid the study of theory and best practice. They range from high cost to no cost and may be completed on-site, online, or as a combination of the two. In what follows, we describe several options that teachers and administrators may find useful.

Online Modules and Courses

Online courses and modules, including MOOCs, allow teachers and other school professionals to study specific, relevant content or pedagogy synchronously or asynchronously. Developed by universities, professional organizations, state and federal departments of education, as well as private entities, some online courses and modules are offered free of charge, while others are fee based. Online courses and modules provide teachers with opportunities to watch video clips, read articles, listen to lectures, interact on discussion boards, or work through case studies and complete brief assessments of their learning. Teachers and other school professionals can acquire background information through various activities and make use of additional resources for continued learning. Asynchronous online modules can be completed at any time and can be paused and continued if necessary. Examples of online courses and modules include those found at ASCD's PD Online (http://pdo.ascd.org/home.aspx?ReturnUrl=%2f). IRIS modules from Vanderbilt University (https://iris.peabody.vanderbilt.edu) and state education agency modules, such as those from the North Carolina Department of Public Instruction (https://www.rt3nc.org/), allow teachers to choose from a wide range of support on instructional and behavioral strategies for the classroom.

An increasing number of universities are developing and offering MOOCs to the general public free of charge. Currently, profit and nonprofit options exist. For example, profit-based Coursera (https://www.coursera.org/)—with contributions from more than 140 renowned universities and educational organizations, including the University of Pennsylvania, Johns Hopkins University, the University of Michigan, Stanford University, the University of California at San Diego, and Duke University—offers a plethora of online courses. Alternatively, Harvard University and Massachusetts Institute of Technology (MIT) founded edX (https://www.edx.org/), a nonprofit organization comprising more than 90 global partners that offers high-quality online courses on a variety of topics developed by world-class universities and institutions. Websites of individual universities and institutions also can be searched for the most up-to-date MOOC offerings. For instance, a listing of MOOCs is available through the MIT Open Courseware website (http://ocw.mit.edu/index.htm).

Professional Development Webinars and Webcasts

Webinars and webcasts give teachers and other school professionals access to an expert on specific content or pedagogical practice through an online presentation or series of presentations. Most webinars and webcasts are an hour or two in length. Webinars and webcasts may be recorded and archived electronically, which allows for later on-demand viewing. Alternatively, they may be offered live, which requires real-time participation. A variety of reputable resources for webinars and webcasts are available to teachers and other school professionals, using live or on-demand access. For example, ASCD offers free and paid webinars (http://www.ascd.org/professional-development/webinars.aspx) on timely and relevant topics that fuel professional learning. Similarly, Learning Forward offers free webinars (https://learningforward.org/learning-opportunities/webinars) on various topics. edWeb.net (https://home.edweb.net/) provides the same; however, by participating in webinars and taking quizzes, teachers and other school professionals can earn personalized continuing education credits. Professional organizations, such as the National Council of Teachers of Mathematics (https://www.nctm .org/Conferences-and-Professional-Development/Webinars-and-Webcasts/) and the Council for Exceptional Children (https://www.cec.sped.org/Professional-Development/Webinars), also offer free and paid webinars and webcasts to members, as does Education Week (http://www.edweek.org/ew/marketplace/webinars /webinars.html). From time to time, the U.S. Department of Education offers free webinars related primarily to policy, rather than content or pedagogy (for an example, see https://www2.ed.gov/policy/elsec/leg/essa/essastwebinar12222015. pdf). Finally, state departments of education, such as the North Carolina Department of Public Instruction (http://www.dpi.state.nc.us/profdev/), routinely make webinars and webcasts available as well.

Professional Learning Communities (PLCs) and Personalized Learning Networks (PLNs)

A slightly more interactive alternative to online modules, courses, and webinars is an online PLC. These web-based sites and platforms are built on the concept of reciprocal information sharing as a way for teachers and other school professionals to strengthen their content knowledge and pedagogical know-how through online interaction and dialogue. In a review of relevant literature, Blitz (2013) found numerous advantages to online or blended PLCs, including heightened sense of community, improved content and pedagogical knowledge, enhanced intent to change classroom practices, and increased flexibility in facilitating professional learning. Perhaps most surprising, however, was Blitz's conclusion that participation in online PLCs yielded greater self-reflection on teaching and learning than did offline (i.e., face-to-face) models.

Practically speaking, online PLCs afford teachers and other school professionals the convenience of engaging in interactive professional development without the time and expense of travel. Teachers and other school professionals create online profiles and join communities or groups developed around a specific topic of study. Teachers and other school professionals can then post their own thoughts, create discussion threads, and search for resources. Teachscape (https://www .frontlineeducation.com/insights/teachscape-login/), which is affiliated with Frontline Education, and edWeb.net (http://home.edweb.net) are online professional development communities that allow educators to gather and share reputable information about content or pedagogy, offering unparalleled convenience because they are available and accessible at any time.

Similar to PLCs, another way to share learning about content or pedagogy is through personalized learning networks (PLNs): customized online communities, developed around a specific topic of study, that allow teachers and other school professionals to learn from and interact with each other, at any time, within a school or around the world (Flanigan, 2011). To create a PLN, teachers and other school professionals assemble a combination of online tools for using social media (e.g., Twitter [https://twitter.com/], Facebook [https://www.facebook.com/]), gathering information about the content or pedagogical practice chosen for study from various electronic publications or online resources (e.g., e-books, webinars, websites), organizing materials (e.g., Diigo [https://www.diigo.com/]or Evernote [https://evernote.com/]), communicating and collaborating (e.g., blogs, wikis, online videoconferencing software), and bookmarking (e.g., subscription-based Pinboard [https://pinboard.in/]) that promote deeper learning or understanding.

Electronic Publications

Books, journals, and articles are examples of electronic publications suitable for technology-enabled study of specific content or pedagogical practice. These publications can be another effective method for learning together about the chosen theory or best practice. E-readers (e.g., Kindle), tablets, and computers can be used to design an e-book study. E-books can be purchased and downloaded through online vendors, such as Amazon (https://www.amazon.com/); checked out electronically via online libraries, such as the World Digital Library (https://www.wdl.org/en/); or accessed for a fee or for free via professional organizations, such as ASCD (http://www.ascd.org/Publications/E-Publications/Electronic_Publications_Overview.aspx). Electronic articles can be obtained by searching Google Scholar (https://scholar.google.com/), and some publishers, such as SAGE (https://journals.sagepub.com/), offer free access to electronic journals and articles on specific topics, albeit often for a limited time. Open-access initiatives are becoming more widely available, so it is important to monitor availability from time to time.

As mentioned earlier, after reading an electronically distributed journal, article, or e-book, teachers and other school professionals, including administrators and eCoaches, can come together either on-site or online, via videoconferencing, and discuss what they have read. This is an opportunity to pose questions, ask for explanations, share examples of classroom application, and expand on existing knowledge to better understand the content or pedagogical practice. Online video-conferencing options, such as Skype (https://www.skype.com/en/), Google Hangouts (https://hangouts.google.com/), or Zoom (https://zoom.us/), provide even greater meeting flexibility. For example, an eCoach, teachers, and other school professionals from different schools or districts can discuss an electronic publication without having to meet on-site.

Podcasts

Concise and convenient, podcasts offer teachers and other school professionals brief audio explanations that can also be an effective way to fuel professional learning about content or pedagogical practice. For example, Reading Rockets offers a podcast series about effective literacy instruction that can be downloaded to a mobile device via iTunes (http://www.readingrockets.org/podcasts/itunes). Science Underground (http://scienceunderground.org/), a two-minute weekly podcast, enables teachers and other school professionals to bolster content knowledge and pedagogical practice aligned with Next Generation Science Standards (NGSS). Also, experts such as Michael Kennedy, of the University of Virginia, have created a series of podcasts on a variety of topics related to special education content knowledge and pedagogical practice (https://vimeo.com/mjk/videos). Podcasts featuring teachers discussing content and pedagogy are also available through Talks with Teachers (http://talkswithteachers.com/).

Reputable Websites

A popular form of knowledge sharing on the Internet, websites offer teachers and other school professionals quick, easy access to information on a variety of topics related to content and pedagogy. Websites may be affiliated with universities, professional organizations, nonprofit or for-profit entities, state and federal government departments of education, or individuals. When considering websites for technology-enabled study, teachers and other school professionals should select those in which the content complements, rather than replaces, more in-depth information available through online modules or courses, MOOCs, e-books, and other electronic publications. For example, information included on a website might offer additional examples of classroom application or include access to newly updated information about the content or pedagogical practice of interest. Figure 1.5 provides examples of reputable websites that teachers and other school professionals could consider when undertaking technology-enabled study.

Social Media

Online social personal and professional media and networks, such as Twitter (https://twitter.com/), Facebook (https://www.facebook.com/), Tumbler (https://www.tumblr.com/), LinkedIn (https://www.linkedin.com/), Classroom 2.0 (http://www.classroom20.com/), and Edmodo (https://www.edmodo.com/) offer teachers and other school professionals access to educational information and opportunities to connect around that information that can fuel professional learning. In the article "Teachers at the Wheel," Carpenter (2016) points out that "social media facilitates

Figure 1.5

Resources for Reputable Websites–Content, Pedagogy, and Culture

Content—What to Teach

Reading/Literacy
Florida State University–Florida Center for Reading Research
(http://www.fcrr.org/resources/)
- Evidence-based intervention guides, checklists, presentations, instructional resources, library, and more

U.S. Department of Health and Human Services and National Institutes of Health
(https://www.nichd.nih.gov/about/org/der/branches/cdbb/Pages/nationalreadingpanelpubs.aspx)
- National Reading Panel publications and reports

Center for Literacy and Disability Studies/University of North Carolina Chapel Hill School of Medicine, Department of Allied Health Sciences
(https://www.med.unc.edu/ahs/clds)
- Products and resources

Mathematics, Science, and Social Studies
National Council of Teachers of Mathematics
(http://www.nctm.org/)
- Classroom resources, publications, standards and positions, research and advocacy, conferences and professional development

National Library of Virtual Manipulatives/funded by the National Science Foundation
(http://nlvm.usu.edu/en/nav/vlibrary.html)
- Interactive web-based virtual manipulatives as well as concept tutorials for grades K–12
- An enhanced version of NLVM is available for a fee through Matti Math (https://www.mattimath.com/)

The National Science Foundation (NSF)
(https://www.nsf.gov/news/classroom/earth-environ.jsp)
- Earth and environment classroom resources

National Geographic
(https://www.nationalgeographic.com/) and (https://kids.nationalgeographic.com/)
- News, stories, video, photography, kids (e.g., videos, games, magazine, interactive world map), and so forth

National Geographic Society–Education
(https://www.nationalgeographic.org/education/classroom-resources/, https://www.nationalgeographic.org/education/professional-development/, and https://www.nationalgeographic.org/activity/wildcam-observations/)
- Classroom resources, professional development resources, blogs, and so on

The American Museum of Natural History/The Hayden Planetarium
(http://www.amnh.org/our-research/hayden-planetarium)
- Blog and resources, including the Digital Universe, a downloadable atlas as well as articles, essays, and letters on astronomy and astrophysics

National Council for the Social Studies
(https://www.socialstudies.org/)
- Conferences and professional learning, publications, resources, standards, and so on

edtechteacher (http://besthistorysites.net/)
- Listing and a brief description of the "Best of History Websites"
(http://besthistorysites.net/general-history-resources/)

Across Curriculum and Grade Levels
PBS Learning Media
(https://unctv.pbslearningmedia.org/)
- Customized dashboard, curriculum, state standards, instructional resources, lesson plans, videos, free interactive adventure games (e.g., Mission US: For Crown or Colony @ https://unctv.pbslearningmedia.org/resource/mu10.vk8soc.7-8.nation.crownorcol/mission-us-for-crown-or-colony/)

Figure 1.5

Resources for Reputable Websites–Content, Pedagogy, and Culture

Pedagogy—How to Teach

Effective Instruction and Assessment

National Center on Universal Design for Learning
(http://www.udlcenter.org/)

- Learn the basics, advocacy, implementation, research, community, and resources

Teaching Works—University of Michigan's High-Leverage Practices
(http://www.teachingworks.org/work-of-teaching/high-leverage-practices)

- Support and resources, publications and presentations

The Council for Exceptional Children (CEC) & CEEDAR Center's High-Leverage Practices (HLPs)
(https://highleveragepractices.org/)

- Informational resources, including videos, for HLPs in four practice areas:
  - ◇ Collaboration
  - ◇ Assessment
  - ◇ Social/Emotional/Behavioral
  - ◇ Instruction

What Works Clearinghouse
(https://ies.ed.gov/ncee/wwc/)

- Intervention reports, practice guides, trainings, videos, infographics, summaries, research reviews, and searchable databases to help teachers and other school personnel find what works based on "high quality" research

Research Institute on Progress Monitoring
(https://www.progressmonitoring.org/)

- Resources, videos, multimedia modules, literature reviews, literature databases, technical reports, and so forth

Center on Response to Intervention at American Institutes for Research
(http://www.rti4success.org/)

- Essential components of RTI, related RTI topics, resources

The Resource Institute for Problem Solving
(http://www.cehd.umn.edu/EdPsych/RIPS/default.html)

- Curriculum-based measurement modules, evidence-based practices, measurement and assessment resources, tiered service and delivery resources

Educational Equity and Culturally Responsive Teaching

Arizona State University's Equity Alliance
(http://www.equityallianceatasu.org/)

- Blogs, publications, resource guides, e-learning, technical assistance, and Learning Carousel (*Note*: The latter offers content regarding evidence-based practices and information about educational equity. More than a thousand down-loadable documents, searchable by category, are available at http://ea.niusileadscape.org/lc.)

Assistive Technology

The Rehabilitation Engineering and Assistive Technology Society of North America (RESNA)
(https://www.resna.org/)

- Assistive technology standards, professional development (e.g., courses, webinars, quizzes), news, research guidelines, and so on

Differentiated Instruction

(http://www.ascd.org/research-a-topic/differentiated-instruction-beyond-ascd.aspx)

- ASCD offers a wealth of online and traditional resources pertaining to differentiated instruction as well as a compilation of resources beyond ASCD, including research and reports, websites, blogs, and Twitter handles.

(continues)

Figure 1.5   (continued)

Resources for Reputable Websites–Content, Pedagogy, and Culture

Climate—How to Reach and Teach the Whole Child

Social, Emotional, Behavioral Support
Positive Behavioral Interventions and Supports
(https://www.pbis.org/)
- Resources (e.g., informational documents, blueprints, videos, presentations) designed for school, family, and community stakeholders when carrying out multitiered, social, emotional, and behavioral supports

Family and Community Engagement
National Center for Parents, Family, and Community Engagement
(https://cssp.org/our-work/project/national-center-for-parents-family-and-community-engagement/)
- Publications and resources, including a blog, aimed at supporting equitable access and outcomes for children and families

Trauma
The National Child Traumatic Stress Network
(https://www.nctsn.org/)
- Resources (e.g., information, fact sheets, tips, training) for professionals, including teachers and other school personnel, who support children experiencing traumatic stress

Poverty
National Center for Children in Poverty
(http://www.nccp.org/)
- Resources (e.g., information, publications, fact sheets, state profiles, data tools, blog) for turning research into practice when supporting children and families in poverty

School and Student Health and Wellness
Institute for Collaboration on Health, Intervention, and Policy—Collaboratory on School and Child Health
(https://csch.uconn.edu/)
- Resources (e.g., multimedia presentations, publications, tools, guides, brief reports, informational archives) for creating healthy, safe, supportive, and engaging environments, including schools and classrooms, for all children

National Center for School Mental Health
(http://csmh.umaryland.edu/)
- Resources (e.g., publications, modules, technical assistance) designed to promote school mental health programs and systems through research, training, and support

School Safety
National Center on Safe Supportive Learning Environments
(https://safesupportivelearning.ed.gov/resources/national-school-safety-center)
- Resources (e.g., webinars, guides, training products, school climate surveys, resource directories, news articles) for use by a variety of stakeholders, including teachers and other school personnel, who are committed to improving learning conditions that foster student success

National School Boards Association—School Safety, Security, and Emergency Preparedness
(https://www.nsba.org/services/school-board-leadership-services/school-safety-and-security)
- Resources (e.g., webinars, videos, research, reports, school safety plans) designed to aid frontline practitioners in ensuring safe and secure learning environments, including emergency preparedness and disaster management

Bullying
National Bullying Prevention Center
(https://www.pacer.org/bullying/)
- Resources (e.g., handouts, templates, posters, videos, event kits, curriculum, book clubs, modules) for preventing bullying, promoting kindness, and leading social change in schools, classrooms, and communities

Figure 1.5

Resources for Reputable Websites–Content, Pedagogy, and Culture

---

Inclusive Education
National Professional Development Center on Inclusion
(https://npdci.fpg.unc.edu/)
- Resources (e.g., evidence-based practices, planning and facilitation tools, assessment instruments, presentations, articles, papers, blogs, discussions, modules) for teachers and other education personnel to use when supporting young children with disabilities in inclusive learning environments

The TIES Center: Increasing Time, Instructional Effectiveness, Engagement, and State Support for Inclusive Practices for Students with Significant Cognitive Disabilities
(https://tiescenter.org/)
- Resources (e.g., publications, technical assistance, toolkits, curriculum resources, instructional resources, professional development modules, briefs, testimony) for use by key stakeholders to support students with significant cognitive disabilities in inclusive learning environments

---

Note: URLs active as of July 2019.

participation, challenges hierarchies, and helps build professional networks that support teacher collaboration and autonomy" (p. 30). Using mixed methods, Visser, Evering, and Barrett (2014) investigated how K–12 teachers used Twitter. Chief among the reported advantages were increased content and pedagogical knowledge, as well as improved classroom practices that were acquired and achieved "through meaningful, interpersonal relationships within a participatory culture" (p. 407). Relatedly, Carpenter and Krutka (2014) surveyed 755 K–12 educators to determine how and why they used Twitter. Professional development was a commonly reported use, with respondents indicating they valued the personalization, immediacy, positivity, and collaboration Twitter afforded. With more than 200 weekly Twitter chats available for teachers and other school professionals to join in each week (Carpenter, 2016), we think that this and other forms of social media offer unique opportunities for strengthening and supporting technology-enabled study.

Determining Which Technology-Enabled Options and Materials Are the Best Fit

Teachers and administrators have many varied and unique options for using technology to build content knowledge and enhance pedagogical practice. Determining the best fit involves assessing readiness and determining sustainability. Simply put, that requires short- and long-term thinking. Allow us here to reiterate a previous point: if technology-enabled approaches to study are to succeed, then it is vital that teachers and administrators take some time to ensure the options selected are not just the shiniest, newest technology options available. Instead, the technology-enabled options and materials selected should be those that fuel deep professional study of specific content or a pedagogical practice more effectively and efficiently with greater convenience. Teachers and other school professionals can use the following eight questions to guide their decision making:

- How ready are teachers and other school professionals to undertake technology-enabled study? Do teachers and other school professionals prefer a blended approach or a completely technology-enabled one?
- How ready are district- and building-level administrators to support teachers and other school professionals as they undertake technology-enabled study?
- What technology-enabled options and materials are available to aid the study of theory and practice of interest? For instance, are online modules available on the topic of interest? What about e-books?
- Of the available technology-enabled options and materials, what are the benefits and liabilities associated with each? Do the benefits outweigh the liabilities? How so?
- What technology know-how do teachers and other school professionals need in order to access and interact with the technology-enabled options for studying the theory and practice of interest? Relatedly, what are their training needs? For instance, do they need a tutorial on using a specific online platform or on social media etiquette?
- What is the quantity and quality of technology support available to teachers and administrators when using technology to study the theory or practice of interest?
- What is the budget for supporting technology-enabled study? Are other funds available through public or private grants to teachers and other school professionals? What technology-enabled options and materials offer the most bang for the buck?
- What is the time frame for technology-enabled study on a selected topic? How will this impact the decisions about which technology options and materials are selected? For example, are options and materials available to support the technology-enabled study of interest, or do they need to be developed internally or externally?

Taking the time to answer these questions can go a long way toward preventing or mitigating the hazards associated with technology-enabled approaches.

Designing an Instructional Plan for Technology-Enabled Study

As can be seen from the foregoing descriptions, teachers and other school professionals have a variety of technology options and materials available to support their study of content or pedagogy. Also, as described previously, when deciding on the topic, the technology-enabled options and materials, and the overall approach that will guide study, there are a number of considerations to weigh. Let's face it: all this decision making can be overwhelming, exhausting, and time sucking. So, why bother? In the words of Benjamin Franklin, "If you fail to plan, you are planning to fail." To make this process positive, productive, efficient, and effective, as we also noted earlier in this chapter, we suggest putting together an instructional design plan that teachers and other school professionals can use to guide technology-enabled study. There is flexibility within the structure, meaning teachers and other school professionals should modify the plan as needed during study. Figure 1.6 presents an instructional design plan for a technology-enabled study of questioning.

Figure 1.6

Instructional Design Plan for Technology-Enabled Study– Questioning Example

Guiding Questions	Sample Instructional Design Planning for Technology-Enabled Study of Specific Content or Particular Pedagogy (20–30 hours recommended)
What is the topic and purpose of study?	Develop or refine pedagogical knowledge in four areas: • *Effective questioning* to enhance students' comprehension during literacy instruction • *Two of Deborah Ball's 19 high-leverage practices related specifically to questioning*—leading a group discussion and eliciting and interpreting individual students' thinking • *Culturally responsive questioning* to meet the needs of diverse students • One of the Council for Exceptional Children's (CEC's) high-leverage social, emotional, and behavioral practices—HLP #7: Establish a Consistent, Organized, and Respectful Learning Environment

Why is the topic of study important?	• The school improvement plan
	  ◊ 100 percent of students will achieve proficiency in literacy.
	• District student achievement data
	  ◊ Currently, student performance data confirm many students, especially those who are diverse, are not achieving proficiency in literacy.
	• Classroom/teacher performance data
	  ◊ Currently, classroom observational data confirm most teachers are using lower-order questioning and minimal discussion during literacy instruction. High-performing students respond frequently and accurately.
	• Pedagogical research
	  ◊ Institute for Education Sciences (IES) researchers Matsumura and colleagues (2013) found the quality of classroom text discussions, including questioning, mediated students' reading achievement.
	• Social/emotional/behavioral research
	  ◊ Results from meta-analytic studies have confirmed many varied benefits for students whose teachers provided social, emotional, and behavioral supports, including 11 percentile point gains in academic achievement (Mahoney, Durlak, & Weissberg, 2018).

(continues)

Figure 1.6   (continued)

Instructional Design Plan for Technology-Enabled Study– Questioning Example

Guiding Questions	Sample Instructional Design Planning for Technology-Enabled Study of Specific Content or Particular Pedagogy (20–30 hours recommended)
What is already known about the topic of study?	Based on theory-of-change/logic-model planning, teachers and other school professionals realize that if they want to increase all K–12 students' proficiency in literacy, they need to develop in-depth knowledge of effective questioning practices as well as how to make questions culturally responsive to their diverse students while creating and maintaining a positive, respectful, organized, and consistent environment for learning.
What content or information is needed to transfer the topic of study to the classroom?	Teachers and other school professionals need to understand and include in their lesson planning for literacy instruction • A range of effective questions from lower to higher order that support rich thoughtful discussion • Two of Deborah Ball's 19 high-leverage practices related specifically to questioning—leading a group discussion and eliciting and interpreting individual students' thinking • Culturally responsive questions • One of the CEC's high-leverage social, emotional, and behavioral practices—HLP #7: Establish a Consistent, Organized, and Respectful Learning Environment

How will technology be used to sup-port the topic of study?	• *E-book study.* Engage in e-book study of effective questioning tactics, using *Questioning for Classroom Discussion* (Walsh & Sattes, 2015).
	• *Electronic discussion guide.* Download the Study Guide for *Questioning for Classroom Discussion* from http://www.ascd.org/publications/books/115012/chapters/ An-ASCD-Study-Guide-for-Questioning-for-Classroom-Discussion@-Purposeful-Speaking, -Engaged-Listening,-Deep-Thinking.aspx
	• *PDF document.* Use the description of HLP #7 from the CEC's high-leverage social, emo-tional, and behavioral practices as a study aid (https://highleveragepractices.org/wp-content/ uploads/2017/06/SEBshort.pdf).
	• *Reputable websites.* Bookmark three websites:
	  ◇ University of Michigan's Teaching Works (http://www.teachingworks.org/work-of-teaching /high-leverage-practices) to review two of Deborah Ball's 19 high-leverage practices related specifically to questioning—leading a group discussion and eliciting and interpreting individual students' thinking
	  ◇ *Create Success!* by Kadhir Rajagopal (http://www.ascd.org/publications/books/111022 /chapters/Culturally-Responsive-Instruction.aspx) to study Chapter 1, "Culturally Responsive Instruction," focusing on the section pertaining to questioning
	  ◇ The CEC's high-leverage practices to review HLP #7: Establish a Consistent, Organized, and Respectful Learning Environment (https://highleveragepractices.org/wp-content /uploads/2017/06/SEBshort.pdf and https://highleveragepractices.org/about-hlps/)
	• *Professional online community platforms.* Use edWeb (https://home.edweb.net/) or PBworks (http://www.pbworks.com/) to create an online PLC for weekly e-book study discussion.
	• *Social media.* Follow Teaching Works on Twitter (https://twitter.com/) and Facebook (https://www .facebook.com/). Engage in weekly Twitter chats using #culturallyresponsivequestioning, #questioningforclassroomdiscussion, and #socialemotionallearning.

How will participants demonstrate understand-ing of the topic of study?	• Create low-stakes chapter quizzes for e-book study using Google Docs (https://www.google.com /docs/about/) or SurveyMonkey (https://www.surveymonkey.com/). • Design and deliver one or two interactive presentations on culturally responsive questioning and two of Deborah Ball's 19 high-leverage practices related specifically to questioning—leading a group discussion and eliciting and interpreting individual students' thinking—with peers /colleagues using Pear Deck (https://www.peardeck.com/), Nearpod (https://nearpod.com/), or Classkick (https://classkick.com/). • Earn digital badges/microcredentials for effective questioning, culturally responsive questioning, two of Deborah Ball's 19 high-leverage practices related specifically to questioning—leading a group discussion and eliciting and interpreting individual students' thinking—and one of the CEC's high-leverage practices (i.e., HLP #7: Establish a Consistent, Organized, and Respectful Learning Environment)—via ASCD or Digital Promise (http://digitalpromise.org/initiative /educator-micro-credentials/).

Creating Norms That Support Technology-Enabled Study

As mentioned previously, individual teachers, other school professionals, or members of school- or district-based teams can use technology to study specific content or pedagogical practice. Whether a team or an individual undertakes technology-enabled study, it is important to dedicate time proactively to creating norms. Doing so can go a long way toward establishing a supportive school climate and culture for technology-enabled study. Failing to do so may result in a number of undesirable outcomes, including inconsistent adoption of a technology-enabled approach, increased conflict, heightened disengagement, or poor results. Conversely, when team members invest time initially to creating norms, they set the stage for shared understanding, mutual respect, increased engagement, and improved results.

Like creating classroom rules and expectations, when creating norms for technology-enabled study, the members of the learning community should participate actively in their development. We recommend the following steps for doing so:

1. *Develop the norms for technology-enabled study in partnership with colleagues and record them.* Electronic options (e.g., Google Docs) work well during this step because everyone can contribute and comment as the norms are developed and revised. If meetings are needed for additional discussion, try a blended format (e.g., meeting online via Google Hangouts or Zoom and reserving face-to-face meetings for dialoguing about the most important content).
2. *Distribute the norms widely so that all teachers and other school professionals have access to them.* Hard copies can be disseminated to those who request them, while all receive access electronically via Google Docs or an online wiki, such as via PBworks (http://www.pbworks.com/).
3. *Revisit the norms periodically, revising as needed.* This will help to foster adherence and promote accountability. Also, as norms should change over time, it is important to keep a pulse on changes in school or district culture, climate, and expectations and revise the norms accordingly.

We will now describe the general considerations when drafting norms for technology-enabled study of theory and practice—legal conduct, professional dispositions, peer support and troubleshooting, and positivity and encouragement.

Legal Conduct

When engaging in technology-enabled study of specific content or pedagogical practice, teachers and other school professionals need to be mindful about legal matters, such as digital copyright, social media policies, privacy protocols, and confidentiality measures. For example, digital copyright protections mean that e-books must be purchased separately and cannot be duplicated and shared electronically. Also, teachers and other school professionals need to understand what school or district policies exist. How free is cyberspeech? What happens when a teacher or other school professional posts or tweets a contradictory point of view regarding school- or district-sanctioned content or pedagogical practice? Would it be considered cybermisconduct? What happens when teachers or other school professionals share personal information online? We have all read stories in the popular press about the firings of education professionals based on a tweet or a Facebook post. When blogging about specific content or a pedagogical practice, teachers and other school professionals need to be sure to credit information sources. To be fully informed, teachers and other school professionals should review reputable resources explaining digital copyright as well as the consequences of violating it. When videoconferencing or uploading content to wikis, teachers and other school professionals also need to consider policies regarding student privacy and confidentiality (Abilock & Abilock, 2016). No doubt, all of these considerations can be overwhelming. Our suggestion to include legal considerations in the norms for technology-enabled study is not intended to frighten teachers and other school professionals; rather it is to ensure they are informed and empowered. For that reason, we recommend inviting district legal counsel to share recent case law and to explain cyberconduct policies (Shipley, 2009).

Professional Dispositions

Crafting norms for technology-enabled study also entails addressing relevant professional dispositions, such as online etiquette and digital citizenship. Just as K–12 students learn about online etiquette and digital citizenship (Zuger, 2016), teachers and other school professionals also need to decide how they should act and interact during the technology-enabled study of theory and practice. This involves reviewing or, if necessary, developing protocols. For example, Zuger (2016) raises a number of questions that should be considered: What is the district or building policy for downloading personal information on a device, such as a tablet or e-reader, that is provided by the district? What happens if a device, such as a teacher's tablet, is found? What is the protocol? Should teachers or other school professionals try to determine whom the device belongs to and return it? What if, while doing so, they encounter questionable content or photos on the device? Alternatively, should lost devices routinely be returned to administrators without attempting to identify the owner? Because of the complexity of these and other issues, the potential for legal issues to emerge, along with the ever-changing nature of technology, we encourage teachers and other school professionals to be resourceful when developing norms for technology-enabled study. For instance, we view partnering with the school media specialist or librarian and technology staff, as well as school district counsel, to develop awareness and provide ongoing training in online etiquette and digital citizenship as vital to developing and institutionalizing these dispositional norms (Preddy, 2016).

Peer Support and Troubleshooting

Although technology-enabled study is more convenient for teachers and other school professionals than traditional, face-to-face approaches, technology glitches can occur at any time. District technology support aside, there will be occasions, especially after hours and on weekends, when teachers and other school professionals need to lend support to one another and engage in troubleshooting. Thus, when developing norms for technology-enabled study, teachers and other school professionals should also consider peer support and troubleshooting. They need to address how and when colleagues will be able and willing to lend support and to assist with troubleshooting, especially when district-level supports are not available. For instance, some teachers and school professionals may be accessible during evening hours and others on weekends. Addressing these expectations in the norms helps alleviate the feelings of anxiety and frustration that often emerge when technology goes awry.

Positivity and Encouragement

Because technology can be as much of a curse as a blessing, creating and sustaining a positive culture for technology-enabled study of theory and practice is vital to its success. Moreover, teachers and other school professionals are busy. There never seem to be enough hours in a day. Some might find the need for in-depth study off-putting, overwhelming, and unreasonable. Countering and overcoming naysayers require that teachers and other school professionals create norms in which colleagues champion technology-enabled professional learning and support one another in staying the course. How so? With relentless enthusiasm, endless curiosity, deep-seated commitment, and a strong sense of esprit de corps.

Contemplating Benefits and Cautions Associated with a Technology-Enabled Approach to Studying Theory and Practice

As we mentioned at the beginning of this chapter, teachers and other school professionals should opt for technology-enabled study that minimizes stress and maximizes professional learning. Also, as mentioned previously, that means teachers and other school professionals should dedicate sufficient time prior to engaging in technology-enabled study of specific content or a pedagogical practice to determine what options best suit their needs. In the sections that follow, we highlight a few benefits and cautions that teachers and school professionals should factor in to their decision making. Doing so will more likely set the stage for success, rather than frustration and failure.

Benefits

While expert-facilitated professional development, via face-to-face workshops, is expensive (often costing $1,000 per day in consulting fees, plus travel expenses, especially when an expert is brought on-site), engaging in an e-book study and meeting online to question the author can save time and money because travel time and expenses are greatly reduced or eliminated altogether. Everyone can attend from anywhere they have access to the Internet. Also, district personnel do not need to spend extra money booking multiple sessions for different schools, nor do they have to find a venue large enough for teachers and other school professionals to attend at the same time.

As noted previously, online modules and some online courses can be accessed at any time, allowing teachers and other school professionals to work through them at their own pace. They can also easily return to the content for review or additional information. Reputable online professional development websites and communities (e.g., edWeb.net or Frontline Education) give teachers access to webinars and to a wide range of perspectives and options for practice. Typically, the content available through these sites is created by teachers, for teachers, so it is practical and easy to understand. Also, teachers can provide one another with comments and tips or pose questions about the specific content or pedagogical practice they are studying. These groups are an effective way for teachers and other school professionals to deepen and broaden their online study by communicating, sharing knowledge and experience, answering questions, and lending support. In this and other ways, online study can also alleviate the professional isolation often experienced by teachers (National Research Council, 2007).

Cautions

First, technology can be complicated and unreliable. If an e-reader or a tablet malfunctions or a website goes down, that information may be temporarily or permanently lost, or teachers and other school professionals may need to find alternative ways to access it. This can lead to frustration or even premature abandonment. Second, investigators at the National Research Council (2007) identified a number of barriers to technology-enabled professional learning for teachers and other school professionals, including shortcomings in knowledge, administrative support, access, time, and financial backing—all of which need to be considered and resolved.

Translating the eCoach's Role into Action During Technology-Enabled Study of Theory and Practice

The eCoach plays a vital and unique role in each of the four components of the eCoaching continuum. Whether teams of teachers and school professionals or individuals undertake technology-enabled study of theory and practice, we offer here a list of possible roles and responsibilities eCoaches could shoulder to create and sustain in-depth learning. To take on these roles, eCoaches need administrator and colleague support, including dedicated release time, clearly delineated job roles and responsibilities, and ongoing training and professional development.

- Take a leadership role in overcoming known obstacles by assessing readiness for technology-enabled study, creating time frames for technology-enabled study, providing resources to increase knowledge of technology-enabled study, securing administrative support, enhancing access to technology, assisting in scheduling, and finding additional financial support when needed.
- Facilitate topic selection, using the five guiding questions to ensure a data-informed, "bottom-up, top-down" approach based on a clear theory-of-change/logic model.
- Offer guidance on determining availability and evaluating the credibility of technology-enabled options and materials that support the study of content or pedagogy.
- Provide information on principles of effective instruction, adult learning theory, and Mayer's (2001) principles for multimedia design.
- Coordinate evaluation of technology-related options and materials and consider goodness of fit, using the eight questions to guide their decision making.
- Construct the instructional design plan for technology-enabled study and modify as needed.
- Co-create norms for technology-enabled study.
- Partner with school librarians, technology support specialists, and legal counsel to provide training in online etiquette, digital citizenship, and technology-related policies and protocols.
- Develop quizzes and digital badges or microcredentials.
- Create modules for training on new and existing technologies that support technology-enabled study.

- Monitor progress of technology-enabled study and evaluate professional learning.

Moreover, just as teachers and other school professionals need to use technology to study content and pedagogy, so do eCoaches. For example, using Coursera, eCoaches may find some modules especially well-suited to their professional learning needs. One such course is entitled "Coaching Skills for Managers Specialization" (https://www.coursera.org/specializations/coaching-skills-manager). Although the course content is geared toward coaching in business, there are individual modules, such as "Coaching Conversations," that eCoaches may find useful and economical. The modules are fee based; however, financial aid is available for those who qualify.

Revisiting Important Ideas

In this chapter, we've described in detail how to go about technology-enabled study of content and pedagogy—what and how to teach. We've also pointed out why doing so is important as well as the known advantages and disadvantages. Before moving on to Chapter 2, let's take a minute to review the important ideas we've shared:

- The primary purpose of using technology to study a theory and practice of interest is to build teachers' and other school professionals' specific content knowledge or particular pedagogical skill with increased effectiveness, improved convenience, and enhanced access to a broader range of experts and resources— all at a lower cost.
- The topic for technology-enabled study should be based on careful consideration of five guiding questions, as well as the relevant factors that pertain to each.
- When considering, selecting, and using technology options and materials to support the study of theory and practice, the aim is to decrease time constraints and alleviate stressors, not compound them.
- There are many varied technology options for teachers and administrators to consider. Examples include online courses and modules, webinars, professional learning communities (PLCs) and personalized learning networks (PLNs), electronic publications, podcasts, reputable websites, and social media.
- Considerations such as readiness, time, budget, technology resources, technology know-how, and technology support should guide team members' and individuals' decision making about which technology-enabled options to pursue when studying the theory or practice of interest.

- An instructional plan based on the five guiding questions and supported by the principles of effective instruction and multimedia design ensures a successful approach to technology-enabled study.
- Norms for technology-enabled study are vital to supporting the success of its undertaking. Joining together to revisit existing norms and to create new ones is time and energy well spent. Failure to do so will likely result in premature abandonment of technology-enabled approaches for in-depth study of specific content or a pedagogical practice.
- Benefits of technology-enabled study, and associated cautions, should be weighed thoroughly and carefully to determine the best approach—traditional, blended, or technology enabled.
- eCoaches shoulder unique roles and responsibilities that are vital to successful technology-enabled study. Like teachers and other school professionals, they need support from administrators and colleagues.

Because it's easy to get overwhelmed and abandon efforts to begin something new, like technology-enabled study of theory or best practice, we close this chapter with an At-a-Glance Checklist—designed to help educators organize their efforts and to make the process more manageable. The more teachers and other school professionals use the checklist, the more efficient and effective they become in preparing for technology-enabled study. Laying the foundation for practical, powerful, impactful professional development has never been easier.

AT-A-GLANCE CHECKLIST

Preparing for Successful Technology-Enabled Study

□ The purpose for technology-enabled study is clear and differentiated.
□ The topic for technology-enabled study is selected based on guiding questions and the important factors to consider for each.
□ Technology-enabled options and materials are identified and based on goodness of fit.
□ An instructional design plan is developed to guide technology-enabled study and can be modified as needed.
□ Norms for technology-enabled study are established and supported.
□ Benefits and cautions of technology-enabled study are considered and choices are made accordingly.
□ eCoaches' roles and responsibilities are clearly articulated and supported.

2

Technology-Enabled Observations

Strengthening the Foundation for Practical, Powerful, Impactful Professional Development

Marcia Rock and Aftynne E. Cheek

We learn more from people who are different from us than from the ones who are the same. —Andy Hargreaves (n.d.)

How can teachers and other school professionals use technology effectively and efficiently to observe themselves, colleagues, or experts not only to support the transfer of newly acquired content knowledge and pedagogical know-how to the classroom, but also to improve their K–12 students' learning?

Understanding the Purpose of Using Technology to Carry Out Observations

Observing colleagues model or demonstrate the content and pedagogy under study—the latter of which includes social, emotional, and behavioral domains aimed at reaching and teaching the whole child—is by no means a novel idea. That said, observation is the second of the four essential components in the coaching and eCoaching continuum. Why? As others have pointed out, observation affords teachers and other school professionals the opportunity to view others carrying out the content or pedagogy under study in real-world classrooms (Joyce & Showers, 1982), which in turn aids in increasing instructional effectiveness (Bell & Mladenovic, 2008; Glickman, Gordon, & Ross-Gordon, 2014). Similar to the traditional on-site variation, technology-enabled observations provide teachers and other school professionals with opportunities to observe real-world models of content or pedagogy using digital resources (Hendry & Oliver, 2012). Why bother with the hassles technology often brings? Simply put, extending teachers' face-to-face, on-site observations to include electronic visits increases access to experts and models from across the building, district, state, region, country, or globe, while saving time and money. We elaborate extensively on the advantages associated with technology-enabled observations near the end of the chapter.

A Developmental Approach and Purpose

Traditional approaches to observation, without technology, are typically organized into three categories—evaluative, developmental, and peer review (Gosling, 2002; Pattison, Sherwood, Lumsden, Gale, & Markides, 2012)—that also apply to the technology-enabled version. In the coaching or eCoaching continuum, during technology-enabled observation, we recommend relying primarily on the developmental approach with some variation. Typically, in the developmental approach, experienced teachers and other school professionals observe less-experienced colleagues and provide feedback (Pattison et al., 2012). We modify this approach by also including opportunities for less-experienced teachers and other school professionals (novices) to observe more-experienced colleagues (experts) and provide feedback. In this way, novices and experts learn from one another, allowing for more reciprocal and less hierarchical professional interactions.

Taking a modified developmental approach to technology-enabled observations of content and pedagogy serves several unique and varied purposes. The primary aim of observation is to make the study of content and pedagogy visible in an applied context—the classroom. As noted in the Introduction, Joyce and Showers (1982) recommended 15–20 observations, which does *not* equate to 15–20 hours. Brief, focused observations are as effective as—if not more so than—lengthy, unfocused ones. The same applies to the technology-enabled version with some variation: that is, to provide teachers and other school professionals with multiple opportunities for viewing classroom applications—models and demonstrations—of the content or pedagogy under study more effectively, conveniently, and efficiently at a lower cost.

Another specific aim of technology-enabled observations is to facilitate the transfer of content or pedagogy from knowledge to practice. Observing oneself or others applying the content or pedagogy under study allows teachers and other school professionals to see what it looks like in the real world and to problem solve when doing so by observing and exploring questions such as "How are K–12 students responding to the content or pedagogy?" "What's working and why?"

"What's not working and why?" and "What needs to be changed, modified, or eliminated altogether and why?"

Finally, when taking a modified developmental approach to technology-enabled observation, the purpose is *not* evaluation. Instead, the aim is to fuel teachers' and other school professionals' growth and development as they learn to apply the content or pedagogy under study. As a result, heightened critical reflection of teaching and learning often ensues (Liang, 2015). In this way, another purpose of professional learning through technology-enabled observations is to tailor opportunities for viewing models and demonstrations so that they address individual teachers' challenges in understanding and applying content or pedagogy under study (Liang, 2015), while also affirming their strengths in understanding and applying the content or pedagogy under study, and pinpointing needs for specific areas of growth (Hamilton, 2013).

Distinctions Between Technology-Enabled and Non-Technology-Enabled Observations

There are clearly commonalities between the technology-enabled and non-technology-enabled versions of observation. That said, important distinctions also exist:

- Traditional observation, without technology, requires on-site, face-to-face observation of the content or pedagogy under study. By contrast, technology-enabled observations of content or pedagogy allow teachers and other school professionals to observe synchronously or asynchronously (Grimm, Kaufman, & Doty, 2014) and can be carried out online or in a blended format.
- Technology-enabled observation of the content or pedagogy under study offers teachers and other school professionals a "window into practice," wherein observers can relax and observe (Zhang, Lundeberg, Koehler, & Eberhardt, 2011, p. 459). Because traditional observation requires teachers or other school professionals to actually visit the classroom, observers often feel like intruders whose mere presence interrupts instruction.
- Traditional observation is typically limited by the constraints of geography, whereas technology-enabled observation gives teachers and other school professionals global access to models and demonstrations of content and pedagogy—a consideration that can prove vital to culturally relevant instruction.
- Technology-enabled observation requires teachers and other school professionals to demonstrate some digital will and skill; traditional options do not. That said, today's early-, mid-, and late-career teachers and other school professionals possess more digital sensibilities and curiosities than ever before.

Ensuring Alignment with the Technology-Enabled Study of Content and Pedagogy

Chapter 1 described how teachers and other school professionals could go about identifying the content or pedagogy for technology-enabled study. In this chapter, we turn our focus to explaining how teachers and other school professionals can ensure alignment between technology-enabled study and technology-enabled observations. The two should support one another. In other words, the content or pedagogy selected for technology-enabled study should also be the focus of technology-enabled observations. That may sound simple and straightforward, but consideration of a few points ensures alignment between the two:

- Identify clearly what and how many exemplars (models and demonstrations of content or pedagogy) are needed. Determine how viewing the models and demonstrations over time strengthens teachers' and other school professionals' understanding of how to apply the content or pedagogy under study in the classroom.

- Secure application exemplars across varying contexts. Doing so allows teachers and other school professionals to gain a deeper understanding of the complexities encountered when applying the content or pedagogy in the classroom under differing conditions with diverse K–12 students.

- Determine the goals and objectives for the technology-enabled observations of content or pedagogy—individually or collectively. As is the case with technology-enabled study, the goals and objectives for technology-enabled observations should be tailored to meet the needs of individuals or teams of teachers and other school professionals. For example, veteran teachers could provide models and demonstrations of the content or pedagogy and request feedback from novices and the eCoach, a form of "flipped" (Grimm et al., 2014) technology-enabled observation, which we describe in the next section, whereas novices engage in self-observation and receive feedback only from the eCoach.

Tailoring the Approach and Considering the Configurations for Technology-Enabled Observations

As mentioned previously, we recommend a modified developmental approach to on-site, blended, or fully technology-enabled observation. Taking that approach, observations may be observer led or teacher led—the latter of which is referred to as a flipped model or demonstration of the content or pedagogy under study (see Grimm et al., 2014). In an observer-led approach, observers identify and observe models and demonstrations of the content or pedagogy under study, relying on guiding questions, such as "How do I carry out the content or pedagogy in the real world?" "What does it look like?" and "What does it sound like?" In the flipped variation, teachers or other school professionals ask colleagues, experts, and novices alike, as well as eCoaches or administrators, to observe and to provide feedback on their use of the content or pedagogy under study. With this approach, the guiding questions become "How am I doing in carrying out the content or pedagogy I've been studying?" "What's working well in my classroom?" "What needs to be further developed or refined?" "How are K–12 students responding?" and "How do I know?"

After ensuring alignment with the content or pedagogy under study and tailoring the approach based on teachers' and other school professionals' unique needs, it is time to determine the configurations as well as roles and responsibilities for models and observers. As we described previously, using a modified developmental approach to technology-enabled observations involves not only novices watching veterans, but also veterans viewing novices. The reciprocal nature of this approach to technology-enabled observations allows teachers and other school professionals to learn from one another. Self-observation, too, is an option. Following are several possible configurations to consider:

- *Veteran/novices.* Veteran teacher or school professional provides the model or demonstration of the content or pedagogy under study; novices observe.
- *Novice/veterans.* Novice teacher or school professional provides the model or demonstration of the content or pedagogy under study; veterans observe.
- *Novice/novices.* Novice teacher or school professional provides the model or demonstration of the content or pedagogy under study; novices observe.
- *Veteran/veterans.* Veteran teacher or school professional provides the model or demonstration of the content or pedagogy under study; veterans observe.
- *Self/self.* Individual teacher or school professional provides the self-model or demonstration of the content or pedagogy under study.

In Figure 2.1, we delineate potential roles and responsibilities for observers as well as for teachers and other school professionals who are providing the model or demonstration of the content or pedagogy under study.

A key question is, "Who should serve as the model for the fully immersed, blended, or on-site real-world classroom observation?" Peers or experts may conduct technology- or non-technology-enabled models and demonstrations. Self-modeling is another option. Regardless of who provides the models and demonstrations of

Figure 2.1

Potential Configurations, Roles, and Responsibilities for Technology-Enabled Observations

Model/ Demonstration Teacher or School Professional	Roles and Responsibilities	Observers: Teachers or Other School Professionals	Roles and Responsibilities
Veteran	• Provide aim/goal of instruction aligned with content or pedagogy under study, including social, emotional, and behavioral domains. • Provide unit/lesson plan(s) • Connect with observers online as planned, rescheduling as needed. • Carry out lesson(s) as planned, modifying as needed in accord with K–12 students' response to instruction.	Novices	• Ensure aim/goal of instruction is aligned with content or pedagogy under study, including social, emotional, and behavioral domains. • Review unit/lesson plan(s) • Connect with model/demo online as planned, rescheduling as needed. • Observe lesson(s) as planned, collecting performance data on content or pedagogy under study, including social, emotional, and behavioral domains, focusing not only on the teacher's delivery but also on students' response to instruction.
Veteran		Veterans	
Novice		Veterans	
Novice		Novices	
Self		Self	

the content or pedagogy under study, with or without technology, they may do so in an embedded or extracted manner. Although definitions of embedded and extracted professional development vary, during technology-enabled observation, we turn to those described most recently by Hamilton (2013) for clarification (also discussed in more detail later in this chapter). Simply put, *embedded* technology-enabled observations are those carried out with teachers or other school professionals who not only possess expert command of the content or pedagogy under study but also are familiar with the unique school culture, professional learning goals, and K–12 students' strengths and needs. By contrast, *extracted* technology-enabled observations are those modeled or demonstrated by experts who, although they have exemplary command of the content or pedagogy under study, are often outsiders who lack the insiders' knowledge of important district, school, or classroom context. In both cases, however, classroom application is central to the model or demonstration. In other words, even when extracted models or demonstrations serve as the source for the technology-enabled observation, they are carried out in the context of real-world classrooms.

Making Technology-Enabled Observations of Content or Pedagogy Work

When translating any approach to real-world practice, a systematic one is useful, productive, and empowering. Technology-enabled observation is no exception. The organizational framework for before, during, and after traditional observation (e.g., as is used during clinical supervision of teaching) works well when applied to the technology-enabled variation in the eCoaching continuum. This three-part organizational framework serves several important functions, including easing scheduling difficulties, minimizing technology issues, facilitating communication, maximizing transfer of learning, and decreasing feelings of stress or anxiety. Figure 2.2 illustrates the framework, elaborating on each component and distinguishing, too, between live (synchronous) and electronically archived (asynchronous) options:

- *Before*. Planning activities and scheduling logistics before undertaking technology-enabled observation sets the stage for success. Before carrying out technology-enabled observations of content or pedagogy, teachers and other school professionals should schedule the logistics, including the focused activities that take place during and after each observation session. Although this detailed planning and preparation might seem burdensome, it is not. No worries when initial plans are thwarted by technology glitches or unanticipated schedule changes. Modifying plans is relatively painless, and all can move forward with the alternatives fairly quickly.

- *During*. Engaging in focused, purposeful activities during technology-enabled observations goes a long way toward ensuring teachers and other school professionals gain deeper understanding of classroom application, which is necessary to support the transfer of newly learned content or pedagogy. The use of templates or protocols, such as those described and provided in the section that follows, often provides teachers and other school professionals with the focus and purpose they need (see Figures 2.4 and 2.5 later in the chapter). The templates or protocols we offer can and should be modified as needed.

- *After*. Providing opportunities for systematic discussion (debriefing) after observations is also important. During this time, teachers and other school professionals share examples illustrating how the content or pedagogy was used during the observations, offer insights regarding effectiveness, discuss matters of ongoing reflection, and engage in thoughtful analysis—all related to practical application of the content or pedagogy under study.

Figure 2.2

Technology-Enabled Observations of Content or Pedagogy–Organizational Framework

	Before Observation	During Observation	After Observation
Live (Synchronous)	• Identify mentor/demonstration teachers or other school professionals willing and able to provide classroom application of content or pedagogy under study, including social, emotional, and behavioral domains. • Arrange dates and times for online or blended observations. • Identify technology for online or blended observations. • Troubleshoot technology for online or blended observations. • Identify and agree upon templates or protocols to use when observing the application of content or pedagogy under study, including social, emotional, and behavioral domains.	• Experts or peers connect online with teachers or other school professionals at a predetermined time. • Experts or peers deliver model/demonstration lesson (microteaching or real world). • Teachers or other school professionals observe and take copious notes, using suggested templates (see Figures 2.4 and 2.5).	• Review observation notes. • Meet online at agreed-upon dates/times with members of PLN or PLC to debrief on the observation. • Share insights and reflections according to agreed-upon protocol. • Continue taking copious notes re: debriefing session.
Electronically Archived (Asynchronous)	• Identify electronically archived video files in which the teachers or other school professionals model/demonstrate classroom applications of content or pedagogy under study, including social, emotional, and behavioral domains. • Arrange dates and times to view electronically archived video files. • Identify technology for viewing electronically archived video files. • Troubleshoot technology for viewing electronically archived video files. • Identify and agree upon templates or protocols to use when viewing electronically archived video files.	• Teachers or other school professionals access agreed-upon electronically archived video files. • Teachers or other school professionals observe the agreed-upon archived video files and take copious notes, using suggested templates (see Figures 2.4 and 2.5).	• Same as described for live variation.

Adapted from Pattison and colleagues, 2012.

Collecting Performance Data and Using Protocols or Templates as a Guide During Technology-Enabled Observations

Why bother with collecting performance data and using templates or protocols as a guide during technology-enabled observations? Simply put, doing so transforms viewings from passive, aimless, and disengaged activities into active, purposeful, and engaged pursuits (Scott, 2013). We discuss both in the sections that follow.

Collecting Relevant Performance Data

To make technology-enabled observations as meaningful and productive as possible, teachers and other school professionals need to decide how they will collect teacher and K–12 student performance data relevant to the content or pedagogy under study. What does the teacher do and say when carrying out the content or pedagogy? How are the students responding? Data collection approaches can be simple or complex. The key to success involves ensuring that the data collected, analyzed, and discussed support deeper, richer application of the content or pedagogy under study. Grimm and her colleagues (2014) recommend generating a focus question to guide data collection, analysis, and discussion. They define a focus question as one that cannot be answered without performance-based data. Let's return to the example for technology-enabled study included in Chapter 1— using effective, culturally relevant questioning while creating and maintaining a positive, respectful, organized, and consistent environment for learning. Related focus questions could include: "During literacy instruction, how does the model of demonstration teacher use thoughtful questioning to lead the group discussion?", "What evidence is there that students are providing higher-order responses based on text-to-text connections when responding?", and "How does the teacher interact with students to establish a caring, respectful, positive classroom climate?" Corresponding data could be collected using tactics such as counting, describing, or scripting.

When collecting performance data during technology-enabled observation, teachers and other school professionals have three options: the old-school way (paper and pencil), the digital way, or the blended approach. The old-school way involves creating templates that are used to record counts, descriptions, or scripts. By comparison, the digital way allows teachers and other school professionals to use technology-enabled data collection tools, such as observation systems, apps, toolkits, and devices (for examples, see Figure 2.3). A blended approach allows for both. Teachers and other school professionals can consider the tools suggested in Figure 2.3 to get the ball rolling when collecting performance data during technology-enabled observations. Many of the observation systems and apps are part of a comprehensive teacher assessment system. Consequently, we recommend thinking about whether and how performance data collected as part of the eCoaching continuum will be integrated into the school or district approach to teacher assessment and evaluation. This issue will be discussed more fully in Chapter 6.

Using Templates or Protocols as a Guide

Although the web-based systems and apps listed in Figure 2.3 include ready-made templates and protocols, not all can be tailored to fit teachers' and other

Figure 2.3

Technology-Enabled Data Collection–Observation Systems, Apps, Toolkits, and Devices

Name	URL
Web-Based Systems and Apps	
iObservation	http://www.iobservation.com/
eWalk	http://www.media-x.com/ewalk/
Edivate	https://www.pd360.com/#login
Observe4success	https://observe4success.com/
TextExpander Touch for iPad	https://itunes.apple.com/us/app/textexpander-3-+-custom-keyboard/id917416298?mt=8
Toolkits and Devices	
Harvard University's Center for Education Policy Research *Best Foot Forward: A Toolkit for Fast-Forwarding Classroom Observations Using Video*	http://cepr.harvard.edu/video-observation-toolkit
Livescribe smartpen	https://www.livescribe.com/en-us/
TeachFX	https://teachfx.com/

school professionals' needs while conducting technology-enabled observations. Also, we echo Grimm and colleagues' (2014) caution that using templates or protocols during technology-enabled or on-site observations can feel awkward and contrived. So, why should teachers and other school professionals take the time to locate, create, or modify templates and protocols? Using templates and protocols as a guide for technology-enabled observations allows teachers and other school professionals to further refine the focus of the observations, to facilitate connections with the content or pedagogy under study, and to fuel professional learning. Figures 2.4 and 2.5 present two sample templates that can be modified as needed.

Considering Extracted and Embedded Sources for Carrying Out Technology-Enabled Observations

Let us reiterate two important points here. First, technology-enabled observation is designed to enhance teachers' understanding and application of the content or pedagogy under study. Second, technology-enabled sources include electronically

Figure 2.4

Technology-Enabled Observations–Observation Template

Technology-Enabled Observation Session:	
Demographics and Logistics	
Model/Demonstration Teacher(s) Name(s) and Grade(s)	
Observer(s)	
Date(s)/Time(s) of Model/ Demonstration Lesson(s)	
Venue	
Technology Required	
Technology Support Available	
Teaching and Learning	
Technology-Enabled Study Topic— Content or Pedagogy	
Learning Goal(s) and Objective(s) for K–12 Students	
Observation Methods	
Data Collection Methods	
Technology Required for Data Collection	
Reflection and Insights	
Ideas to Promote Transfer of Content/ Pedagogy	
What worked well?	
What evidence supports this?	
What did not work well?	
What evidence supports this?	
What should be changed and why?	
What evidence supports this?	

Adapted from Pattison and colleagues, 2012.

Figure 2.5

Technology-Enabled Observations–Observer Template

Technology-Enabled Observation Session:	
Technology-Enabled Study Topic—Content or Pedagogy, Including Social, Emotional, and Behavioral Domains	
Links to Existing Knowledge and Practice	
Existing content or pedagogical know-how, including social, emotional, and behavioral domains, related to the technology-enabled topic of study: *What do I already know about the content/ pedagogy, including social, emotional, and behavioral domains?*	
Examples of current classroom use—content or pedagogy, including social, emotional, and behavioral domains: *How am I currently using the content/pedagogy during instruction, including social, emotional, and behavioral domains?*	
Goal(s)/objective(s) for observation specific to content/pedagogy (including social, emotional, and behavioral domains) of technology-enabled study: *What will I learn through this observation that will improve my knowledge or use of the content/pedagogy, including social, emotional, and behavioral domains?*	
Technology-Enabled Observation of Content or Pedagogy, Including Social, Emotional, and Behavioral Domains	
Preparing for the Lesson	
Lesson Introduction	
Lesson Goals and Objectives	
Lesson Development	
Interaction Between Teacher(s) and K–12 Students	
K–12 Students' Response to Instruction	
Evidence of Content or Pedagogy *How was the topic for technology-enabled study included in the lesson?*	
Lesson Closure	
Instructional Assessment—Formative or Summative	

(continues)

Figure 2.5   (continued)

Technology-Enabled Observations–Observer Template

Group Debriefing and Systematic Reflection of Technology-Enabled Observation	
Points Relevant to Technology-Enabled Topic of Study—Content or Pedagogy, Including Social, Emotional, and Behavioral Domains *Strengths:* *Needs:* *Questions:*	
Sample Application(s) for Own Classroom Use: *How do I plan to use the content/pedagogy (including social, emotional, and behavioral domains) now that I have observed others?*	
Insight(s)/Reflection	

Adapted from Pattison and colleagues, 2012.

archived video repositories and synchronous (live) online visits, which may be extracted (external) or embedded (internal) in nature, as described earlier.

Electronically Archived Video Files

One extracted source for technology-enabled observation involves viewing prerecorded video models of the content or pedagogy online, via paid or no-cost repositories, such as ASCD's Professional Learning Solutions (http://www.ascd.org /professional-development.aspx), YouTube (www.youtube.com), TeacherTube (www.teachertube.com), the Council for Exceptional Children and the CEEDAR Center's High-Leverage Practices (https://highleveragepractices.org/videos/), the Teaching Channel (https://www.teachingchannel.org/), or the Research for Better Teaching Video Library (http://www.rbteach.com/products-resources /video-library/all). Relying on this source, in accord with the pre-observation plan, teachers and other school professionals observe selected video models individually or together in small groups. Then, following the observations, they engage in debriefings about the content or pedagogy under study. During debriefing, the discussion should be goal driven and theory informed (Tekkumru-Kisa & Stein, 2017). This means the debriefing discussion should provide teachers and other school professionals with opportunities to monitor, select, and connect the observation video clips with the study of theory and practice described in Chapter 1 (i.e., the what), as well as the theory of change that supports it (i.e., the why).

Let's consider again the example of effective, culturally sensitive questioning during literacy instruction. Teachers and other school professionals could select video models showcasing how to use "I wonder . . ." questions during literacy instruction and view clips, such as "Before, During and After Questions: Promoting Reading Comprehension and Critical Thinking," posted by The Balanced Literacy Diet (https://www.youtube.com/watch?v=Sd1FlXxpVIw) on YouTube. In all, 55 video models (at the time of this writing) pertaining to effective comprehension questioning during literacy instruction are available through the Balanced Literacy Diet channel on YouTube (https://www.youtube.com/watch?v=psakx RT9hdA&list=PL5178787DB725559D). Teachers and other school professionals could choose to view and debrief on those clips most closely aligned with those they are learning about during the technology-enabled e-book study of *Questioning for Classroom Discussion: Purposeful Speaking, Engaged Listening, Deep Thinking* by Jackie Acree Walsh and Beth Dankert Sattes (2015). Opportunities for personalization are also present here. Not all teachers and other school professionals need to view the same video clips. Instead, they should select those most relevant to deepening their understanding about classroom application.

An embedded variation of electronically archived video files includes those made by peers. Again, in accord with the pre-observation plan, teachers and other school professionals identify colleagues who are carrying out the content or pedagogy under study and schedule a series of lessons to record and archive electronically for later viewing individually or in small groups. Then, following the observations, they engage in debriefings about the content or pedagogy under study. This approach requires video/audio recording and digital storage devices to capture and archive the lesson series. Low- and high-tech options abound at varying price points, which will be described briefly in the section that follows and more fully in Chapter 3 as well as in the Appendix. Options for video/audio recording that may be more readily available and cost effective include mobile devices, such as smartphones, iPads, iPod Touches, electronic tablets, or desktop or laptop computers with web cameras. Alternatively, video/audio recording devices may include a Flip Video camera or a camcorder. More sophisticated and costly web-based systems—such as Edthena (https://edthena.com/) or IRIS Connect (http://www.irisconnect.com/)—are available, too, offering both video/audio recording and digital storage capabilities. Secure cloud-based systems, such as Tresorit (https://tresorit.com/) or Dropbox (https://www.dropbox.com/), are useful for electronic archival of video files. Alternatively, password-protected external hard drives, ranging from 2GB to 8TB, can be purchased through a variety of vendors, such as Amazon, Office Depot, Staples, or Costco, for the same purposes.

Yet another embedded option for viewing electronically archived video files includes those based on self-observation. Similar to the previously mentioned approaches, in accord with the pre-observation plan, teachers and other school professionals identify when they are carrying out the content or pedagogy under study in their own classrooms, recording and electronically archiving the lesson series for later viewing. Depending on comfort level and trust, the lesson series is debriefed individually, with an eCoach, or in small groups. This approach, too, requires video/audio recording and digital storage devices to capture and archive the lesson series. That said, because self-observation can be too close to the bone for some teachers and other school professionals, we suggest proceeding with thought and care.

In "What You Learn When You See Yourself Teach," Jim Knight (2014) offers six guidelines when using video for self-observation:

- Because watching one's classroom video footage can be difficult, teachers and other school professionals should ensure a psychologically safe climate, characterized by trust, respect, humility, and support.
- The decision to use video self-observation should be made by individual teachers and other school professionals, rather than through a mandate handed down by eCoaches or administrators. Doing so helps to create and sustain a psychologically safe climate.
- The complexities inherent in teaching and learning are best supported by fostering intrinsic motivation—a deep, driving desire to improve—rather than by imposing extrinsic motivation, which is fueled by exerting outward pressure and embarrassment.
- Clear policies should be in place to ensure that teachers and other school professionals are in charge of the video files. The aim is self-observation, so that the individual teacher or school professional retains decision-making authority when it comes to whether colleagues, eCoaches, or administrators share viewing privileges.
- eCoaches and administrators should model self-observation, showcasing their own video files to demonstrate how they are using content or pedagogy under study to improve their professional practice.
- Efforts to promote self-observation should begin slowly and on a small scale. Trying to go too quickly with too many teachers or other school professionals often results in sloppy, fragmented implementation, which in turn yields lackluster results, resulting in frustration, failure, and premature abandonment.

Thoughtful consideration of Knight's guidelines ensures that the power of profound professional learning through technology-enabled self-observation remains intact.

Synchronous (Live) Online Observations

Not too long ago, the thought of watching colleagues or experts model or demonstrate the content or pedagogy under study online would have been considered too futuristic. In the digital age, that is no longer the case. Thanks to online videoconferencing platforms, such as Google Hangouts (https://hangouts.google.com/), Skype (https://www.skype.com/), and Zoom (https://zoom.us/), which have become personal and professional staples in many homes and businesses, online observations can be conducted any time with ease in real time (live), using embedded or extracted models. Doing so offers teachers and other school professionals the option for real-time viewings when schedules permit, while eliminating barriers, such as time and distance, that often plague on-site observations.

As was the case with the asynchronous sources described previously, when opting for the live version, teachers and other school professionals use the pre-observation plan to select and observe models/demonstrations, illustrating classroom application of the content or pedagogy, online in real time—individually or in small groups. Then, following the live, online observations, they engage in debriefings about the content or pedagogy under study using the same online videoconferencing platform they used for observations. The basic technologies needed for carrying out live, online observations include mobile devices, such as smartphones or tablets, or laptop/desktop computers with internal or external web cameras. Online videoconferencing platforms such as Google Hangouts, Skype, or Zoom also need to be downloaded and in good operating order. Teachers and other school professionals need to decide in advance whether the live, online observations will be captured and archived electronically for later viewing. If so, additional technologies, such as screen or video call recording software/applications, are required. Again, we describe these and other options briefly in the next section, and they will be described more fully in Chapter 3 as well as in the Appendix.

Considering the Technology Options for Carrying Out Technology-Enabled Observations

In addition to considering sources for technology-enabled observations, teachers and other school professionals need to review the technology options available for carrying out, recording, and archiving remote observations.

Remote Classroom Viewing with or Without Video Recording

- *Live streaming.* Some teachers and other school professionals might wish to explore live streaming as a means to carry out synchronous technology-enabled observations. Live streaming typically involves surveillance-type video camera systems in classrooms. Although this might conjure a negative "Big Brother" connotation, we encourage teachers and other school professionals to reserve judgment and to explore some of the options. Through Telestream's (http://www.telestream.net/) guide entitled *Classroom Live Streaming on a Budget*, teachers and other school professionals can obtain information about necessary technology; components such as cameras, microphones, audio mixers, and computer hardware and software; as well as information about the cost of each component, including options for live streaming service (i.e., where the live stream will be sent) available from YouTube and IBM Watson Media (https://video.ibm.com/).

- *Laptop or desktop computers*. Most teachers and other school professionals have laptop or desktop computers in their classrooms. So, it makes sense to use them to carry out technology-enabled observations. PC or Apple platforms can be used for conducting remote observations, synchronously or asynchronously, as long as they have webcam and audio capabilities.

- *Mobile devices*. Many teachers and other school professionals have access to mobile devices such as smartphones or tablets. These devices make conducting remote, synchronous or asynchronous, classroom observations easy, too. Cameras and audio are required for viewing purposes.

- *Webcams and microphones*. If computers or mobile devices lack sufficient internal camera/video or audio capabilities, then it becomes necessary to add them as external accessories. Teachers and other school professionals can do so by perusing options and purchasing accessories through popular vendors, such as Amazon or eBay.

- *Online videoconferencing platforms*. Online telecommunications technologies allow teachers and other school professionals to visit classrooms in real time by transmitting audio and video remotely from different locations. Online videoconferencing platforms are available that range from no or low cost to high cost. Examples include Google Hangouts, Skype, Zoom, OoVoo (http://www.oovoo.com/), and Go To Meeting (http://www.gotomeeting.com/). One feature teachers and other school professionals need to consider is whether multiple observers will be viewing the real-time classroom applications of content or pedagogy from different remote locations. Some platforms offer this as an option for an added cost, while others do not. As we noted earlier, another feature that warrants consideration is whether teachers and other school professionals wish to electronically capture and archive the live, online observation sessions for later viewing and debriefing. If so, apps need to be added to protect private recording and controlled sharing. Popular examples include Snagit (https://www.techsmith.com/screen-capture.html), Camtasia (https://www .techsmith.com/video-editor.html), and Apowersoft (http://www.apowersoft .com/free-online-screen-recorder). Some platforms, such as Skype, also offer plugins, which include Pamela (http://www.pamela.biz/en/products/) for PC or Call Recorder (http://www.ecamm.com/mac/callrecorder/) for Mac.

- *Video-based online professional development systems.* Video-based online systems such as Edthena or IRIS Connect offer teachers and other school professionals learning and collaboration systems that allow for private video capture, upload, editing, annotation, and sharing. Packages can be customized to meet differing needs and budgets. Through these secure web-based platforms, teachers and other school professionals access integrated video technology for planning, reflection, and analysis before, during, and after observations—all of which can be done individually, with an eCoach, or with selected colleagues in a private online professional learning community.

- *Swivl* (https://cloud.swivl.com/). Swivl is a robotic platform for video. Teachers and other school professionals can use Swivl for remote classroom observations as well as video capture. To connect online, teachers or other school professionals need to use Skype or Google Hangouts, both of which are Swivl compatible. The Swivl base serves as a dock for iOS mobile devices, Android mobile devices, or video cameras. Teachers and other school professionals insert a device, such as a smartphone or tablet, in the robotic platform, which rotates by tracking a lanyard the teacher wears during classroom instruction. Similarly, Revolve Robotics (https://www.revolverobotics.com/) offers easy-to-use robotic-based technology for carrying out video calls when observing from a distance.

- *Wearable digital camcorders.* Body-worn camcorders allow for hands-free, real-time, point-of-view video/audio streaming in the classroom as well as immediate sharing and video capture. Wearable mini mobile camcorders vary in size and price. Options include camcorders embedded in eyeglasses or in buttons and necklaces, as well as those that can be snapped on ball caps, headbands, or shirts. Teachers and other school professionals can view demos, review capabilities, and purchase wearable camcorders through online vendors such as Pivothead (http://www.pivothead.com/), Soloshot (https://shop.soloshot.com/), GoPro (https://gopro.com/), or MeCam (http://mecam.me/).

- *Flip Video cameras.* Although Flip Video cameras have been discontinued and largely replaced by mini camcorders and mobile devices, some people still prefer them for video capture because of their ease of use and simple USB interface with laptop or desktop computers. Teachers and other school professionals can purchase Flip Video cameras online through vendors such as Amazon or eBay.

Video Storage

When teachers and other school professionals electronically capture synchronous or asynchronous observations, they also need to consider how they will archive the observations for later viewing. External hard drives or cloud- or web-based options are available. Cost and storage capability (an important consideration, especially for large video files) vary.

- *External hard drives.* Teachers and other school professionals can purchase external computer hard drives, ranging from 2GB to 8TB, through a variety of vendors, such as Amazon, Office Depot, Staples, or Costco. External drives can be password protected and housed in locked offices to minimize risk and maximize privacy and confidentiality of the video files.
- *Cloud- or web-based repositories.* Secure cloud-based systems, such as Tresorit (https://tresorit.com/) or Dropbox (https://www.dropbox.com/), as well as private web-based channels, such as those available through YouTube, offer alternatives to external hard drives for electronic archival of video files. That said, some teachers and other school professionals might find cloud- or web-based systems troubling when it comes to ensuring privacy and confidentiality.

Video Viewing

- *Private conference room, classroom, or office.* Private, confidential venues are a must for teachers and other school professionals to view live or electronically archived observations as well as during debriefings of the same. Teachers and other school professionals need to think ahead during pre-observation planning and activities to identify such venues. Conference rooms, classrooms, and offices suffice as long as privacy can be maintained.
- *Laptop or desktop computer.* Although mobile devices could be used to view live or electronically archived observations, we do not recommend them because of the small screen size. Instead, we suggest opting for the largest screen possible, which is often available on a desktop or laptop computer or by adding an even larger monitor as a second screen.

Determining Which Technology Sources and Options Are the Best Fit for Observations

As was the case with technology-enabled study, because many varied technology sources and options are available to support technology-enabled observations, it is important for teachers and other school professionals to dedicate some time to determining which offer the best fit based on current and future professional learning needs. To assist teachers and other school professionals in determining goodness of fit, we offer guiding questions in the next several sections. Taking time to work through these questions goes a long way toward saving time and money, and preventing future frustration. That's time well spent, indeed!

Readiness of Observers and Model/Demonstration Teachers

- How comfortable are teachers and other professionals with the idea of using technology to observe themselves, one another, or expert models as they carry out the content or pedagogy under study in classrooms?
- What are the training needs of teachers and other school professionals related to carrying out high-quality technology-enabled observations? What do they already know? What do they need to know? What is the budget and timeline for training?
- Do guidelines and policies exist regarding privacy and confidentiality of technology-enabled approaches to observations, or do they need to be developed?

Time, Money, and Capabilities

- What is the available budget?
- What technologies are already available? What technologies need to be purchased?
- Are extracted video files, illustrating models and demonstrations of content or pedagogy available for free or is a fee required, such as a subscription cost?
- How long are the extracted or embedded video files?
- What is the cost of the technology required for synchronous or asynchronous observations?
- What bells and whistles are included in the technology for synchronous or asynchronous observations (e.g., remote control camera, zoom lens, video-editing capabilities)?
- In terms of maintenance and sustainability, how often are upgrades available and at what cost?

Quality of Sources

The questions provided in this section are adapted, in part, from Sherman, Dlott, Bamford, and McGivern (2003).

- Is the content or pedagogy modeled or demonstrated in the synchronous or asynchronous observations appropriate for the needs of the target audience— teachers and other school professionals engaged in professional learning? In other words, is it aligned with their technology-enabled study?
- Are the models and demonstrations of content or pedagogy culturally and ethnically sensitive, free of bias, and reflective of diverse audiences?

- Are the goals and objectives of the technology-enabled observations clear, challenging, and appropriate for the teachers and other school professionals who are viewing?
- Are the technology-enabled observations followed by debriefings and discussions about how the content or pedagogy under study can be applied in different classrooms?
- What is the quality of the video and the audio? Is the audio distorted or garbled? Is the video pixelated?
- Is too much polish evident in the electronically archived video files? In other words, have they been edited too much? (Moon & Michaels, 2016)
- Do the synchronous or asynchronous technology-enabled observations selected reflect a real-world case study approach to the transfer of content or pedagogy, rather than a sanitized, one-shot, best-practice example? (Moon & Michaels, 2016)

Technology Support

- What district and school technology supports are in place to support teachers and other school professionals as they carry out technology-enabled observations?
- How accessible are district and school technology support personnel when teachers and other school professionals are carrying out technology-enabled observations?
- What technology troubleshooting and support are available through the contracted vendors, and how will that be coordinated with that which is typically available through the school or district? For example, should difficulties arise during technology-enabled observations, should teachers or other school professionals contact the school or district support personnel first or the vendor?

Building on the Instructional Plan for Technology-Enabled Observations

Chapter 1 introduced the need for teachers and other school professionals to put together a blueprint, referred to as an instructional plan, as a guide for engaging in technology-enabled study. In this chapter, we stress the importance of teachers and other school professionals building on the instructional plan. In doing so, they delineate how technology-enabled observations will be embedded to facilitate the transfer of new knowledge to the classroom. Using the example from Chapter 1, we illustrate how this can be accomplished by highlighting in gray the relevant parts of the plan in Figure 2.6. Taking a few minutes

Figure 2.6

Instructional Design Plan for Technology-Enabled Study and Observation–Questioning Example

Guiding Questions	Sample Instructional Design Planning for Technology-Enabled Study and Observation of Specific Content or Pedagogy
What is the topic and purpose of study?	Develop or refine pedagogical knowledge in four areas: • *Effective questioning* to enhance students' comprehension during literacy instruction • *Two of Deborah Ball's 19 high-leverage practices related specifically to questioning*—leading a group discussion and eliciting and interpreting individual students' thinking • *Culturally responsive questioning* to meet the needs of diverse students • One of the Council for Exceptional Children's (CEC's) high-leverage social, emotional, and behavioral practices—HLP #7: Establish a Consistent, Organized, and Respectful Learning Environment

Why is the topic of study important?	• The school improvement plan
	  ◊ 100 percent of students will achieve proficiency in literacy.
	• District student achievement data
	  ◊ Currently, student performance data confirm many students, especially those who are diverse, are not achieving proficiency in literacy.
	• Classroom/teacher performance data
	  ◊ Currently, classroom observational data confirm most teachers are using lower-order questioning and minimal discussion during literacy instruction. High-performing students respond frequently and accurately.
	• Pedagogical research
	  ◊ Institute for Education Sciences (IES) researchers Matsumura and colleagues (2013) found the quality of classroom text discussions, including questioning, mediated students' reading achievement.
	• Social/emotional/behavioral research
	  ◊ Results from meta-analytic studies have confirmed many varied benefits for students whose teachers provided social, emotional, and behavioral supports, including 11 percentile point gains in academic achievement (Mahoney et al., 2018).

What is already known about the topic of study?	Based on theory-of-change/logic-model planning, teachers and other school professionals realize that if they want to increase all K–12 students' proficiency in literacy, they need to develop in-depth knowledge of effective questioning practices as well as how to make questions culturally responsive to their diverse students while creating and maintaining a positive, respectful, organized, and consistent environment for learning.
What content or information is needed to transfer the topic of study to the classroom?	Teachers and other school professionals need to understand and include in their lesson planning for literacy instruction • A range of effective questions from lower to higher order that support rich thoughtful discussion • Two of Deborah Ball's 19 high-leverage practices related specifically to questioning—leading a group discussion and eliciting and interpreting individual students' thinking • Culturally responsive questions • One of the CEC's high-leverage social, emotional, and behavioral practices—HLP #7: Establish a Consistent, Organized, and Respectful Learning Environment
How will technology be used to support the topic of study and observation of the same?	• *E-book study.* Engage in e-book study of effective questioning tactics, using *Questioning for Classroom Discussion* (Walsh & Sattes, 2015). • *Electronic discussion guide.* Download the Study Guide for *Questioning for Classroom Discussion* from http://www.ascd.org/publications/books/115012/chapters/An-ASCD-Study-Guide-for-Questioning-for-Classroom-Discussion@-Purposeful-Speaking,-Engaged-Listening,-Deep-Thinking.aspx • *PDF document.* Use the description of HLP #7 from the CEC's high-leverage social, emotional, and behavioral practices as a study aid (https://highleveragepractices.org/wp-content/uploads/2017/06/SEBshort.pdf).

(continues)

Figure 2.6   (continued)

Instructional Design Plan for Technology-Enabled Study and Observation–Questioning Example

Guiding Questions	Sample Instructional Design Planning for Technology-Enabled Study and Observation of Specific Content or Pedagogy
	• *Reputable websites.* Bookmark three websites: 　◇ University of Michigan's Teaching Works (http://www.teachingworks.org/work-of-teaching/high-leverage-practices) to review two of Deborah Ball's 19 high-leverage practices related specifically to questioning—leading a group discussion and eliciting and interpreting individual students' thinking 　◇ *Create Success!* by Kadhir Rajagopal (http://www.ascd.org/publications/books/111022/chapters/Culturally-Responsive-Instruction.aspx) to study Chapter 1, "Culturally Responsive Instruction," focusing on the section pertaining to questioning 　◇ The CEC's high-leverage practices to review HLP #7: Establish a Consistent, Organized, and Respectful Learning Environment (https://highleveragepractices.org/wp-content/uploads/2017/06/SEBshort.pdf and https://highleveragepractices.org/about-hlps/) • *Professional online community platforms.* Use edWeb (https://home.edweb.net/) or PBworks (http://www.pbworks.com/) to create an online PLC for weekly e-book study discussion. • *Social media.* Follow Teaching Works on Twitter (https://twitter.com/) and Facebook (https://www.facebook.com/). Engage in weekly Twitter chats using #culturallyresponsivequestioning, #questioningforclassroomdiscussion, and #socialemotionallearning. • *Online video conferencing + robotic platform for video streaming and capture.* Use Skype (https://www.skype.com) with Call Recorder (http://www.ecamm.com/mac/callrecorder/) and Swivl (https://cloud.swivl.com/) to observe and electronically capture models and demonstrations of teachers using effective, culturally sensitive questioning during literacy instruction. • *YouTube.* Teachers and other school professionals select video models showcasing how to use "I wonder . . ." questions during literacy instruction and view clips, such as "Before, During and After Questions: Promoting Reading Comprehension and Critical Thinking," posted by The Balanced Literacy Diet (https://www.youtube.com/watch?v=Sd1FlXxpVIw) on YouTube. In all, there are 55 video models pertaining to effective comprehension questioning during literacy instruction available through The Balanced Literacy Diet channel on YouTube (https://www.youtube.com/watch?v=psakxRT9hdA&list=PL5178787DB725559D) that could be reviewed for models and demonstrations showcasing effective, culturally relevant questioning.
How will participants demonstrate understanding of the topic of study and the models and demonstrations observed?	• Create low-stakes chapter quizzes for e-book study using Google Docs (https://www.google.com/docs/about/) or SurveyMonkey (https://www.surveymonkey.com/). • Design and deliver one or two interactive presentations on culturally responsive questioning and two of Deborah Ball's 19 high-leverage practices related specifically to questioning—leading a group discussion and eliciting and interpreting individual students' thinking—with peers/colleagues using Pear Deck (https://www.peardeck.com/), Nearpod (https://nearpod.com/), or Classkick (https://classkick.com/). • Earn digital badges/microcredentials for effective questioning, culturally responsive questioning, two of Deborah Ball's 19 high-leverage practices related specifically to questioning—leading a group discussion and eliciting and interpreting individual students' thinking—and one of the CEC's high-leverage practices (i.e., HLP #7: Establish a Consistent, Organized, and Respectful Learning Environment)—via ASCD or Digital Promise (http://digitalpromise.org/initiative/educator-micro-credentials/).

to add this information also helps teachers and other school professionals ensure alignment between technology-enabled study and technology-enabled observations.

Creating Norms That Support Technology-Enabled Observations

Carrying out technology-enabled observations as part of the eCoaching continuum requires teachers, other school professionals, coaches, administrators, and other key stakeholders to think differently about professional development. As was the case with technology-enabled study, if technology-enabled observations are to be embraced, institutionalized, and valued, then some thought and effort must be dedicated to establishing and sustaining new norms. When creating new norms, all teachers and other school professionals need to weigh in. In Chapter 1, the steps and some technology tools for undertaking this process were outlined. In the sections that follow, we describe a few issues, unique to technology-enabled observations, that teachers and other school professionals should ponder when discussing and generating new norms. If norms are not developed and maintained, teachers and other school professionals are at risk for becoming self-absorbed and mistrustful of administrators and colleagues. Under these less-than-ideal circumstances, professional paralysis often erupts, leaving teachers and other school professionals unable to focus on improving their own content knowledge and pedagogical know-how, let alone their students' learning (Scott, 2013).

Psychological Safety

We agree with Knight (2014): observing oneself, colleagues, or even experts can induce anxiety in even the most experienced, capable, and confident teachers or other school professionals. The demands of not only learning new content or pedagogy but also figuring out how to implement it in the classroom can leave early-, mid-, and late-career professionals feeling overwhelmed, frustrated, and inadequate. As we mentioned previously, it is important for teachers and other school professionals to intentionally create a psychologically safe climate. Pattison and his colleagues (2012) found that although medical students reported fear of criticism as common during peer observations, those feelings were mitigated by opportunities to dialogue before the observations—often in as few as two meetings. Consequently, scheduling time for teachers and other school professionals who are modeling or demonstrating the content or pedagogy to meet with observers may go a long way toward promoting trust and alleviating fear.

Privacy and Confidentiality

Although surveillance cameras have become the norm in 21st century schools and society, when it comes to using cameras for professional development purposes, such as technology-enabled observations, concerns about privacy and confidentiality are bound to erupt (Liang, 2015). Rather than dismissing these apprehensions, teachers, other school professionals, administrators, and eCoaches need to address them fully. We suggest the first step in doing so is to partner with school district counsel to review relevant district or school policies. Such policies need to address privacy and confidentiality for both teachers and students. For instance, policies should address specifically why, how, with whom, and under what conditions live and electronically archived video data will be shared. If policies do not exist, then a task force should be assembled to create them in cooperation with technology support professionals and school district counsel.

Growth Mindset

Achieving the promise of technology-enabled observations for improving teaching and learning outcomes requires teachers and other school professionals to shift from isolated, siloed professional development practices to unified, job-embedded approaches wherein everyone is a learner (Coggshall, Rasmussen, Colton, Milton, & Jacques, 2012; Hamilton, 2013).

Creating a culture for professional development wherein teachers and other school professionals adopt and embrace a job-embedded, learner-centered approach means that administrators and eCoaches need to "walk the talk," routinely modeling how they are using technology-enabled observations to accomplish their professional learning goals. Also, administrators and eCoaches need to refrain from using technology-enabled observations as a "Big Brother" tactic to spy on, gather evidence, and remove struggling teachers or other school professionals. Finally, to truly embrace a job-embedded, learner-centered approach, teachers and other school professionals, including administrators and eCoaches, need to guard against opting for models/demonstrations and videos that are "too polished" (Moon & Michaels, 2016). Instead, they need to plan for and carry out a series of models/ demonstrations or video-based observation sessions wherein the "messiness" of teaching and learning is captured and opportunities for in-depth debriefing and reflection are the norm, rather than the exception.

Contemplating the Benefits and Cautions Associated with Technology-Enabled Observations

As with any approach to professional learning, there are benefits and cautions associated with technology-enabled observations. Here we review the most salient to help teachers and other school professionals make informed decisions about the speed, scope, and scale with which they move forward with technology-enabled observations.

Benefits

Benefits of technology-enabled observations are similar to those associated with traditional on-site observations. For instance, Hamilton (2013) reported that peer-to-peer observations (P2POs) resulted in increased respect for colleagues that allowed observers to "get into the heads of" those who provided the models and demonstrations of content and pedagogy. Improvements in professionals' content knowledge and pedagogy have been reported, too (Pattison et al., 2012).

Similarities aside, some compelling distinctions warrant mention. When opting for technology-enabled observations, teachers and coaches are no longer limited by the constraints imposed by time and distance (Rock et al., 2009; Rock et al., 2012). For example, remote observations, whether synchronous or asynchronous, offer teachers and other school professionals broader access to models and demonstrations of the content or pedagogy under study. They can access experts or colleagues located across the building, district, state, region, country, or globe. Also, technology-enabled observations allow teachers and other school professionals to electronically capture and archive video models/demonstrations, which provides ongoing access for repeated analysis and reflection. Liang (2015) pointed out that technology-enabled observations result in decreased reactivity, meaning teachers and students are less likely to change their behavior because observers are no longer physically present in the classroom. Similarly, observing remotely typically reduces interruptions to classroom instruction. Knight (2014) reported yet another advantage: objectivity improved during analysis and debriefing because discussions were grounded in video and other performance-related data, rather than on individuals' recollections of what transpired during teaching and learning. Technology-enabled observations, such as those based on electronically archived video files, offer teachers greater convenience in that repeated viewings can take place wherever and whenever they choose, insofar as privacy and confidentiality can be preserved.

Although initial investments in technology may appear prohibitive, costs can be reduced over time—especially when efficiency and effectiveness are considered. For example, the time and money spent in travel to classroom sites for ongoing observations may be offset by technology-enabled alternatives. Moreover, storing electronically archived video models on an external hard drive or a secure cloud server creates a rich database of models/demonstrations that teachers, school professionals, and eCoaches can view and share confidentially and privately with others as needed to strengthen and refine transfer of professional learning to the classroom.

Cautions

Technology-enabled observations require teachers and other school professionals to possess differing levels of technological know-how, including securing online videoconferencing accounts and operating equipment. For instance, teachers and other school professionals must learn how to use and adjust the web camera to acquire the best viewing angle. Adjusting the camera angle is important because it impacts the observer's ability to adequately see and hear the teacher and the students in the classroom. Although technology-enabled peer observations may alleviate the intrusiveness of having adults (observers) physically present in the classroom, students should be acclimated to having technological equipment, including video cameras or webcams, in the classroom. Also, equipment failures and connection problems can occur at any time. Although minimal time is lost when using online videoconferencing platforms, teachers must possess troubleshooting know-how, demonstrate flexibility, and consider alternative options in the event of technology issues (e.g., rescheduling for another date and time).

Also, school and district policies for addressing issues such as privacy, confidentiality, and power differentials are a must. When paired with collegial discussion and administrative reassurance, these policies go a long way toward mitigating fear and anxiety (Liang, 2015; Pattison et al., 2012). In describing potential benefits, we noted that cost could be a drawback, albeit initially. Consequently, school and district budgets for the eCoaching continuum, in general, and technology-enabled observations, specifically, must be considered. Doing so requires teachers and other school professionals to think not only about initial purchase prices but also about ongoing costs for updates, technology support, renewal licenses, maintenance, repairs, and so forth. In their Education Week article "Is Today's Video-Based Teacher PD Missing the Picture?" Jean Moon and Sarah Michaels (2016) point out that video models and demonstrations can be "too polished," resulting in superficial professional learning. Moreover, if electronically archived video files are edited too heavily, they can be "leading" and promote misunderstanding of the content or pedagogy under study (Moon & Michaels, 2016). The absence of existing design criteria for what constitutes "educative" technology-enabled observations, too, means that teachers and other school professionals need to rely on professional learning data to guide decision making (Moon & Michaels, 2016). Finally, technology-enabled observations, whether synchronous or asynchronous, present some viewing limitations. Observers cannot always see all students, cannot smell the classroom, and cannot always control the camera (Liang, 2015).

Translating the eCoach's Role into Action During Technology-Enabled Observations

As pointed out in Chapter 1, the eCoach plays a vital and unique role in each of the four components of the eCoaching continuum. Whether teams of teachers and school professionals or individuals undertake technology-enabled observations, we offer a list of possible roles and responsibilities eCoaches could shoulder to foster learning transfer. To do so, eCoaches need administrator and colleague support, including dedicated release time, clearly delineated job roles and responsibilities, and ongoing training and professional development.

- Take a leadership role in overcoming known obstacles by assessing readiness for technology-enabled observations, creating time frames for technology-enabled observations, providing resources to increase knowledge of technology-enabled observations, securing administrative support, enhancing access to technology, assisting in scheduling, and finding additional financial support when needed.
- Assist in identifying extracted or embedded models or demonstrations relevant to the content or pedagogy under study.
- Offer guidance on determining availability of technology-enabled options, equipment, software, apps, and so forth that support observations of content or pedagogy.
- Coordinate evaluation of technology-related options, equipment, software, and apps, and consider goodness of fit, using guiding questions.
- Build on the instructional design plan for technology-enabled observations and modify as needed.
- Co-create norms for technology-enabled observations.
- Partner with school librarians, technology support specialists, and legal counsel to provide training in relevant policies, such as privacy and confidentiality.
- Locate, adapt, or generate templates or protocols for focused observations.
- Develop digital badges or microcredentials.

- Create modules for training on new and existing technologies and approaches that support technology-enabled observations.
- Monitor progress of technology-enabled observations and assess professional learning.

Moreover, just as teachers and other school professionals need to use technology to observe relevant content and pedagogy, so do eCoaches. For example, returning to the example provided in Chapter 1, after viewing the "Coaching Conversations" module in Coursera (https://www.coursera.org/specializations /coaching-skills-manager), eCoaches could electronically archive debriefing observations that included coaching conversations with teachers and other school professionals and view them to self-assess learning transfer.

Revisiting Important Ideas

In this chapter, we've described in detail how to carry out technology-enabled observations of content and pedagogy—what and how to teach, as well as how to reach and teach the whole child. We've also pointed out why doing so is important, as well as the known benefits and cautions. Before moving on to Chapter 3, let's take a minute to review the important ideas we've shared:

- Clarify and communicate the purposes for carrying out technology-enabled observations of the content or pedagogy under study, which include reaching and teaching the whole child.
- Take a developmental approach, opting for both embedded and extracted models and demonstrations.
- Ensure alignment between technology-enabled study and technology-enabled observations.
- Tailor the technology-enabled observations to teachers and other school professionals' unique learning needs about the content or pedagogy, including social, emotional, and behavioral domains aimed at teaching and reaching the whole child.
- Use differing configurations comprising veterans, novices, and self as models/ demonstrations and observers. Be sure, too, to define the roles and responsibilities for each.
- Make technology-enabled observations work, in part by adopting a three-part organizational framework comprising focused activities before, during, and after the technology-enabled observations.
- Collect performance data and use protocols and templates as a guide to focus learning transfer and gain deeper meaning from technology-enabled observations.

- Make use of electronically archived as well as live, online observations.
- Consider equipment, software, apps, and so forth in accord with budgets and professional learning needs.
- Determine the best technology fit, in part based on answers to guiding questions.
- Build on the blueprint, also referred to as the instructional plan, developed in Chapter 1 by adding the technology-enabled observations that support the content or pedagogy under study, including social, emotional, and behavioral domains aimed at reaching and teaching the whole child.
- Create and sustain norms that support technology-enabled observations, including fostering psychological safety, ensuring privacy and confidentiality, and embracing a growth mindset.
- Contemplate the benefits and cautions carefully and make decisions about how to proceed with technology-enabled observations accordingly.
- Ensure that the eCoach's roles and responsibilities are clearly articulated and supported by administrators, teachers, and other school professionals during technology-enabled observations.

To help prevent teachers and other school professionals from becoming overwhelmed by the information we've presented in this chapter, we offer an At-a-Glance Checklist. As noted in Chapter 1, using the checklist will empower teachers and other school professionals to move forward with technology-enabled observations effectively and efficiently. Realizing the power of technology-enabled observations requires that you understand 10 simple things!

AT-A-GLANCE CHECKLIST

Preparing for Successful Technology-Enabled Observations

☐ The purpose for technology-enabled observations is clear and differentiated.

☐ The content or pedagogy, including social, emotional, and behavioral domains, selected for technology-enabled observations aligns with that selected for technology-enabled study.

☐ The three-part organizational framework—before, during, and after—is developed and used, in part to make technology-enabled observations work.

☐ Differing configurations—novice, veteran, self—and contexts are used as models and demonstrations for technology-enabled observations.

☐ Performance data are collected and templates and protocols are used during technology-enabled observations to promote transfer and deepen learning.

☐ Technology-enabled options, equipment, software, apps, and so on are identified based on goodness of fit.

☐ The instructional design plan is expanded to guide technology-enabled study and observations and can be modified as needed.

☐ Norms for technology-enabled observations are established and supported.

☐ Benefits and cautions of technology-enabled observations are considered, and choices are made accordingly.

☐ eCoaches' roles and responsibilities are clearly articulated and supported.

3

Technology-Enabled
One-on-One, In-Ear Coaching
Framing Professional Development
in Real-Time Instruction

Marcia Rock and Kara B. Holden

What we want for our students we should want for our teachers:
learning, challenge, support, and respect. —Andy Hargreaves (n.d.)

How can teachers and other school professionals use technology effectively and efficiently to provide one-on-one, in-ear coaching aimed not only at strengthening their content knowledge and pedagogical know-how but also at improving their K–12 students' performance?

Understanding the Purpose of Using Technology to Carry Out One-on-One, In-Ear Coaching

No doubt, targeting content and pedagogy for in-depth study and observation allows teachers and other school professionals to bolster existing knowledge. Translating knowledge of what and how to teach, however, requires different tactics—namely, those that promote transfer. One-on-one (1:1), real-time, in-ear coaching is one such tactic.

Practice and Carry Out the Content

The primary purpose for using technology during real-time eCoaching is to provide teachers and other school professionals opportunities to carry out the content or pedagogy they have studied and observed, with immediate feedback from an online, in-ear coach during classroom instruction. Simply put, when it comes to transfer techniques, 1:1, real-time, in-ear coaching allows an eCoach to provide more support to more teachers when it counts the most—at the point of performance. An effective and efficient transfer tactic, no doubt!

Immediate, Discreet Feedback

Using a few simple technology components, such as a Bluetooth earpiece, a computer or a mobile device, a camera, and an online videoconferencing platform, the eCoach provides immediate, discreet feedback that only the teacher or other school professional can hear. The discreet nature of the immediate real-time feedback provided by the eCoach is intended not only to facilitate transfer of learning to practice but also to empower teachers and other school professionals. For instance, the Hawthorne effect, more commonly referred to as the observer effect, is greatly diminished by not having a coach physically present in the classroom. Also, the teacher's self-efficacy, which Bandura (1997) described as an individual's belief in his own ability to succeed, is cultivated. In this context, we mean that the teacher's belief, motivation, and willingness to carry out newly learned content or pedagogy is enhanced when he does so within an authentic classroom setting, experiencing immediate success with K–12 students' learning or behavior along with immediate encouragement from the eCoach.

Share Authentically in Instructional Leadership

Another purpose for engaging in 1:1, real-time eCoaching is to provide teachers and other school professionals with opportunities to share authentically in instructional leadership. Shared instructional leadership involves the eCoach and the teacher or other school professional working collaboratively to carry out newly learned content or pedagogy in the classroom to maximize instructional effectiveness, enhance an empowered classroom learning environment, and improve student outcomes (Rock, Zigmond, Gregg, & Gable, 2011). That said, opportunities for shared instructional leadership are abundant throughout the eCoaching continuum, not just during 1:1 coaching. What is unique about shared leadership during technology-enabled real-time coaching is that it provides the eCoach and the teacher or other school professional with opportunities to engage not only in joint lesson delivery but also in collaborative lesson planning. This shared approach allows teachers and other school professionals to coconstruct effective instruction and then to codevelop situational awareness with an eCoach (Rock et al., 2011). In this way, the eCoach plays two vital roles. First, he or she partners in planning lessons that incorporate newly learned content or pedagogy. Second, she provides immediate feedback that focuses, in part, on describing how students are responding to the newly incorporated content or pedagogy. This approach helps the teacher or other school professional to carry out what's working well while immediately modifying what's not. Again, this shared focus on proactive lesson planning, coupled with real-time feedback during teaching and learning, is purposeful. It is focused specifically on improving student outcomes—a hallmark of shared instructional leadership.

An Educational Engineer in the Ear

A related purpose unique to technology-enabled, real-time coaching is that the approach provides teachers and other school professionals with an educational engineer in the ear—again, at the point of performance (Rock et al., 2011). Why is an educational engineer in the ear needed? Transferring content or pedagogy that has been studied extensively and even observed repeatedly over time into real-world classrooms rarely goes smoothly for teachers and other school professionals. In many instances, what has been studied and observed is the ideal. Yet, when translating content or pedagogy, teachers and other school professionals are often faced with myriad seemingly insurmountable realities that are at odds with the ideal. During 1:1, in-ear coaching, an eCoach often purposefully and gently guides the teacher or other school professional in navigating these tensions in real time.

The eCoach offers an outside eye and ear by naming and noticing potential problems and pitfalls, suggesting approaches to avoiding or overcoming them, and describing how students are responding to instruction. Let's continue with the example of effective questioning, in particular the high-leverage practice of actively engaging all students during group discussion. For instance, the eCoach might say, "Oh, my. We've lost most of the students. A few are asleep, many are engaging in off-topic conversations with their neighbors, some are doodling, and only two have raised a hand to answer questions. Let's try a strategy we learned through our study and observation of Walsh and Sattes (2015) *Questioning for Classroom Discussion*. Let's see what happens when we put the students in the driver's seat by instructing them to use a think-pair-share tactic to generate at least three follow-up questions for ongoing discussion. That way the students can take the lead, interact with one another, and participate in answering." After the teacher or other school professional carries out the eCoach's suggestion, then the eCoach comments immediately on how the students are responding. The eCoach might say, "That's it! Now that the students are in the driver's seat, only one appears a little groggy or disinterested. All the others are now engaged and on topic with their partners." Through this example, we illustrate the eCoach as an educational engineer in the ear who avoids judging or blaming the teacher or other school professional and instead provides on-the-spot, just-in-time troubleshooting aimed at enhancing teaching and learning (Rock et al., 2011).

Online Companionship

Another purpose for technology-enabled 1:1, in-ear coaching is related to online companionship. To be effective in his role as a virtual companion, the eCoach acts as a "supportive other," *not* as a "big brother" or a "nagging mother" (see Rock et al., 2011). Online companionship is important because teaching can be a lonely, isolating endeavor. When serving as a supportive other, the eCoach acts as an online companion by encouraging the teacher or other school professional as he works to transfer what has been studied and observed. When doing so, the eCoach communicates, "You are not alone. We are in this together." In this way, the purpose of real-time, in-ear coaching is to "inspire and build up" teachers and other school professionals (Rock et al., 2011, p. 44). That said, the purpose of online companionship is *not* cheerleading. Instead, the encouragement, feedback, guidance, and companionship the eCoach provides is intended to be strategic, supportive, and intentional in ensuring ongoing commitment and fostering independence in carrying out the studied and observed content or pedagogy.

Making Technology-Enabled One-on-One, In-Ear Coaching Work

First and foremost, technology-enabled 1:1, in-ear coaching requires an effective eCoach who understands not only how to maximize the effectiveness of real-time coaching but also how to minimize the liabilities. There are some knowledge and skill sets that elbow (face-to-face) coaches and eCoaches share, but a few distinguishing eCoach characteristics require consideration.

Characteristics of an Effective eCoach

An effective eCoach understands how eCoaching works and helps others, including administrators, realize its power and value. Also, if the promise of 1:1, in-ear coaching is to be realized, then teacher, student, and eCoach performance data must be captured and archived electronically. Doing so allows the eCoach to use the

WHY BOTHER? REASONS FOR REAL-TIME, IN-EAR COACHING

- Provides opportunities for real-world practice with discreet feedback
- Supports transfer of learning
- Reduces the Hawthorne effect
- Empowers frontline practitioners
- Cultivates shared instructional leadership
- Offers educational engineering in the ear
- Serves as a supportive other

performance data as a guide for reflection. In turn, he uses the insights gained through that reflection to continually inform his real-time coaching.

An effective 1:1, real-time eCoach possesses four key characteristics:

- *Technological know-how.* Identifying eCoaching technology options, connecting online in real time, and troubleshooting eCoaching technology issues.
- *Content and pedagogical expertise.* Possessing expert knowledge of curriculum, content, and pedagogy; understanding adult learning principles and motivation; and grasping school climate and culture.
- *Interpersonal skills.* Establishing trust and respect; prioritizing and negotiating goal setting, monitoring, and evaluation; communicating and resolving conflict; leading change; and possessing important personal attributes.
- *Technical competence.* Planning and assessing; observing and collecting data; providing immediate and delayed feedback; and using the eCoaching continuum (i.e., in-depth study of content or pedagogy, peer observation of best practice, 1:1 coaching, and group coaching).

A basic equation—knowledge + will + skill = an effective 1:1 eCoach—captures these characteristics well. The sections that follow address them in more detail:

Technological know-how. Carrying out technology-enabled 1:1, in-ear coaching successfully requires the eCoach to have some basic technological know-how. Before getting under way, the eCoach needs to work with district or school technology support personnel, teachers, and other school professionals to identify the technology options they prefer. Later in this chapter, we describe in detail not only the eCoaching technology options for 1:1, in-ear coaching, but also the considerations that should be taken into account when deciding among them. Although school or district technology support personnel shoulder responsibility for having in-depth knowledge of the technology options, eCoaches should also be familiar with them.

Once everyone has settled on the technology, ordering and installing the components are among the next orders of business. Again, the eCoach works with technology support and other relevant school personnel to ensure the desired technology components are ordered and installed in a timely manner. In our experience, some district administrators prefer that technology support staff shoulder sole responsibility for installation. Others prefer that teachers, school professionals, and eCoaches install the necessary technology, using detailed written procedures provided by the vendor or technology support staff. Whether technology support staff are involved directly or indirectly in installation, they should be at the ready to lend troubleshooting and expert support should problems arise during installation.

After installation, it is always wise to test the technology. We recommend scheduling a few (i.e., three to five) sessions wherein eCoaches and teachers or other school professionals practice connecting online. Doing so allows the eCoach and the teachers or other school professionals to ensure the discreet audio, webcam, and online videoconferencing components are in good working order. An added benefit is that the K–12 students become acclimated to this approach, in which the eCoach visits their classroom online rather than in person.

Under real-time conditions during 1:1 eCoaching, the eCoach typically needs to lend troubleshooting assistance to teachers and other school professionals in three essential areas: audio (Bluetooth), video (webcam), and Internet connectivity (online videoconferencing). Although technology support staff can and should also lend support with technology troubleshooting when problems arise during 1:1, in-ear coaching, we recommend reserving their involvement for chronic issues that cannot be remedied quickly or easily. When difficulties erupt during eCoaching, more often than not they are relatively simple and straightforward to address and can usually be resolved quickly. On rare occasions when that's not the case, such as when the Internet is down, a Bluetooth earpiece has not been charged, or the laptop has contracted a virus and expert technology support is warranted, the session can simply be rescheduled without losing valuable time and money to travel. The Appendix provides guidelines for getting started and connecting online as well as tips for installation and troubleshooting. Please be mindful, however, that the guidelines will vary based on the type of technology used for online 1:1, in-ear coaching. That means additional guidelines should be developed as needed with support from school or building technology professionals.

Content and pedagogical expertise. Providing support effectively in real time during planning and at the point of transfer requires the eCoach, like a face-to-face coach (Polly, Mraz, & Algozzine, 2013), to have substantive command of the curriculum, content, and pedagogy under study. In a Reading First study undertaken by L'Allier and Elish-Piper (2007), hierarchical linear modeling (HLM) analysis confirmed significant gains in elementary students' reading achievement when their teachers received job-embedded support from coaches with advanced training and preparation in literacy. Advanced knowledge and expertise allows the 1:1 eCoach to assess and prioritize what (if any) content and pedagogical changes need to be made and why, and then to tailor his immediate feedback accordingly. In this way, the immediate feedback supports the teacher or other school professional in making those changes in real time. Simple and straightforward? Not so much. This complex cycle of real-time assessment and decision making happens in seconds. Thus, an effective 1:1 eCoach not only must access her content and pedagogical expertise rapidly and repeatedly throughout the course of a lesson but also must decide in the moment what to address immediately through real-time feedback and what to address later through coplanning. That said, because even an eCoach with advanced training and preparation may not possess the desired level of content and pedagogical expertise across all curriculum areas and grade levels, it is reasonable to expect him to partner with other eCoaches in and beyond the school district who do.

As does a face-to-face coach (L'Allier, Elish-Piper, & Bean, 2010; Polly et al., 2013), an effective 1:1 eCoach also draws on knowledge and understanding of adult learning principles and motivation. Among the foundational adult learning theorists, Knowles (1980) and Mezirow (1997, 2000) offer insights eCoaches should find instructive. Although the two have generated distinct concepts and theories (e.g., andragogy and transformative learning, respectively), common themes emerge. For instance, Knowles and Mezirow assert that past experience, prior knowledge, ongoing reflection, critical thinking, and intrinsic motivation play vital roles in adult learning. Initially, Knowles maintained that self-direction was a central tenant of adult learning. In his later work, however, he revised this position, emphasizing instead the importance of adopting a continuum of expert- and self-directed learning activities. Neither Knowles nor Mezirow is without critics. And neither offers exhaustive, empirically validated theories of adult learning. Instead, taken together, they provide a framework for better understanding the unique (and not so unique) characteristics of adult learners. Although an in-depth discussion of adult learning theories and motivation is beyond the aim and scope of this book, it is incumbent on the eCoach to ensure that he possesses sufficient command of both. For instance, during 1:1, in-ear coaching, the eCoach must gauge how much immediate feedback will support or thwart the teacher's or other school professional's motivation and momentum in translating his or her goals for effective instruction and positive behavior support into concrete classroom action.

School climate has been described as the atmosphere, culture, resources, and social networks included in it (Loukas & Murphy, 2007). Because school climate and culture impacts teacher commitment (see Firestone & Pennell, 1993), including whether and how effectively content and pedagogy translate into classroom practice (Firestone, 1996), 1:1 eCoaches should be mindful of its importance. For example, the eCoach should be familiar with school- or districtwide initiatives, such as a balanced literacy approach, a "hands-on and minds-on" approach to science, or schoolwide positive behavior interventions and supports. As Rock and her colleagues (2013) pointed out, when the eCoach is well versed in school climate and culture, including prevailing school- or districtwide initiatives, she can provide immediate feedback during 1:1, real-time eCoaching that supports it, making the experience more rewarding and successful than not. Over time, these successful

1:1 eCoaching experiences accumulate, contributing to the establishment or maintenance of a positive school climate and culture. Underscoring the importance of a positive school culture, Collie, Shapka, and Perry (2012) found that it significantly predicted greater teacher commitment in three ways: through general professional commitment, future professional commitment, and organizational commitment.

Interpersonal skills. Effective eCoaches tap in to their interpersonal skills to create a safe psychological climate. Although the purposes we have described for carrying out 1:1, real-time eCoaching are varied, unique, and compelling, the idea of receiving immediate feedback in one's ear while teaching creates understandable and considerable unease for some. In fact, more than 45 years ago, Herold, Ramirez, and Newkirk (1971) recognized the role anxiety played in on-site, in-ear coaching. To mitigate the potentially adverse effects of anxiety associated with in-ear coaching, Herold and colleagues recommended advising coachees that approximately three to four sessions are needed to be able to successfully process multiple forms of incoming auditory stimuli (i.e., teacher talk, student talk, eCoach talk) seamlessly, without anxiety and frustration. We offer this as a general guideline, rather than a hard, steadfast rule. Individual teacher preferences vary: some wish to jump right in, finding practice sessions a waste of valuable time, while others prefer a gradual approach, welcoming a few practice opportunities. We have found it best to ask each teacher whether he prefers practice sessions.

Effective 1:1 eCoaches are excellent communicators. Walkowiak (2016) identified five essential communication skills associated with effective face-to-face coaches that also apply to the interpersonal skill set needed by eCoaches:

- *Effective 1:1 eCoaches collaborate with administrators to define roles, responsibilities, and expectations.* Together, they communicate these to teachers and other school professionals. When defining roles, responsibilities, and expectations, the eCoach and his administrators consider the following questions: What does the eCoach do? How much of the eCoach's time will be dedicated to each of the four components included in the continuum, including 1:1, real-time eCoaching? What does the eCoach *not* do? How will the eCoach be evaluated? What opportunities will the eCoach have for ongoing professional development? Does one size fit all when it comes to eCoaches' roles and responsibilities? No. Not surprisingly, Denton and Hasbrouk (2009) found that workloads vary considerably among face-to-face coaches. Factors such as school size, grade levels, student achievement, teacher capacity, and district/school reform initiatives influence the frequency and intensity of the workload and should be considered on an individual basis. As Fullan and Knight (2011) cautioned, failing to clearly define eCoaches' roles and responsibilities, especially those that are the most intensive—like 1:1, in-ear coaching—is a surefire route to failure.

- *Effective eCoaches establish trust with administrators, teachers, and other school professionals.* Establishing trust allows the 1:1 eCoach to facilitate changes in classroom practices, to encourage teachers and other school professionals to take instructional risks, and to demonstrate empathy when job-related stressors abound. Through extensive case study analysis, Lowenhaupt, McKinney, and Reeves (2014) revealed that face-to-face literacy coaches established trust in three ways—building relationships, demonstrating symbolic gestures (e.g., sending Kleenex for the classroom if needed), and creating safe (i.e., warm, welcoming) spaces for immediate and delayed feedback—all of which are relevant to eCoaches.

- *Effective eCoaches value the ideas of teachers and other school professionals.* Providing 1:1, real-time feedback in a teacher's ear during classroom instruction requires a humble, rather than a know-it-all, approach. In this way, 1:1, real-time eCoaching is coteaching. The eCoach works with the teacher or other school professional in real time to figure out what will make the biggest impact on instruction and positive behavior interventions and supports for students and provides in-ear feedback the teacher can use immediately to make that happen. Walkowiak (2016) points out that, when doing so, the coach should "suggest slight changes, rather than a complete overhaul of the lesson" (p. 15). In this way, the eCoach communicates value for the teacher's original ideas. We agree. Moreover, we see this as particularly important during 1:1, real-time eCoaching because providing immediate feedback that requires a major overhaul to the lesson would prove paralyzing, rather than empowering, to the teacher.

- *Effective eCoaches use focused goal setting, monitoring, and evaluation to make decisions with teachers and other school professionals that positively impact instruction and positive behavior interventions and supports.* This allows the eCoach to tailor the immediate feedback he provides during 1:1, real-time coaching not only according to the content or pedagogy that was studied and observed, but also according to how it is meeting the needs of the teacher or other school professional and students. Walkowiak (2016) suggests that the latter is vital for promoting professional growth. Specifically, narrowing the focus of the feedback helps teachers and other school professionals minimize overload, while customizing the immediate, in-ear feedback based on unique classroom context maximizes effective transfer.

- *Effective eCoaches use K–12 student performance data (e.g., examples of understanding and misunderstanding) to engage in conversation, inform immediate feedback, and guide goals* not only for the teacher or other school professional but also for the eCoach. In this way, the process of 1:1, real-time eCoaching becomes reciprocal rather than one sided.

In addition to being excellent communicators, effective eCoaches are leaders of instructional change (see Polly et al., 2013). In an *Educational Leadership* article entitled

"Coaches as System Leaders," Fullan and Knight (2011) argued that as champions of effective instruction, coaches play an important role in school reform within the context of 1:1, real-time eCoaching, we see the eCoach demonstrating leadership, not only in these ways but also in another capacity that involves taking on a political role. How so? By tailoring the immediate feedback provided during 1:1, real-time eCoaching to encourage teachers' use of effective instruction and positive behavioral interventions and supports while helping them understand why doing so is important from a policy point of view. Coburn and Woulfin (2012) found that effective face-to-face literacy coaches did this and more. In fact, the literacy coaches even helped teachers understand which aspects of the Reading First policy could and should be ignored.

Effective eCoaches also possess important personal attributes. In a national survey of middle and high school literacy coaches, Blamey, Meyer, and Walpole (2008) found that optimism, patience, resilience, flexibility, and determination ranked among the most desired attributes. They pointed out, too, that respondents indicated effective coaches champion perseverance while embracing their dual role as expert and learner—notions popularized as grit (see Duckworth & Gross, 2014) and a growth mindset (see Dweck, 2006). We see great relevance in eCoaches adopting these attributes as well. For example, during 1:1, real-time eCoaching, effective eCoaches use reassurance to alleviate anxiety and demonstrate patience, perseverance, and positivity when troubleshooting technology-related issues. Effective eCoaches also value others' time—something as simple as scheduling sessions a week in advance can alleviate anxiety and go a long way toward communicating respect. Overall, a 1:1 eCoach demonstrates warmth, encouragement, compassion, reassurance, humor, and understanding while maintaining high standards for transfer to practice.

Technical competence. Effective eCoaches also possess a variety of technical skills. Assessing how students are responding to instruction and tailoring feedback around that is paramount to effective literacy coaching (L'Allier et al., 2010). Similarly, rather than evaluating the teacher's or other school professional's instructional skill set, the 1:1 eCoach focuses on providing feedback that describes how well instruction is meeting students' needs. Consequently, he must be well versed in data collection and data-informed decision making related to content, pedagogy, and positive behavioral interventions and supports. Chapter 6 will address how eCoaches can and should go about doing this effectively. Overall, the technical skills 1:1 eCoaches need include the following:

- Planning and assessing
- Observing and collecting data
- Providing immediate and delayed feedback
- Using the eCoaching continuum (i.e., in-depth study of content or pedagogy, peer observation of best practice, 1:1 coaching, and group coaching)

How 1:1, Real-Time eCoaching Works

Now that we've identified the characteristics of an effective 1:1 eCoach, it's time to turn attention to explaining how 1:1, real-time eCoaching works. Originally, because in-ear coaching was based largely on wired FM radio technology with limited transmitting capability, it was carried out on-site. The coach wore a portable transmitting device equipped with a microphone, and the teacher or other school professional wore a portable receiving device equipped with an earpiece. While teaching, the coach provided discreet feedback that only the teacher or other school professional could hear. Located in the rear of the classroom, or in a nearby hallway, the coach was somewhat intrusive. An example of discreet, in-ear coaching conducted on-site through two-way radios can be viewed at https://www.teachingchannel.org/videos/teaching-coaching-models. In this video, a coach and a first-year teacher engage in a coaching session using the two-way radios. Also, the two provide intermittent commentary about the experience. Although we encourage teachers, other school professionals, administrators, and eCoaches to carry out in-ear coaching online, rather than on-site, we recognize that this option can help some frontline professionals take the first step in revolutionizing their practice because it can be easier to get under way.

Recognizing the pitfalls associated with on-site, in-ear coaching and finding the promise of online videoconferencing captivating, Rock and her colleagues pioneered the research and development of an online variation in 2009. Formerly referred to as virtual coaching, Rock and her colleagues (2014) defined eCoaching as "a relationship in which one or more persons' effective teaching skills are intentionally and potentially enhanced through online interactions with another person" (p. 2). Rather than relying on FM radio technology, Rock and her colleagues cobbled together a few essential off-the-shelf components that allowed the eCoach and the teacher or other school professional to connect online in real time. An example of a discreet, in-ear coaching session using online technology can be viewed at http://www.youtube.com/watch?v=stRSmdX661Y. In this video example, an eCoach located remotely connects with a teacher via an iPhone app (i.e., FaceTime). Typically, eCoaching sessions like this one that are carried out online are captured and archived electronically. Then, when needed, the eCoach can select a portion or portions of it to share with the teacher or other school professional. This approach offers the eCoach and the teacher or other school professional rich footage for shared conversation based, in part, on the discreet, in-ear feedback provided during a lesson as well as from the online debriefing afterward.

Applying the Three-Part Organizational Framework to One-to-One, In-Ear Coaching

Chapter 2 provided a three-part organizational framework for making technology-enabled observations of content and pedagogy work. We suggest taking a similar approach to 1:1, real-time eCoaching. The steps that support technology-enabled, online in-ear coaching are similar to those needed for face-to-face delivery. So, the three-part organizational framework works well for both. In the sections that follow, we describe each component of the organizational framework.

Before

First, the eCoach and the teacher or other school professional connect online or on-site to arrange a session or series of sessions lasting 20–30 minutes in which the eCoach observes and provides immediate, in-ear feedback during real-time instruction. Typically, the eCoach and the teacher or other school professional also set up time to meet before (i.e., preplanning) and after (i.e., debriefing) the 1:1, real-time eCoaching session (Rock et al., 2009). During preplanning, the eCoach and the teacher might connect online, via Skype or another videoconferencing platform, to review the lesson plan and objectives for student learning. The eCoach and the teacher or other school professional also review previously set goals or establish new ones for learning transfer. These goals indicate how the teacher or other school professional will incorporate the content or pedagogy studied and observed previously to bolster student learning. Then they discuss preferences for how the eCoach will provide immediate feedback during the lesson using on-site or online BIE technology. For example, the eCoach and the teacher or other school professional might agree on the use of a signal system (using a series of keywords or predetermined codes). Alternatively, they might opt for the eCoach to employ a running dialogue. Finally, the eCoach and the teacher or other school professional might decide to conduct a few trial runs to practice connecting online or on-site in real time. Doing so ensures the technology is in good working order prior to the 1:1, real-time eCoaching session.

IMPORTANCE OF THE 4:1 RATIO

As noted, the eCoach can offer immediate feedback in the form of a running commentary (Rock et al., 2009, 2012, 2014) or a signal system (Scheeler, McKinnon, & Stout, 2012). At present, no research has indicated that one approach is more effective than the other. We prefer the commentary approach for two reasons. First, creating signals seems to add unnecessarily to planning and preparation time. Second, recalling signals in the moment seems to add unnecessarily to the extraneous cognitive processing load, not only for the teacher or other school professional but also for the eCoach. Regardless of whether the eCoach uses a commentary or a signal approach when providing immediate feedback, there is reason to suspect that providing four positive comments for every one corrective or instructive remark (also referred to as the 4:1 ratio; see Daniels & Bailey, 2014) results in greater changes in desired performance.

During

When providing 1:1, in-ear coaching, the eCoach may use on-site or online technology. Regardless, the eCoach focuses the feedback she delivers electronically in the teacher's ear by describing the teaching and learning that unfolds in the classroom. When emphasizing the latter, the eCoach names and notices how students respond to instruction. When pinpointing teaching, the eCoach comments on instructional practices, such as stimulating prior knowledge during discussion and, if necessary, suggests alternatives to enhance students' responding (e.g., How have you stimulated students' prior knowledge so far? Try offering students some think time before asking for responses to open-ended questions."). Throughout, the eCoach encourages the teacher by pointing out what curriculum, instructional, and behavioral tactics he employs effectively (e.g., "Terrific job using text-to-text connections as a way to help students extend their understanding during discussion!").

One of the most frequently asked questions we receive about 1:1, real-time eCoaching is, "How do you know what to say and when to say it?" To answer that question, we turn to the literature and draw on our professional experience in carrying out more than 800 1:1, in-ear coaching sessions. Let's start with the literature. In a recent review of coaching, Kretlow and Bartholomew (2010) found that one of the top three critical components of effective coaching is feedback.

What is feedback? In a seminal meta-analysis of the feedback literature, Kluger and DeNisi (1996) defined feedback as "actions taken by (an) external agent(s) to provide information regarding some aspect(s) of one's task performance" (p. 255). More recently, Park, Schmidt, Scheu, and DeShon (2007) differentiated between normative and diagnostic feedback, positing that the former refers to social comparisons, while the latter pertains to directives that include guidance, cues, correction, or explanation. During eCoaching, because feedback is delivered immediately during classroom instruction and intended to strengthen teacher practice and to improve students' academic and behavioral performance, the feedback is more diagnostic than normative.

The dimensions or principles of effective feedback have also been identified and explored by past researchers, albeit more so in organizational psychology than in education. To date, researchers have found that to be effective, feedback must be situational (i.e., individualized) and task specific (deVilliers, 2013). Feedback must be reliable, meaning that an individual with considerable expertise and credibility (see Larson, 1984; deVilliers, 2013) should provide it. DeVilliers noted that when providing feedback, it should be manageable (i.e., based on prior knowledge, digestible—not too much information). Larson (1984) described effective feedback cues specifically as indicators of situational deviation from the norm (p. 65), while Casey and McWilliam (2011) referred to them more generally as antecedents. Other dimensions of feedback thought to yield differing outcomes include the timing (i.e., immediate versus delayed) (deVilliers, 2013), the type (i.e., positive or negative, questioning, encouraging, instructing/correcting) (Fishbach, Eyal, & Finkelstein, 2010; Scheeler, McAfee, & Ruhl, 2004), the focus (i.e., relevant, meaningful, specific) (Casey & McWilliam, 2011; deVilliers, 2013), and the acceptance (i.e., use) (Bracken & Rose, 2011; Kinicki, Prussia, Wu, & McKee-Ryan, 2004; Kulhavy; 1977; Markose, 2011).

Types of feedback. The immediate feedback an eCoach offers during 1:1, in-ear coaching falls into one of four categories—encouraging, questioning, corrective, and instructive (Fishbach et al., 2010; Scheeler et al., 2004):

- *Encouraging.* "Praise contingent on demonstration of a specific teaching behavior is provided" (Scheeler et al., 2004, p. 399). For example, "Terrific! Nice job providing students with stems to scaffold their collaborative skills and engage all in the social studies discussion."
- *Questioning.* "A sentence posed in interrogative form to get information or to clarify specific teaching behaviors" (Random House Unabridged Dictionary, 2006, as cited in Rock et al., 2009). For example, "Is that a worksheet or a graphic organizer the students are using to respond to the discussion questions?"
- *Corrective.* "The type and extent of errors and specific ways to correct the error" (Scheeler at al., 2004, p. 399). For example, "Please try paying more attention to the student when she is cooperative and participating in the discussion according to the new norms you established with the class, rather than when she is not."
- *Instructive.* "Information related to predetermined specific teaching behaviors is offered" (Scheeler, et al., 2004, p. 399). For example, "Round-robin responding (i.e., calling on one student at a time), while discussing use-of-knowledge skills, is a low-access instructional strategy. To give all students an opportunity to demonstrate use-of-knowledge skills correctly and simultaneously during discussion, embed some of the stems or prompts we studied in your questions. Then, ask them to get out their response boards, jot down their answers, and share them with all after you give the class a signal."

Timing of feedback. When providing immediate feedback during 1:1, in-ear coaching, the eCoach can offer it while the teacher or students are talking or during silence (see Rock et al., 2009). To date, no evidence exists indicating that one is more effective than the other. Consequently, we encourage eCoaches to provide the immediate feedback when it is needed the most, rather than to wait for the "ideal" moment during a 1:1, real-time eCoaching session. Why? The ideal moment may never materialize, and the opportunity for impact will likely be missed.

Scaffolding of feedback. During 1:1, in-ear coaching, the eCoach also needs to scaffold the feedback she provides. When scaffolding feedback, the eCoach gradually, systematically, and intentionally facilitates teachers' and other school professionals' autonomy, self-management, and empowerment. Engin (2013) described scaffolded feedback in five levels that ranged from more to less directive and specific, with one being the most open ended and least directive and five being the opposite (see Figure 3.1). These levels varied from moment to moment, during postobservation feedback sessions. We see Engin's levels as useful and purposeful when providing eCoaching feedback in real time during classroom instruction.

Goal monitoring. As mentioned previously, the immediate feedback the eCoach provides in real time should be specific to the predetermined goals, and it should be limited in focus—namely, to describing how students are responding as the teacher endeavors to transfer newly learned content or pedagogy that he has studied and observed. To ensure objectivity, the eCoach collects relevant teacher and student performance data either in real time or by reviewing archived electronic video files. We describe how to do this later in this chapter and the topic will be addressed in greater depth in Chapter 6.

Troubleshooting online or on-site in real time. During 1:1, real-time eCoaching, technological issues arise. The eCoach needs to help the teacher or other school professional troubleshoot as efficiently and effectively as possible. If the problem cannot be remedied quickly, we suggest rescheduling the session so that valuable instructional time is not squandered. Again, extensive troubleshooting guidelines will be offered in the Appendix.

After

Prior to signing off, the eCoach says goodbye to the teacher or other school professional and the K–12 students. Also, the eCoach needs to digitally archive the electronically recorded session. The latter is done by uploading the file to a secure cloud-based server or an external hard drive.

Most important, after the 1:1, in-ear coaching session, the eCoach needs to engage the teacher or other school professional in debriefing, reflection, and goal evaluation. Debriefings can be carried out in various ways: after the lesson, but prior to concluding the videoconference call; during a scheduled debriefing session that takes place within 24 hours of the session; or a combination of the two. During separately scheduled debriefings, the eCoach and the teacher or other school professional might connect online, via Skype or another videoconferencing platform, or on-site to review the in-ear coaching session. Throughout the debriefing conversation, the eCoach points out areas of observed strength—specifically as they pertain to the transfer of content and pedagogy studied and observed

Figure 3.1

Feedback Levels, Descriptions, and Examples

Level of Feedback	Description
	Example
1 = Open-ended	Level 1 feedback is aimed at inviting the teacher to reflect on how he used the content or pedagogy, including social, emotional, and behavioral domains, during instruction. This level of feedback is best provided during a quick postlesson debriefing or during teacher silence when the K–12 students are engaged independently in the lesson. Providing this open-ended feedback in-ear during instruction (i.e., while the teacher and students are talking) is likely to disrupt the flow of the lesson.
	eCoach: "What do you think went well during the five-stages-of-discussion technique you used in this lesson?"
2 = Targeted, specific, open-ended question	Level 2 feedback is intended for clarifying and is generally based on recall. This level of feedback is best provided during a quick postlesson debriefing or during teacher silence when the K–12 students are engaged independently in the lesson. Providing this targeted, specific, open-ended questioning feedback in-ear during instruction (i.e., while the teacher and students are talking) is likely to disrupt the flow of the lesson, especially if it is used frequently.
	eCoach: "How did you embed stems and prompts to scaffold students' use-of-knowledge skills during discussion?"
3 = Forced choice (yes/no)	Level 3 feedback is geared toward guiding the teacher to a specific response. This level of feedback is best provided during a quick postlesson debriefing or during teacher silence when the K–12 students are engaged independently in the lesson. Providing this forced-choice (yes/no) questioning feedback in-ear during instruction (i.e., while the teacher and students are talking) is also likely to disrupt the flow of the lesson, especially if it is used frequently. That said, this kind of feedback can be posed rhetorically as a prompt during 1:1, real-time eCoaching either while the teacher and students are talking or during silence. However, the eCoach should do so judiciously.
	eCoach: "Did you model how to respond to stems and prompts when scaffolding students' use-of-knowledge skills during discussion?"
4 = Slot-fill prompt	Level 4 feedback is designed to allow the teacher or other school professional to fill in the blank. This resembles a cloze procedure in reading. Asking the teacher to fill in the blank during instruction (i.e., while the teacher and students are talking) is also likely to disrupt the flow of the lesson, especially if it is used frequently. That said, this kind of feedback can also be posed rhetorically as a prompt during 1:1, real-time eCoaching either while the teacher and students are talking or during silence. Again, however, the eCoach should do so judiciously.
	eCoach: "During class discussion, you wanted students to demonstrate dispositions such as . . . ?"
5 = Directive or corrective	Level 5 feedback is offered in the spirit of expert guidance, support, or assistance. Using this approach, the eCoach tells the teacher or other school professional what the problem is and how it should be addressed. Although this level of feedback is well suited for immediate delivery while the teacher and students are talking or during silence, it is the most prescriptive and should be used sparingly.
	eCoach: "Asking the students, 'How do you know you provided a credible response?' is expecting too much too soon. None of the students are responding to the question. Recall that we learned during the book study that teachers need to scaffold students' use-of-knowledge skills. One way to do so is by providing stems or prompts. Let's try asking them, 'Did you find your answer online through a Google search, in your textbook, or in an academic article you searched for in the library?'"

Adapted from Engin, 2013, p. 14.

previously. Next, the eCoach poses questions for guided reflection. Then, together they evaluate previously established goal attainment and identify one or two goals to guide future teaching and learning. Finally, they conclude by scheduling the next in-ear coaching session. If the debriefing is carried out after the lesson, but prior to concluding the videoconference call, then the same process occurs but in an abbreviated manner.

Evaluating the Effectiveness of One-on-One, In-Ear Coaching

Evaluating the effectiveness of 1:1, in-ear coaching is best accomplished by routinely evaluating the eCoach's, the teacher's, and the students' performance through multiple measures. This intermittent, data-informed, teacher- *and* student-oriented approach allows the eCoach and the teacher to objectively monitor the impact of the 1:1, real-time eCoaching, not only for the teacher or other school professional but also for students. Using formative and summative tactics also enhances the eCoach's capacity to make ongoing adjustments to her 1:1, real-time eCoaching—maximizing effectiveness over the short and long runs, based not on a sole instrument or a limited perspective, but rather on multiple measures and differing perspectives (Lawley & Linder-Pelz, 2016).

Monitoring the eCoach's Effectiveness

Teachers and other school professionals should have regular opportunities to evaluate the eCoach. Two psychometrically sound instruments for doing so include the eCoach Evaluation Survey, which is adapted from the Coaching Evaluation Survey developed by the Florida PS/RtI Statewide Project (http://floridarti .usf.edu), and the Examining eCoach Feedback Survey, which is adapted from the Examining Evaluator Feedback Survey (Cherasaro, Brodersen, Reale, & Yanoski, 2015), available from https://ies.ed.gov/ncee/edlabs/projects/project.asp?project ID=333. Prior to adapting and administering one of these instruments, eCoaches, teachers, other school professionals, and administrators should look them over and decide which one best meets their needs. Teachers and other school professionals can complete these instruments anonymously in approximately 15–20 minutes at least twice each year (e.g., in December and May). eCoaches should use the data obtained through these measures to assess strengths and needs as well as to set, monitor, and evaluate their eCoaching performance goals.

Monitoring Teacher and K–12 Student Performance

As noted earlier, in addition to providing immediate feedback, the 1:1, real-time eCoach should objectively monitor the teacher's and K–12 students' performance. Why? Objective measures of teacher and student performance provide evidence not only of learning transfer but also of real-world impact. The eCoach can peruse various sources of student performance data. For example, the eCoach can draw on eCoaching session data that reflect student impact goals, such as those that confirm positive changes in students' academic responding or engagement during classroom instruction. The eCoach can also review students' achievement, using change scores on standardized district, building, grade, or class achievement measures. Similarly, when it comes to teacher performance data, the eCoach can extract eCoaching session data. For instance, the eCoach can collect real-time data on specific goals that reflect changes in the teacher's use of effective instructional or behavioral practices during classroom instruction. Also, the eCoach can look over changes in state, district, or building teacher evaluation data (e.g., walk-through data, or Danielson or Marzano data).

Collecting Performance Data and Using Protocols or Templates as a Guide During Technology-Enabled One-on-One, In-Ear Coaching

Chapter 6 will discuss in detail how to collect and use data to support formative and summative evaluation. Here we briefly describe how eCoaches can collect teacher and K–12 student data during 1:1, real-time eCoaching.

Published Protocol or Templates

There are several commercially produced or published protocols or templates the eCoach can use during 1:1, real-time eCoaching to collect performance data. These include those produced by Danielson (https://www.danielsongroup.org/framework/), Marzano (http://www.marzanoevaluation.com/evaluation/causal_teacher _evaluation_model/), Pianta (http://teachstone.com/classroom-assessment-scoring -system/), and others—just to name a few. If a school or district has adopted one of these published protocols or templates, then the eCoach is wise to use all or part of them. Fidelity checklists are also popular. These instruments allow the eCoach to determine how well the teacher is carrying out specific content or pedagogical tactics.

Homegrown Versions

Alternatives to commercially produced or published protocols include "create-your-own" templates. Homegrown approaches allow eCoaches and teachers or other school professionals to produce customized data sheets that are goal oriented, standards informed, curriculum based, and content and pedagogy focused. Using Google docs (https://docs.google.com/), eCoaches, teachers, and other school professionals can create homegrown versions quickly, easily, and collaboratively. For example, they can design a data sheet template that includes the five stages of the discussion process, an element of the high-leverage practice of leading a group discussion. The eCoach then uses this template as a checklist during 1:1, real-time eCoaching sessions, to provide feedback and to monitor goal-related progress, including students' participation in each stage of discussion. Homegrown versions can also be used in conjunction with commercially available or published protocols or templates.

Whether published or homegrown options are employed, the aim is to use the data to better understand students' responsiveness to the content or pedagogy studied and observed previously (e.g., productive discussion, effective instruction, positive behavior interventions and supports). This means that the eCoach and teacher or other school professional need to review the data collected during eCoaching, in part, by comparing and contrasting it not only with content and pedagogical goals but also within the overarching theory of change, described in Chapter 1. In this way, the essential question that guides data collection and discussion is, "What's working for whom, under what conditions, and why?" For example, the data may reveal that the teacher is consistently incorporating many of the recommended scaffolding techniques to increase students' participation in productive discussion. However, he has not yet established culturally sensitive norms and dispositions, so the majority of students in this high-needs school remain disengaged during class discussion.

Considering Options for Carrying Out Technology-Enabled One-on-One, In-Ear Coaching

Considering the equipment needed for carrying out 1:1, real-time eCoaching requires consideration of what the eCoach needs, as well as what the teacher or other school professional needs. Simply stated, the eCoach needs technology that allows her to connect, see, hear, coach, and record. And the teacher or other school professional needs technology that allows him to connect, see, hear, and talk. The necessary "off-the-shelf" technology components for eCoaches and teachers may be assembled using stationary or mobile configurations. Higher-end and higher-cost, all-inclusive systems, as well as online and on-site versions, are available for consideration, as well.

Online–Off-the-Shelf, On-a-Budget Stationary or Mobile Configurations

Although on-site BIE technology has been used successfully for 1:1, real-time eCoaching for more than 50 years across various disciplines (see Bowles & Nelson, 1976; Giebelhaus & Cruz, 1994; Korner & Brown, 1952; Van der Mars, 1988), as noted previously, Rock and her colleagues were the first to successfully pioneer an online version in 2009. Their advanced online BIE technology relies on affordable off-the-shelf components, including a laptop or desktop computer, a Bluetooth earpiece, a Bluetooth adapter (if necessary), a wide-angle webcam, and an online videoconferencing app or platform (e.g., Skype, FaceTime, Adobe Connect). An "on the go" variation can be assembled, too, using a mobile device (e.g., smartphone, tablet, iPhone, iPad, iPod Touch), a robotic platform, a Bluetooth earpiece, and a videoconferencing app or platform. The coach or teacher(s) can record 1:1, real-time eCoaching sessions by using the option included in the system or by adding low-cost apps. Secure cloud-based or external storage (i.e., a hard drive) also needs to be accessed to electronically archive, share, and annotate the video files. Each of these components were delineated and described in Chapter 2. Here we list them as a reminder, describing only the Bluetooth earpiece and adapter, because that is what makes the discreet feedback possible. In short, eCoaches, teachers, and other school professionals use the same technology components that they do for remote classroom viewing with or without video recording.

In addition, the teacher pairs the Bluetooth earpiece with the computer, mobile device, or all-inclusive system. Then, she is ready for online 1:1, real-time eCoaching.

- *Bluetooth earpiece.* Pairing a Bluetooth earpiece with the computer, mobile device, or video-based online professional development system (see Chapter 2 and the next item in this list), allows the teacher or other school professional to discreetly hear the eCoach's feedback during real-time instruction. Bluetooth earpieces can be purchased through online or brick-and-mortar vendors, such as Plantronics (https://www.plantronics.com/us/en) and Staples, respectively. The cost for a Bluetooth earpiece can be as low as $20 or $30, with the average being approximately $60. If teachers and other school professionals share the Bluetooth earpiece, then antiseptic wipes should be used to clean it prior to each use.

- *Bluetooth adapter (if the laptop or desktop computer is not Bluetooth enabled).* If the laptop or desktop computer used for 1:1, real-time eCoaching is not Bluetooth enabled, but does have USB capability, then an external adapter can be added. The adapter looks like a travel or thumb drive. Installing the software and inserting the adapter into the USB port allows the Bluetooth earpiece to be paired with the computer. The cost for a Bluetooth adapter begins at about $20. Bluetooth adapters can be purchased through online or brick-and-mortar vendors, such as Best Buy (http://www.bestbuy.com/site/insignia-bluetooth-4-0 -usb-adapter-black/5655065.p?skuId=5655065).

- *Additional components (outlined in Chapter 2).* Other components include online videoconferencing platforms, webcams, robotic platforms, wearables, video call recorders, and secure storage (cloud-based or external hard drive).

Online–All-Inclusive High-End, High-Priced Systems

Costlier web-based, high-tech options, such as IRIS Connect and Edthena, have also become available. Both are video-based, professional development systems that are all inclusive and allow for discreet 1:1, real-time eCoaching as well as video archival, sharing, and annotation. Similar to the lower-cost online BIE technology, with these systems the coach and teacher(s) connect online, in real time, at a previously agreed-upon time. Then, the 1:1, real-time eCoaching with discreet in-ear feedback sessions ensue by pairing a Bluetooth earpiece with the desired system. These systems were described in Chapter 2 as well. Descriptions and demonstrations of IRIS Connect and Edthena can be obtained through their websites (http://www.irisconnect.com/ and https://www.edthena.com/). Pricing and contract information can be also obtained by requesting direct quotes through these websites. Costs for systems like these vary, typically ranging from $5,000 to $15,000.

On-Site

On-site options include not only low-cost two-way radios (with an earpiece), but also pricier alternatives that include language translation systems, such as Talk System by Talk Technologies, and assistive listening devices, such as the Williams Sound Personal FM Listening System. Whether a lower- or higher-cost option is employed, the eCoach positions himself in the classroom, or in a nearby hallway or classroom, and speaks into one device while the teacher or other school professional discreetly receives the feedback through a second device attached to a wired or wireless headset or ear bud. Following are brief descriptions of the on-site options:

- *Two-way radios (with an earpiece).* Two-way radios are handheld devices that allow the teacher and the eCoach to communicate in real time. Using push-to-talk technology, the eCoach provides immediate feedback to the teacher during classroom instruction. Connecting an earpiece to the radio allows the teacher to discreetly receive the eCoach's feedback. Costs for two-way radios vary, from as low as $20 to more than $100. Motorola offers several different device options that can be purchased through the company's website (https://www.motorola solutions.com/en_us/products/two-way-radios-story.html). Discounted two-way radios can also be purchased through vendors such as Amazon or Walmart.

- *Personal FM listening systems.* Assistive listening devices, such as the Williams Sound Personal FM Listening System, also allow the teacher and the eCoach to communicate, offering listen-only or two-way modes of communication. Descriptions of professional devices can be viewed online through Williams Sound (https://www.williamssound.com/catalog/pfm-pro-rch) but must be purchased through a regional vendor (https://www.williamssound.com/wtb-us). The cost for a personal FM listening system is approximately $600–$700 per unit. A personal FM listening system functions like two-way radios when it is used for 1:1, real-time eCoaching. Some schools might have personal FM listening systems on hand. We suggest checking with colleagues who provide speech and language services to determine availability for long- or short-term use.

- *Language translation systems.* Language translation systems, such as Talk System by Talk Technologies, have been used traditionally with interpreting programs. Like two-way radios and personal FM listening systems, language translation systems allow the eCoach to provide feedback in real time and the teacher to receive it discreetly during classroom instruction. The system can be purchased online through TalkTechnologies (https://talktech.com/interpretation -system-talksystem/). Quotes must be requested online; however, the cost for this system is typically around $1,000. Some schools might have previously purchased language translation systems. We suggest consulting colleagues who provide support to English language learners and their families to determine availability for long- or short-term use.

Determining Which Technology Options Are the Best Fit for One-on-One, In-Ear Coaching

Online and on-site options exist, at various price points, for carrying out 1:1, in-ear coaching in real time. One size does not fit all. Administrators, eCoaches, teachers, and other school professionals should determine which options best meet their needs. In the next several sections, we offer important considerations and corresponding questions. Also, we suggest involving district or school technology support personnel in these discussions. Doing so is important because they can help others understand technology-related specifications, guidelines, limitations, and so forth.

Budget

- What is the initial budget (i.e., dollar amount) available for purchasing the technology components or systems needed for 1:1, in-ear coaching?
- What is the ongoing or longer-term budget for maintaining the technology components or systems needed for 1:1, in-ear coaching? For instance, consider not only replacement parts and software updates but also day-to-day items such as sanitary wipes to clean Bluetooth earpieces.

Compatibility

Of the available technology options, which are compatible with existing district, school, or classroom technology? For example, if teachers and other school professionals already have tablets or iPads, then they can add a Bluetooth and a Swivl for a reasonable cost without having to purchase new laptop or desktop computers, which can be far costlier.

Availability

How much time is required for delivery and installation? What if the technology components or systems are delayed significantly or require an inordinate amount of time and labor for installation?

Dependability and Responsibility

- How dependable are the technology options? For instance, some Bluetooth earpieces are made by companies with higher dependability and customer satisfaction ratings than others. Be sure to check out reviews online prior to purchase.
- What if the technology is defective or falls into a state of disrepair? Who is responsible for the cost of replacing or repairing the technology—the vendor, the district, the eCoach, or the teacher or other school professional?

Mobility and Other Features

- How important is mobility? For instance, if the teacher or other school professional works in an early childhood setting, then it is vital that the eCoaching technology selected for one-on-one, in-ear coaching allows the teacher and her students to move about regularly and for the eCoach to be able to move with them, albeit online.
- How important is it that the eCoach be able to operate the camera remotely to zoom in closely on the teacher or students, or to focus on a certain spot in the classroom? If such features are important, then they should be considered prior to purchase.

Comfort and Familiarity

- How familiar are administrators, eCoaches, teachers, and other school professionals with the required technology components or systems? On-site systems, such as two-way radios, may be familiar and reduce cost and time initially, but they impose restrictions (i.e., the Hawthorne effect) over time.
- Similarly, the use of cloud-based storage, albeit secure, might cause great concern to some, so opting for secure external storage drives to electronically archive 1:1, real-time eCoaching video files might be a better choice.

Technology Support

- What external technology support is available through the vendor when the products (i.e., components or systems) are purchased? Is the support included in the purchase price, or is it an add-on? How long is the support provided?
- What internal technology support is available through district or school personnel?
- How accessible are internal or external technology supports during 1:1, real-time eCoaching sessions? Who should be contacted first: internal (i.e., school or district) or external (i.e., vendor) technology support personnel?

Building on the Instructional Plan for Technology-Enabled One-on-One, In-Ear Coaching

Chapters 1 and 2 described the need for teachers and other school professionals to put together a blueprint, which was referred to as an instructional plan, as a guide for engaging in technology-enabled study and observation. It is important for teachers and other school professionals to continue building on the plan by delineating how 1:1, real-time eCoaching will be used intentionally to facilitate transfer of the content or pedagogy that has been studied and observed, as shown in the last row of text (highlighted in gray) in Figure 3.2. Taking a few minutes to add this information also helps teachers and other school professionals to ensure alignment among technology-enabled study, observation, and 1:1, real-time, in-ear coaching.

Creating Norms That Support Technology-Enabled One-on-One, In-Ear Coaching

Teachers and other school professionals are familiar and comfortable with traditional approaches to professional development, such as studying and observing.

Figure 3.2

Expanded Instructional Design Plan That Includes 1:1, Real-Time, In-Ear Coaching–Questioning Example

Guiding Questions	Sample Instructional Design Planning for Technology-Enabled Study, Observation, and 1:1, Real-Time, In-Ear Coaching of Specific Content or Pedagogy, Including Social, Emotional, and Behavioral Domains
What is the topic and purpose of study?	Develop or refine pedagogical knowledge in four areas: • *Effective questioning* to enhance students' comprehension during literacy instruction • *Two of Deborah Ball's 19 high-leverage practices related specifically to questioning*—leading a group discussion and eliciting and interpreting individual students' thinking • *Culturally responsive questioning* to meet the needs of diverse students • One of the Council for Exceptional Children's (CEC's) high-leverage social, emotional, and behavioral practices—HLP #7: Establish a Consistent, Organized, and Respectful Learning Environment

Why is the topic of study important?	• The school improvement plan
	  ◊ 100 percent of students will achieve proficiency in literacy.
	• District student achievement data
	  ◊ Currently, student performance data confirm many students, especially those who are diverse, are not achieving proficiency in literacy.
	• Classroom/teacher performance data
	  ◊ Currently, classroom observational data confirm most teachers are using lower order questioning and minimal discussion during literacy instruction. High-performing students respond frequently and accurately.
	• Pedagogical research
	  ◊ Institute for Education Sciences (IES) researchers Matsumura and colleagues (2013) found the quality of classroom text discussions, including questioning, mediated students' reading achievement.
	• Social/emotional/behavioral research
	  ◊ Results from meta-analytic studies have confirmed many varied benefits for students whose teachers provided social, emotional, and behavioral supports, including 11 percentile point gains in academic achievement (Mahoney et al., 2018).

What is already known about the topic of study?	Based on theory-of-change/logic-model planning, teachers and other school professionals realize that if they want to increase all K–12 students' proficiency in literacy, they need to develop in-depth knowledge of effective questioning practices as well as how to make questions culturally responsive to their diverse students while creating and maintaining a positive, respectful, organized, and consistent environment for learning.
What content or information is needed to transfer the topic of study to the classroom?	Teachers and other school professionals need to understand and include in their lesson planning for literacy instruction • A range of effective questions from lower to higher order that support rich thoughtful discussion • Two of Deborah Ball's 19 high-leverage practices related specifically to questioning—leading a group discussion and eliciting and interpreting individual students' thinking • Culturally responsive questions • One of the CEC's high-leverage social, emotional, and behavioral practices—HLP #7: Establish a Consistent, Organized, and Respectful Learning Environment

Figure 3.2

Expanded Instructional Design Plan That Includes 1:1, Real-Time, In-Ear Coaching–Questioning Example

Guiding Questions	Sample Instructional Design Planning for Technology-Enabled Study, Observation, and 1:1, Real-Time, In-Ear Coaching of Specific Content or Pedagogy, Including Social, Emotional, and Behavioral Domains
How will technology be used to support the topic of study and observation of the same?	• *E-book study.* Engage in e-book study of effective questioning tactics, using *Questioning for Classroom Discussion* (Walsh & Sattes, 2015). • *Electronic discussion guide.* Download the Study Guide for *Questioning for Classroom Discussion* from http://www.ascd.org/publications/books/115012/chapters /An-ASCD-Study-Guide-for-Questioning-for-Classroom-Discussion@-Purposeful -Speaking,-Engaged-Listening,-Deep-Thinking.aspx • *PDF document.* Use the description of HLP #7 from the CEC's high-leverage social, emotional, and behavioral practices as a study aid (https://highleveragepractices. org/wp-content/uploads/2017/06/SEBshort.pdf). • *Reputable websites.* Bookmark three websites: ◊ University of Michigan's Teaching Works (http://www.teachingworks.org /work-of-teaching/high-leverage-practices) to review two of Deborah Ball's 19 high-leverage practices related specifically to questioning—leading a group discussion and eliciting and interpreting individual students' thinking ◊ *Create Success!* by Kadhir Rajagopal (http://www.ascd.org/publications /books/111022/chapters/Culturally-Responsive-Instruction.aspx) to study Chapter 1, "Culturally Responsive Instruction," focusing on the section pertaining to questioning ◊ The CEC's high-leverage practices to review HLP #7: Establish a Consistent, Organized, and Respectful Learning Environment (https://highleveragepractices.org /wp-content/uploads/2017/06/SEBshort.pdf and https://highleveragepractices .org/about-hlps/) • *Professional online community platforms.* Use edWeb (https://home.edweb.net/) or PBworks (http://www.pbworks.com/) to create an online PLC for weekly e-book study discussion. • *Social media.* Follow Teaching Works on Twitter (https://twitter.com/) and Facebook (https://www.facebook.com/). Engage in weekly Twitter chats using #culturallyresponsivequestioning, #questioningforclassroomdiscussion, and #socialemotionallearning. • *Online videoconferencing and robotic platform for video streaming and capture.* Use Skype (https://www.skype.com) with Call Recorder (http://www.ecamm.com/mac/ callrecorder/) and Swivl (https://cloud.swivl.com/) to observe and electronically capture models and demonstrations of teachers using effective, culturally sensitive questioning during literacy instruction. • *YouTube.* Teachers and other school professionals select video models showcasing how to use "I wonder . . ." questions during literacy instruction and view clips such as "Before, During and After Questions: Promoting Reading Comprehension and Critical Thinking," posted by The Balanced Literacy Diet (https://www.youtube.com /watch?v=Sd1FlXxpVIw) on YouTube. In all, 55 video models pertaining to effective comprehension questioning during literacy instruction are available through the Balanced Literacy Diet channel on YouTube (https://www.youtube.com/watch? v=psakxRT9hdA&list=PL5178787DB725559D). These videos could be reviewed for models and demonstrations showcasing effective, culturally relevant questioning.

(continues)

Figure 3.2   (continued)

Expanded Instructional Design Plan That Includes 1:1, Real-Time, In-Ear Coaching–Questioning Example

Guiding Questions	Sample Instructional Design Planning for Technology-Enabled Study, Observation, and 1:1, Real-Time, In-Ear Coaching of Specific Content or Pedagogy, Including Social, Emotional, and Behavioral Domains
How will participants demonstrate understanding of the topic of study and the models and demonstrations observed?	• Create low-stakes chapter quizzes for e-book study using Google Docs (https://www.google.com/docs/about/) or SurveyMonkey (https://www.surveymonkey.com/). • Design and deliver one or two interactive presentations on culturally responsive questioning and two of Deborah Ball's 19 high-leverage practices related specifically to questioning—leading a group discussion and eliciting and interpreting individual students' thinking—with peers/colleagues using Pear Deck (https://www.peardeck.com/), Nearpod (https://nearpod.com/), or Classkick (https://classkick.com/). • Earn digital badges/micro-credentials for effective questioning, culturally responsive questioning, two of Deborah Ball's 19 high-leverage practices related specifically to questioning—leading a group discussion and eliciting and interpreting individual students' thinking—and one of the CEC's high-leverage practices (i.e., HLP #7: Establish a Consistent, Organized, and Respectful Learning Environment)—via ASCD or Digital Promise (http://digitalpromise.org/initiative/educator-micro-credentials/).
*How will participants demonstrate **transfer** of the topic of study and the models and demonstrations observed?*	• Engage in 10 to 15 one-on-one, real-time eCoaching sessions, demonstrating effective questioning, culturally responsive questioning, and high-leverage questioning practices. • Provide evidence of positive K–12 student engagement and impact in each session.

Some have participated in face-to-face coaching, too. Receiving discreet, immediate feedback from an eCoach during classroom instruction, however, is far from routine. Consequently, if 1:1, real-time eCoaching is to achieve widespread adoption and fulfill its promise as an effective learning transfer technique, then it is important for administrators, eCoaches, teachers, and other school professionals to establish new norms, not only to support it initially but also to maintain it over time.

School Environment for Feedback

On a macro level, school professionals need to take stock of the contextual and situational factors associated with feedback, such as whether administrators and teachers in the school building value and seek feedback aimed at improving instruction and enhancing K–12 student outcomes. Diagnosing contextual and situational factors is vital to maximizing the positive effects and minimizing the negative effects of feedback provided during 1:1, real-time eCoaching. Administrators and eCoaches can objectively and systematically assess whether the school has a feedback-friendly environment through surveys. One such psychometrically sound, multifaceted measure is the Feedback Environment Scale (FES) (Steelman,

Levy, & Snell, 2004). Principals and eCoaches administer the FES, which takes approximately 15–20 minutes to complete, to teachers and other school professionals during dedicated release time. They then use the data obtained to identify strengths and to prioritize areas where changes are needed. Finally, they work with teachers and other school professionals to generate a schoolwide plan for maintaining or transforming the overall environment for feedback.

Individual Teachers' Orientation to Feedback

On a micro level, the eCoach also needs to systematically and objectively assess individual teachers' orientation (i.e., receptiveness) to feedback. One psychometrically sound instrument for doing so is the Feedback Orientation Scale (FOS) (Linderbaum & Levy, 2010). Results from the FOS indicate an individual's receptiveness to feedback. A strong orientation to feedback indicates an individual is likely to value and use it. By contrast, a low orientation indicates the opposite. The good news when it comes to 1:1, real-time eCoaching is that an individual's orientation to feedback can be changed. For instance, the eCoach and the teacher use the FOS data to prioritize strengths and needs and to set goals to strengthen (or maintain) an individual teacher's orientation to feedback. To do so, they might structure a book club around the *New York Times* best seller *Thanks for the Feedback: The Science and Art of Receiving Feedback Well* (Stone & Heen, 2014). Finally, based on that reading, together they coconstruct plans to strengthen (or maintain) the teacher's orientation to feedback.

Privacy and Confidentiality

Feedback environment and orientation aside, teaching and learning has been viewed as a private, solitary act that takes place in individual teachers' classrooms behind closed doors. The introduction and evolution of face-to-face and online coaching have changed that. Yet important questions remain regarding privacy and confidentiality—especially when coaching sessions are carried out online in real time and sessions are captured electronically. Who controls the video files? Who has permission to view them? How will the files be used? Answers to these and other questions are not always forthcoming or readily available. We suggest that administrators, eCoaches, teachers, and other school professionals begin by reviewing existing, relevant district or building policy (e.g., regarding video and audio recording of students and teachers). Based on the presence or absence of such policies, they can then generate new or modify existing, relevant district or building policy, as needed. Initially, for example, they need to determine whether the school's or district's current permission form for audio and video recording students suffices. If not, they need to create a new one. Finally, because the video files captured during 1:1, real-time eCoaching can be considered part of a student's educational record, we recommend reviewing existing and relevant state and federal policies, such as the Family Educational Rights and Privacy Act (FERPA) (20 U.S.C. § 1232g; 34 CFR Part 99). As pointed out in previous chapters, school district lawyers should be consulted and invited not only to join in discussions but also to review newly created forms or policies. Being proactive in these ways helps to create a more transparent and trusting culture.

Contemplating the Benefits and Cautions Associated with Technology-Enabled One-on-One, In-Ear Coaching

As was the case with the previous two components of the eCoaching continuum, there are benefits and drawbacks associated with 1:1, real-time eCoaching. We review them briefly here, to give teachers and other school professionals the information they need to make informed decisions about moving eCoaching from the sidelines to online.

Benefits

With the use of online technology options, the eCoach's physical presence in the classroom is no longer required. When the eCoach provides immediate feedback discreetly and remotely, he no longer presents a potential distraction to students. Also, scheduling disruptions are minimized because online technologies (e.g., e-mail, instant messaging, videoconferencing) allow teachers and eCoaches to rearrange sessions quickly and easily, while also reducing time and travel demands. Most important, the teachers who participated in Rock and her colleagues' (2009, 2012, 2014) studies reported that 1:1, real-time eCoaching carried out online prompted an unparalleled cycle of spontaneous "in-action" reflection. Relatedly, capturing and storing video files from in-ear coaching sessions permits later review and analysis—an especially useful feature that aids in promoting "on-action" reflection and capturing teacher and K–12 student growth. Because both are known attributes of effective teachers, this combination of "in-action" and "on-action" reflection (Schön, 1983) is invaluable.

Cautions

In-ear coaching requires teachers and other school professionals to process multiple forms of incoming auditory stimuli, while the eCoach analyzes and comments on visual and auditory stimuli. Both must do so with speed and accuracy. Thus, teachers need time to adjust to in-ear coaching, and eCoaches need to become proficient in providing discreet and immediate feedback. The former requires about three or four sessions (Rock et al., 2012), while the latter remains to be determined. eCoaches and teachers also need to consider the installation demands of on-site and online in-ear coaching technologies. These demands vary considerably and are often contingent on technology knowledge and skill as well as the availability of building or district support. As is the case with all technology, connectivity issues arise from time to time. Having troubleshooting guidelines and tips on hand (see the Appendix) goes a long way toward reducing frustration and increasing success. Technology support services should be available through the school or district and comprehensive enough to include assistance with audio, video, and online access. To ensure privacy and confidentiality, parent or guardian permissions must be secured prior to electronic video capture and archival. Finally, as was pointed out in the Introduction, although effect sizes are large for face-to-face and technology-enabled coaching, if the other components of the eCoaching continuum are not in place, then its power and promise will be thwarted. For instance, teachers and other school professionals will become dependent on the eCoach if they have not dedicated adequate time to technology-enabled study and observation.

Translating the eCoach's Role into Action During Technology-Enabled One-on-One, In-Ear Coaching

As emphasized in previous chapters, the eCoach plays a vital and unique role in each of the four components of the eCoaching continuum. Here we offer a list of possible roles and responsibilities eCoaches could shoulder in facilitating 1:1, real-time, in-ear coaching to foster learning transfer. To do so successfully, eCoaches need administrator and colleague support, including dedicated release time, clearly delineated job roles and responsibilities, and ongoing training and professional development.

- Take a leadership role in helping administrators, teachers, and other school professionals understand the unique and compelling reasons for engaging in 1:1, real-time eCoaching.
- Prepare a checklist that includes the characteristics of effective 1:1, real-time eCoaches. Use it as a tool for self-assessment and to help identify and develop more eCoaches.
- Carry out live 1:1, in-ear coaching demonstrations so that administrators, teachers, other school professionals, and other coaches can see what it looks like. Capture the demonstrations electronically so that others can access them as needed.

- Practice connecting online and troubleshooting using the guidelines included in the Appendix.
- Adopt the three-part organizational framework for carrying out 1:1, real-time eCoaching.
- Develop greater understanding of how to provide effective feedback in real time.
- Download the Coaching Evaluation Survey developed by the Florida PS/RtI Statewide Project (http://floridarti.usf.edu) and the Examining Evaluator Feedback Survey (https://ies.ed.gov/ncee/edlabs/projects/project.asp?project ID=333). Then adapt them by changing the wording to reflect language relevant to 1:1, real-time eCoaching. Share with administrators, teachers, and other school professionals for review and discussion. Decide together whether one or both instruments will be used to evaluate the eCoach and how often.
- Offer guidance on determining the availability of technology-enabled options, equipment, software, apps, and so forth that support 1:1, real-time eCoaching.
- Coordinate the evaluation of technology-related options, equipment, software, and apps, and consider goodness of fit using guiding questions.
- Build on the instructional design plan for 1:1, real-time eCoaching and modify as needed.
- Schedule and carry out 1:1, real-time eCoaching sessions with teachers and other school professionals.
- Co-create norms for 1:1, real-time eCoaching.
- Secure psychometrically sound instruments, such as the Feedback Environment Scale and the Feedback Orientation Scale. Then adapt, administer, score, and interpret the results. Join with administrators, teachers, and other school professionals in using the results to create a positive climate for feedback acceptance and use.
- Partner with school librarians, technology support specialists, and legal counsel to provide training in relevant policies, such as FERPA's video stipulations.
- Locate, adapt, or generate data collection templates or protocols for focused 1:1, real-time eCoaching.
- Develop digital badges/microcredentials for 1:1, real-time eCoaching.
- Create modules for training on new and existing technologies and approaches that support 1:1, real-time eCoaching.
- Monitor progress of 1:1, real-time eCoaching and assess professional learning.

Just as teachers and other school professionals use technology to engage in 1:1, real-time eCoaching to facilitate learning transfer, so do eCoaches. For example, returning to the example provided in Chapters 1 and 2, after viewing the "Coaching

Conversations" module in Coursera (https://www.coursera.org/specializations /coaching-skills-manager), and electronically archiving debriefing observations that include coaching conversations with teachers and other school professionals and viewing them to self-assess learning transfer, an eCoach could participate in 1:1, real-time, in-ear coaching to receive feedback from another coach.

Revisiting Important Ideas

In this chapter, we've described in detail how to carry out technology-enabled 1:1, real-time coaching to foster teachers' transfer of content and pedagogy. We've also pointed out why doing so is important, as well as the known benefits and cautions. Prior to moving on to Chapter 4, let's take a minute to review the important ideas we've shared:

- Clarify and communicate to key stakeholders the unique, varied, and compelling purposes for carrying out 1:1, real-time, in-ear coaching—on-site or online.
- Consider the characteristics of an effective 1:1, real-time eCoach—including technological know-how, advanced knowledge and expertise, interpersonal skills, and technical skills.
- Ensure alignment among technology-enabled study, technology-enabled observations, and technology-enabled 1:1, real-time, in-ear coaching.
- Tailor the technology-enabled 1:1, in-ear coaching sessions to teachers and other school professionals' unique learning needs about the content or pedagogy.
- Make technology-enabled 1:1, in-ear coaching work, in part, by adopting a three-part organizational framework, comprising focused activities before, during, and after the online or on-site eCoaching sessions.
- Collect performance data and use commercially produced or homegrown protocols and templates as a guide to focus learning transfer and gain deeper meaning from 1:1, real-time eCoaching.
- Consider online or on-site variations for carrying out 1:1, real-time eCoaching.
- Consider equipment, software, apps, and so forth in accord with budgets and professional learning needs.
- Determine the best technology fit, in part based on answers to the guiding questions provided.
- Build on the blueprint, also referred to as the instructional plan, developed in Chapters 1 and 2, by adding 1:1, real-time eCoaching that supports the transfer of content or pedagogy that has been studied and observed previously.
- Make good use of the guidelines for connecting online and troubleshooting that are provided in the Appendix.

- Create and sustain norms that support 1:1, real-time eCoaching, including creating a school environment conducive to feedback, fostering teachers' positive orientations to feedback, and ensuring privacy and confidentiality for all.
- Contemplate the benefits and cautions carefully and make decisions about how to proceed with 1:1, real-time eCoaching.
- Ensure that the eCoach's roles and responsibilities regarding 1:1, real-time eCoaching are clearly articulated and supported by administrators, teachers, and other school professionals.

We know this chapter is chock-full of important information. To help prevent teachers and other school professionals from becoming overwhelmed by the information we've shared, we offer an At-a-Glance Checklist. Using the checklist will empower teachers and other school professionals to move forward with 1:1, real-time eCoaching effectively and efficiently. Realizing the power of 1:1, real-time eCoaching requires that you understand just 12 simple things!

AT-A-GLANCE CHECKLIST

Preparing for Successful Technology-Enabled One-on-One, In-Ear Coaching

> ☐ The purpose for 1:1, real-time eCoaching is clear, unique, and compelling.
> ☐ The content or pedagogy selected for 1:1, real-time eCoaching aligns with that which was selected for technology-enabled study and observation.
> ☐ eCoaches possess the characteristics needed to be effective.
> ☐ The three-part organizational framework (before, during, and after) is developed and used, in part to make 1:1, real-time eCoaching work.
> ☐ Immediate feedback is provided effectively with consideration given to type, timing, scaffolding, and so forth.
> ☐ Performance data are collected and templates or protocols are used during 1:1, real-time eCoaching to promote transfer and deepen learning.
> ☐ Technology-enabled options, equipment, software, apps, and so forth are identified based on goodness of fit.
> ☐ The instructional design plan is expanded to guide technology-enabled study + observations + 1:1, real-time eCoaching and can be modified as needed.
> ☐ Norms for 1:1, real-time eCoaching are established and supported.
> ☐ Benefits and cautions associated with 1:1, real-time eCoaching are considered, and choices are made accordingly.
> ☐ eCoaches are evaluated using psychometrically sound instruments.
> ☐ eCoaches' roles and responsibilities are clearly articulated and supported.

4

Technology-Enabled Group Coaching
Sustaining Professional Development Through Collective Inquiry

Marcia Rock and Jennie Jones

We must use collegiality not to level people down but to bring together their strength and creativity. —Andy Hargreaves (n.d.)

How can teachers and other school professionals use technology effectively and efficiently to engage in group coaching, not only to engage in collective reflection and solve problems of professional practice that erupt when transferring content knowledge and pedagogy, but also to improve their K–12 students' performance?

Understanding the Purpose of Technology-Enabled Group Coaching

Like technology-enabled 1:1, in-ear coaching, the group variation centers on learning transfer. In this way, the primary purpose of using technology to carry out group coaching is to bring teachers, other school professionals, eCoaches, and administrators together online or in a blended environment in real time to engage in collective inquiry, which is characterized by shared reflection *on* and focused investigation *of* the problems that emerge when putting into practice newly learned content or pedagogy, including social, emotional, and behavioral domains. However, unlike technology-enabled 1:1, real-time coaching, which is didactic, in group coaching, several professionals put their heads together in supportive, encouraging, and instructive ways not only to reflect jointly and routinely on practice but also to systematically explore and solve problems of practice. In doing so, they approach reflection and problems of practice collectively and objectively, while also being mindful *not* to become mired in the problem. Fusco, O'Riordan, and Palmer (2015) help us further differentiate the purpose of group coaching from the other three components of the eCoaching continuum (i.e., study, observation, and 1:1, real-time coaching): "We have observed that, rather than skill development, it seems that the group coaching effectiveness lies in its ability to remove obstacles to actual skill deployment" (p. 144).

A second and integrally related purpose for undertaking technology-enabled group coaching is to link teacher learning to student learning, not only through shared systematic problem solving but also through routine critical reflection (see Goodwin, Low, & Ng, 2015). Thus, like a professional learning community (PLC), the overall aim of technology-enabled group coaching is to improve student outcomes by adjusting the content or pedagogical practices (including social, emotional, and behavioral domains) that were studied, observed, and coached 1:1, based on observation and discussion of K–12 students' learning during group coaching meetings (Blitz, 2013). As such, technology-enabled group coaching supports tenets of situated learning within communities of professional practice (see Lave & Wenger, 1991)—that is, by working with others not only to reflect routinely on practice but also to solve problems of practice, improvements in teaching and learning are "situated" within authentic contexts (i.e., classroom, school) and facilitated by colleagues (Curry, 2008).

A third purpose for engaging in technology-enabled group coaching is to foster a culture of collaboration (Goodwin et al., 2015). When groups of teachers join in facilitating the transfer of content and pedagogy (including social, emotional, and behavioral domains) with an eye to solving problems of practice and increasing student achievement, they deprivatize classroom practice and promote a shared responsibility for teaching and learning (Vanblaere & Devos, 2016). How so? Drawing on tenets of community psychology, during technology-enabled group coaching, teachers, other school professionals, eCoaches, and administrators access new resources (i.e., one another, internal or external experts) by engaging intentionally in inquiry, dialogue, reflection, and collaboration within the community of practice. This "heads together" process enables them to think about content or pedagogy in new ways and ultimately to transfer it to classroom practice more effectively and efficiently (Stelter, Nielsen, & Wikman, 2011). Also, through transparent, open discussion and inquiry, which are the hallmarks of technology-enabled group coaching, teachers, other school professionals, eCoaches, and administrators purposively support one another's learning to maximize their students' learning and achievement (Goodwin et al., 2015).

A fourth purpose for technology-enabled group coaching is to create the infrastructure that supports ongoing implementation of the eCoaching continuum. Without technology-enabled group coaching, the content and pedagogy (including social, emotional, and behavioral domains) learned and transferred previously through the other three components of the eCoaching continuum (i.e., study, observation, 1:1 coaching) cannot be sustained over time. That said, maximizing effectiveness and ensuring ongoing sustainability of technology-enabled group coaching requires thoughtful, intentional alignment with the previously discussed components of the eCoaching continuum (see Chapters 1–3).

Determining Frameworks and Facilitators for Technology-Enabled Group Coaching

All components of the eCoaching continuum, including technology-enabled group coaching, are practice based (i.e., job embedded). Fettig and Artman-Meeker (2016) identify three components included in practice-based coaching models: "shared goals and action planning, focused observation, and reflection and feedback" (p. 149). Taken together, the three components are situated within a collaborative coaching framework aimed at supporting the effective transfer of content and pedagogy to improve students' learning and achievement.

When applying principles of practice-based coaching to technology-enabled group coaching, an expert facilitator leads a group, which may vary in size (e.g., generally from 4 to 12 teachers or other school professionals), as members reflect on practice, in part, by identifying and discussing problems that have emerged when putting into practice the content or pedagogy studied, observed, and coached previously. Technology-enabled group coaching typically takes place once or twice a month in sessions lasting as little as 20–30 minutes (Fettig &

WHY BOTHER? REASONS FOR TECHNOLOGY-ENABLED GROUP COACHING

- Support transfer of content and pedagogy, using principles of community psychology, practice-based coaching, and situated learning
- Link teacher learning to student learning
- Deprivatize classroom practice and promote shared responsibility for teaching and learning
- Encourage systematic problem-solving and critical reflection
- Foster a culture of collaboration
- Solve problems of practice in real-world contexts with peer support to increase K–12 student achievement
- Create infrastructure that supports the sustainability of the eCoaching continuum

Artman-Meeker, 2016) or as long as two hours (Curlette & Granville, 2014). During each session, the facilitator and the participants carry out a live, technology-enabled observation, view an electronically archived video file, or share automated teacher performance data captured in real time, illustrating the content or pedagogy (including social, emotional, and behavioral domains), as well as any relevant problem of practice. Then they use a structured protocol to review relevant teacher and K–12 student data; discuss the content or pedagogy (including social, emotional, and behavioral domains), along with any resulting problem of practice; and reflect on what adjustments need to be made in the classroom to maximize students' learning and achievement. As needed, between technology-enabled group coaching sessions, teachers and other school professionals can conduct additional study, observation, and coaching (whether 1:1 or self) of the content or pedagogy (including social, emotional, and behavioral domains) of interest as it pertains to enhancing transfer and further investigating the problem of practice.

In accord with the three earlier-described components of practice-based group coaching, online or hybrid PLCs (see Blitz, 2013) offer teachers, other school professionals, eCoaches, and administrators a familiar framework for carrying out technology-enabled group coaching. In online, hybrid, or face-to-face PLCs, teachers, other school professionals, administrators, and eCoaches work together to find, share, and develop teaching practices that enhance their effectiveness and benefit student learning (Blitz, 2013; DuFour, 2004; Hord, 1997). Popular PLC group coaching approaches that are well suited to the online or technology-enabled variation include critical friends groups (CFGs; Dunne & Honts, 1998) and grand rounds (City, 2011), also referred to as instructional rounds or teacher rounds.

Critical Friends Group (CFG) Framework

When a CFG model (Bambino, 2002; Dunne & Honts, 1998) is adopted for technology-enabled group coaching, a teacher or other school professional shares automated teacher feedback data, uploads a video clip, posts examples of student work (or behavior), or invites a predetermined group of colleagues to observe live online as he puts into practice the content or pedagogy (including social, emotional, and behavioral domains) under study. Then, using a secure web-based platform, such as edWeb (http://home.edweb.net/), group members and the facilitator meet online and use CFG protocols to reflect, explore the problem of practice, pose essential questions, structure interactions, and improve their practice (Curlette & Granville, 2014). For instance, drawing on our previous example based on Walsh and Sattes's (2015) *Questioning for Classroom Discussion*, if a teacher or other school professional is working to consistently embed higher-order questioning into productive discussion, the group might select Blooming Questions (https://www.nsrfharmony.org/wp-content/uploads/2017/10/blooming_questions _0.pdf) as a guide for engaging in protocol-driven structured conversations. Why? Because it includes questions geared specifically toward maximizing the effective use of higher-order questioning strategies that were studied and practiced previously within the context of the eCoaching continuum. Next, the teachers or other school professionals use the TeachFX app (https://teachfx.com) to collect automated feedback data on teacher and student talk, including higher-order questioning, during targeted classroom discussions. Then, through a private discussion board or a secure online videoconferencing platform (e.g., Skype, Google Hangout, Zoom), group members share their automated teacher feedback data and use the CFG protocols to take turns questioning and forming hypotheses about the problem of practice and using the automated teacher feedback data to guide reflection. Whether technology enabled or not, the goal of CFGs remains the same—to generate a cycle of reflection, action, and feedback that results in improved student and teacher performance (see Bambino, 2002; Franzak, 2002) and aligns with the content or pedagogy (including social, emotional, and behavioral domains) that has been studied, observed, and coached previously. When it comes to capturing the gist of CFGs, we think Deborah Bambino (2002) got it right. In an *Educational Leadership* article entitled "Critical Friends," she concluded, "The work involves friends who share a mission, offer strong support, and nurture a community of learners" (p. 27). For more detailed "how-to" information, resources, and training opportunities related to CFGs, teachers, other school professionals, eCoaches, and administrators can visit the National School Reform Faculty Harmony Education Center website (http://www.nsrfharmony.org/about-us/faq).

Instructional Rounds Framework

If grand or instructional rounds (City, 2011) are employed for technology-enabled group coaching, a similar inquiry-based approach is used. Typically, a teacher or other school professional first poses a problem of practice—related to the content or pedagogy (including social, emotional, and behavioral domains) that has been studied, observed, and coached—to his online or hybrid professional network. Then, members of the online or hybrid professional network, the majority of whom are peers, carry out a series of live classroom observations using a webcam, view electronically archived video files, or share relevant, automated teacher-student performance data. Based, in part, on the performance data, network members debrief to collectively investigate the problem of practice, share their collective knowledge and skills, and generate potential solution-centered strategies. That said, the goal of "rounding" is *not* to fix teachers. Instead, it is to "understand what's happening in classrooms and hold one another accountable"

(City, 2011, p. 37). The ultimate aim is to learn from one another and generate solutions collaboratively using practice-based evidence and evidence-based practices that result in improved student and teacher performance (City, 2011). Each "case" or problem of practice comprises two parts: practice-centered inquiry and learning-centered inquiry. In Figure 4.1, we provide examples based on Walsh and Sattes' *Questioning for Classroom Discussion* (2015).

Facilitation Options

Who leads? During technology-enabled group coaching, CFGs and instructional rounds can be facilitated by the eCoach, experts, or peers. The keys to success are to ensure that the facilitator has leadership skills, has up-to-date content and pedagogical expertise, and has been trained in the protocols used to structure group conversation and problem solving. If the eCoach serves as the facilitator, we suggest gradually reducing her responsibility for doing so because the ultimate aim of technology-enabled group coaching is to strengthen the infrastructure that supports the sustainability of the eCoaching continuum, in part by leveraging professional capital.

Figure 4.1

Problems of Practice Illustrating Practice-Centered Inquiry and Learning-Centered Inquiry

Practice-Centered Inquiry Teacher Focused	Learning-Centered Inquiry K–12 Student Focused
How well did you use the critical habits of mind—appreciative listening, valuing student contributions, focused thinking, and fair-mindedness—during classroom interactions to spark and sustain equitable, interactive discussion? (see Walsh & Sattes, 2015, p. 62)	How did the students respond after you intentionally used the critical habits of mind—appreciative listening, valuing student contributions, focused thinking, and fair-mindedness? Did the students engage in and sustain equitable, interactive discussion? (see Walsh & Sattes, 2015, p. 62)
How well did you intentionally model and scaffold learning how to discuss, using think-pair-share (i.e., quietly generate individual response, wait for teacher's cue, exchange response with partner) with students? (see Walsh & Sattes, 2015, p. 107)	How did the students respond after you intentionally modeled and scaffolded learning how to discuss, using think-pair-share (i.e., quietly generate individual response, wait for teacher's cue, exchange response with partner) with them? How did the students actively discuss and share accountability during the think-pair-share? (see Walsh & Sattes, 2015, p. 107)
How well did you use Ink Think to provide students with structured experiences to listen, talk, and learn with peers rather than on their own? (see Walsh & Sattes, 2015, p. 112)	How well did students listen, talk, and learn with their peers during Ink Think? (see Walsh & Sattes, 2015, p. 112)

Note: Focusing collective inquiry on teacher practices *and* K–12 student learning allows teachers and other school professionals to investigate what needs to be adjusted or changed not only to strengthen teacher practice but also to enhance K–12 student outcomes.
Adapted from Walsh & Sattes, 2015.

Making Technology-Enabled Group Coaching Work

The CFG and Instructional Rounds Frameworks in Action

Although video archives illustrating technology-enabled group coaching are not currently accessible online, illustrations of CFGs and instructional rounds are available. While viewing these clips, it is important to consider that the observations and discussions would occur online or in a blended format, using the technologies described later in this chapter, rather than on-site. The Leadership Institute of Riverside County offers a YouTube video titled "Tuning Protocol: Fine Tuning Our Classroom Practice with Presenting Teacher Donn Cushing" (https://www.youtube.com/watch?v=OnI5MMLC5MA). In this clip, a team of high school teachers engages in group coaching using a CFG discussion protocol. More in-depth information regarding training on the CFG protocol is also available online (www.nsrfharmony.org). To view a clip of instructional rounds in which high school administrators and staff observe classrooms and engage in discussion regarding problems of practice, see http://youtu.be/qD2Yes0Ulu4. An additional YouTube clip illustrating group coaching through instructional rounds is available at http://youtu.be/uQsPYyvDd3s.

Before, During, and After Framework

Chapters 2 and 3 included a three-part organizational framework for making technology-enabled observations and online 1:1, in-ear coaching work. In what follows, we present a similar approach suitable for technology-enabled group coaching.

Before. First and foremost, successful technology-enabled group coaching is predicated on planning and preparation. Planning and preparation begin with network members selecting a group problem-solving framework (e.g., CFG, instructional rounds) and engaging in training as needed. Next, they secure the protocols and templates needed to structure conversations and reflections, so that members engage in focused, productive group problem solving. Three relevant resources are as follows:

- For specific group problem-solving protocols, see Chapter 5 ("Protocols for Addressing Issues and Problems") in ASCD's *Protocols for Professional Learning* (Easton, 2009).
- For CFG protocols and training information, visit http://www.nsrfharmony.org/about-us/faq.
- For training information and protocols needed for instructional rounds, see *Instructional Rounds in Education: A Network Approach to Improving Teaching and Learning* (City, Elmore, Fiarman, & Teitel, 2009).

Group members then identify problems of practice specific to the content or pedagogy (including social, emotional, and behavioral domains) they previously studied and observed, and on which they received 1:1, real-time, in-ear coaching. In particular, they identify the greatest challenges they have encountered related to the content or pedagogy they targeted for improvement or refinement. For instance, continuing with our example based on Walsh and Sattes's (2015) *Questioning for Classroom Discussion,* group members might select student engagement during interactive discussion as the problem of practice they wish to explore through technology-enabled group coaching. After agreeing on the problem of practice, group members then set SMART goals relevant to solving the problem of practice. Generally, SMART goals are specific, measurable, attainable, relevant, and time sensitive. SMART goals will be covered in greater depth in Chapter 6, when formative and summative assessment within and across the eCoaching continuum is described. When members have generated a few (i.e., one to three) SMART goals to guide technology-enabled group problem solving, they connect online in real time to observe the problem of practice, to view an archived video clip that illustrates it, or to use an app such as TeachFX (https://teachfx.com) to collect automated teacher-student performance data.

During. While conducting technology-enabled group coaching, members use the selected framework (e.g., CFG, instructional rounds) and relevant protocols to structure conversations and share relevant performance data (as described above in the Before section), which allows members to engage in focused, productive, data-informed group problem solving. During this time, group members also use agreed-upon templates to systematically track the SMART goals and to monitor the effectiveness of the solutions proffered. If desired, they can also collectively troubleshoot the problem of practice as it occurs in real time. When carrying out the technology-enabled variation of group coaching, the selected framework for peer problem solving is carried out online or in a blended/hybrid format. This allows peers and experts, who possess unique (and often highly specialized) content and pedagogical expertise (including social, emotional, and behavioral domains), to join together regardless of geography, expanding the pool of peers and experts to draw on when identifying and solving real-world problems of practice.

After. Charteris and Smardon (2013) argued that digital tools can be used to facilitate deep professional learning among peers. We agree. By creating digital archives that allow for on-demand review and playback, group members have opportunities for "a second look, second think." Doing so, Charteris and Smardon maintain, promotes more extensive dialogue, which ultimately leads to greater reflection and insight. Moreover, after using technology-enabled group coaching to solve a problem of practice, members can debrief and reflect on videos or automated "talk" data (e.g., TeachFX) that were captured and archived electronically, during group problem solving and decision making. This allows network members to view group dynamics objectively and to identify interpersonal interactions that would benefit from improvement. Finally, group members should use SMART goal monitoring data obtained during technology-enabled group coaching to determine whether the originally established SMART goal has been attained—in terms of both teacher practice and student learning.

Collecting Performance Data and Using Protocols or Templates as a Guide During Technology-Enabled Group Coaching

In this chapter, we offer a brief overview of how data can be collected and used to capture the impact of technology-enabled group coaching. Chapter 6 provides an in-depth discussion, including templates and examples, of the use of such data throughout the entire eCoaching continuum.

Published Protocols and Templates

Earlier in this chapter, we noted that published protocols and templates are available for selected approaches to technology-enabled group coaching, such as CFGs and instructional rounds. Regardless of the framework selected for technology-enabled group coaching, corresponding protocols should provide guidance to team members for structured conversation and focused, data-informed problem solving. Templates should include space for recording the problem of practice and room for tracking progress and impact. Taking time to identify and use the best-fitting protocols and templates benefits group members not only by improving the structure for focused conversation and decision making but also by decreasing frustration that often results from squandered time, energy, and paperwork.

Homegrown Versions

If team members opt for a general, rather than a specific, framework that does not include corresponding protocols or templates, then they likely need to create their own. When doing so, process and content should be included. In addition, some protocols and templates are developed to facilitate a structured approach to shared problem solving, whereas others are designed to monitor and evaluate its effectiveness (as outlined in Figure 4.2). Both protocols and templates should be developed and used as a guide for practical, powerful, and impactful technology-enabled group coaching.

Figure 4.2

Critical Components of Homegrown Protocols and Templates

Facilitation and Organization of Technology-Enabled Group Coaching	Focused Problem Solving for Technology-Enabled Group Coaching
Structural aspects of technology-enabled group coaching include meeting preparation, conduct, closure, and follow-up.	Format includes identification, monitoring, and documentation of effectiveness.
Prepare for structured group coaching conversation(s): • Use technology to conduct observations or view illustrations of the case, identify problems of practice, collect data on teacher and K–12 student performance • Schedule a series of meetings to carry out group coaching conversations, using online or blended/hybrid options	Identify content or pedagogically focused problem of practice (including social, emotional, and behavioral domains) concisely and precisely

Conduct structured group coaching conversation(s), using online or blended/hybrid options:
• Establish and convey team norms and expectations
• Carry out group coaching conversations, as scheduled, using online or blended/hybrid options
• During case/problem analysis:
  ◇ Demonstrate active listening
  ◇ Ask deep, probing questions
  ◇ Pose clarifying questions, when needed
  ◇ Identify potential barriers
  ◇ Offer potential solutions for consideration
	Generate SMART goal(s) specific to the problem of practice:
	• Specific
	• Measurable
	• Action oriented
	• Relevant
	• Time limited

Close structured group coaching conversation(s) using online or blended/hybrid options: • Summarize problem reviewed and solutions generated • Prioritize next steps • Schedule follow-up observations • Identify time frames and individual responsibilities • Agree on criteria for success and secure shared commitment	Establish criteria for success (i.e., positive impact) in two ways: • Teacher performance • K–12 student performance, including engagement

Follow up after structured group conversation(s) using online or blended/hybrid options:
• Carry out observations, centered on the solutions offered for the problem of practice
• Collect agreed-upon evidence/data
• Determine engagement and impact
• Debrief on team problem solving and decision making, using archived video clips captured while conducting structured group coaching conversation(s)
• Repeat the cycle
	• Observe the problem of practice
	• Identify potential barriers *and* solutions to the problem of practice
	• Identify the various types of evidence that will be collected to monitor the solution(s):
	  ◇ Teacher performance data
	  ◇ K–12 student performance data (including engagement data)
	• Carry out additional observations and collect agreed-upon evidence of impact
	• Review evidence, determine engagement and impact, and generate future SMART goals

Hold one another accountable!	

Monitoring and Documenting Students' Responsiveness to Solutions

Regardless of whether published or homegrown versions of protocols and templates are used, an important aim of technology-enabled group coaching is to monitor and document K–12 students' responsiveness to solutions generated through CFGs or instructional rounds. In this way, the outcomes achieved support the overarching theory of change for professional development, based on the eCoaching continuum, which was discussed in Chapter 1.

Considering Options for Carrying Out Technology-Enabled Group Coaching

Deciding on the options for carrying out technology-enabled group coaching requires eCoaches, administrators, teachers, and other school professionals to think about how they could use technology in ways that allow them to observe, capture teacher and student performance data, and discuss problems of practice more effectively and efficiently. When observing and discussing problems of practice, eCoaches, administrators, teachers, and other school professionals need to have access to technology that allows them to see or hear one another— privately and confidentially, as well as to upload automated performance data, evidence, or artifacts securely online for shared review, reflection, and analysis.

Videoconferencing Platforms and Video-Based Online Professional Development Systems

Both videoconferencing platforms and video-based online professional development systems options offer eCoaches, teachers, administrators, and other school professionals opportunities to observe, electronically capture, and discuss problems of practice online. Free, low-cost, and high-cost options for consideration were identified in Chapters 2 and 3.

Web-Based Professional Learning Communities and Wikis

Online PLCs (Dede, 2004) and wikis offer eCoaches, teachers, administrators, and other school professionals web-based digital tools for posting problems of practice, uploading evidence and artifacts, engaging in structured dialogue, and communicating regularly. Free and fee-based options are available, depending on the amount of storage and features desired. These options were reviewed in Chapters 1 and 2.

Webcams, Swivl, and Wearable Digital Camcorders (e.g., MeCam)

These and other camera variations offer eCoaches, teachers, administrators, and other school professionals ways to observe problems of practice together in real time without being on-site. Alternatively, these cameras can be used to electronically capture lessons and problems of practice that can be shared, discussed, and analyzed by group members at a later time and date. Basic descriptions of each were provided in Chapter 2.

Video Viewing and Storage

As described in Chapter 2, teachers, eCoaches, administrators, and other school professionals need options not only for viewing synchronous or asynchronous videos of classroom instruction but also for storing them when captured electronically. They also need private space for discussing problems of practice, whether online or on-site.

Desktops, Laptops, or Mobile Devices

Desktop or laptop computers and mobile devices, such as iPads, iPhones, smartphones, and tablets, allow eCoaches, teachers, administrators, and other school professionals to conduct web-based videoconferencing with one another, to participate in online PLCs, to carry out online observations in real time, and to capture lessons electronically and archive them for later viewing.

Apps

There's an app for that! Some school district professionals have gone so far as to develop instructional round apps, based on FileMaker Go 12, for iPad. View an illustration online at http://youtube/4k0aLbgy7YU.

Determining Which Technology Options Are the Best Fit for Group Coaching

As was the case with technology-enabled study, observation, and 1:1 coaching, administrators, eCoaches, teachers, and other school professionals should determine which options best suit their needs for technology-enabled group coaching. In the next several sections, we offer important considerations and corresponding questions. As suggested in previous chapters, we recommend involving district or school technology support professionals in these discussions. Doing so is important because these individuals are often invaluable in helping everyone understand technology-related specifications, guidelines, limitations, security issues, and so forth.

Blended or Online

- Will the technology-enabled group coaching (e.g., CFG, instructional rounds) be conducted completely online or in a hybrid capacity?
- How important is it to adopt a completely online approach?
- When is an online approach needed?
- When is face-to-face interaction needed and why?

Budget

- What is the initial budget (i.e., dollar amount) available for purchasing the technology needed for carrying out online or hybrid group coaching?
- What is the ongoing or longer-term budget for maintaining the technology needed for group coaching? For instance, are annual subscriptions required to maintain access to the secure wiki space or online videoconferencing platform?

Privacy and Confidentiality

- How secure are the technology, the connections that support it, and the content shared with the group through it?
- How will group members connect (e.g., Internet, intranet, virtual private network [VPN], firewalls)?
- Are messages or browsers to be encrypted?
- Are additional security measures needed, such as a two-step log in?

Familiarity and Compatibility

- How familiar are administrators, eCoaches, teachers, and other school professionals with the technology needed for online or hybrid group coaching? Platform fatigue can set in quickly, so it is important to make use of those that are compatible with existing district, school, or classroom technology. For example, if teachers and other school professionals already have tablets or iPads for the other three components of the eCoaching continuum (i.e., studying, observing, and 1:1, real-time, in-ear coaching), then it's important to ensure that the wiki used for group coaching is accessible on the tablet or iPad, too.

Technology Know-How and Support

- What internal technology support is available through district or school personnel?
- What external technology support is available? Is the support provided free of charge or at a price? How long is the free or paid support provided?
- How accessible are internal or external technology supports during group coaching sessions?

- Who should be contacted first: internal or external technology support personnel?
- How can technology support personnel assist in minimizing risks associated with group members connecting online?

Building on the Instructional Plan for Technology-Enabled Group Coaching

The preceding chapters described why and how teachers and other school professionals could put together a blueprint, referred to as an instructional plan, as a guide for engaging in technology-enabled study, observation, and 1:1 coaching. In this chapter, we emphasize that it is important for teachers and other school professionals to continue building on the plan by delineating how technology-enabled group coaching will be used intentionally to facilitate transfer of the content or pedagogy that has been studied, observed, and coached individually. The manner in which this can be accomplished is outlined in the last row in Figure 4.3. Taking a few minutes to add this information also helps teachers and other school professionals ensure alignment among the components of the eCoaching continuum.

Creating Norms That Support Technology-Enabled Group Coaching

Although working in teams is not foreign to teachers or other school professionals, participating in technology-enabled group coaching for the purpose of improving classroom practice and enhancing student outcomes often requires some adjustment. Creating a climate and a culture that support technology-enabled group coaching is one of the first steps toward easing that adjustment. This means that time must be devoted to establishing and maintaining new norms for learning from one another to achieve improved student performance.

Instructional, Shared, and Transformational Leadership

If the power of peer problem solving is to be realized, then the complementary and vital roles that instructional, shared, and transformational leadership play in supporting it must be recognized. Using multilevel analyses, Vanblaere and Devos (2016) concluded that instructional leadership is essential to deprivatizing classroom practice, whereas transformational leadership is fundamental to fostering a collective responsibility for improving teaching and learning. Deprivatization and collective responsibility are, without question, new norms that must be established

Figure 4.3

Expanded Instructional Design Plan That Includes Technology-Enabled Group Coaching–Questioning Example

Guiding Questions	Sample Instructional Design Planning for Technology-Enabled Study, Observation, 1:1, Real-Time, In-Ear Coaching, and Group Coaching of Specific Content or Pedagogy
What is the topic and purpose of study?	Develop or refine pedagogical knowledge in four areas: • *Effective questioning* to enhance students' comprehension during literacy instruction • *Two of Deborah Ball's 19 high-leverage practices related specifically to questioning*—leading a group discussion and eliciting and interpreting individual students' thinking • *Culturally responsive questioning* to meet the needs of diverse students • One of the Council for Exceptional Children's (CEC's) high-leverage social, emotional, and behavioral practices—HLP #7: Establish a Consistent, Organized, and Respectful Learning Environment

Why is the topic of study important?	• The school improvement plan
	  ◇ 100 percent of students will achieve proficiency in literacy.
	• District student achievement data
	  ◇ Currently, student performance data confirm many students, especially those who are diverse, are not achieving proficiency in literacy.
	• Classroom/teacher performance data
	  ◇ Currently, classroom observational data confirm most teachers are using lower-order questioning and minimal discussion during literacy instruction. High-performing students respond frequently and accurately.
	• Pedagogical research
	  ◇ Institute for Education Sciences (IES) researchers Matsumura and colleagues (2013) found the quality of classroom text discussions, including questioning, mediated students' reading achievement.
	• Social/emotional/behavioral research
	  ◇ Results from meta-analytic studies have confirmed many varied benefits for students whose teachers provided social, emotional, and behavioral supports, including 11 percentile point gains in academic achievement (Mahoney et al., 2018).

What is already known about the topic of study?	Based on theory-of-change/logic-model planning, teachers and other school professionals realize that if they want to increase all K–12 students' proficiency in literacy, they need to develop in-depth knowledge of effective questioning practices as well as how to make questions culturally responsive to their diverse students while creating and maintaining a positive, respectful, organized, and consistent environment for learning.
What content or information is needed to transfer the topic of study to the classroom?	Teachers and other school professionals need to understand and include in their lesson planning for literacy instruction • A range of effective questions from lower to higher order that support rich thoughtful discussion • Two of Deborah Ball's 19 high-leverage practices related specifically to questioning—leading a group discussion and eliciting and interpreting individual students' thinking • Culturally responsive questions • One of the CEC's high-leverage social, emotional, and behavioral practices—HLP #7: Establish a Consistent, Organized, and Respectful Learning Environment

(continues)

Figure 4.3   (continued)

Expanded Instructional Design Plan That Includes Technology-Enabled Group Coaching–Questioning Example

Guiding Questions	Sample Instructional Design Planning for Technology-Enabled Study, Observation, 1:1, Real-Time, In-Ear Coaching, and Group Coaching of Specific Content or Pedagogy

How will technology be used to support the topic of study and observation of the same?	• *E-book study.* Engage in e-book study of effective questioning tactics, using *Questioning for Classroom Discussion* (Walsh & Sattes, 2015).
	• *Electronic discussion guide.* Download the Study Guide for *Questioning for Classroom Discussion* from http://www.ascd.org/publications/books/115012/chapters /An-ASCD-Study-Guide-for-Questioning-for-Classroom-Discussion@-Purposeful -Speaking,-Engaged-Listening,-Deep-Thinking.aspx
	• *PDF document.* Use the description of HLP #7 from the CEC's high-leverage social, emotional, and behavioral practices as a study aid (https://highleveragepractices.org /wp-content/uploads/2017/06/SEBshort.pdf).
	• *Reputable websites.* Bookmark three websites:
	  ◊ University of Michigan's Teaching Works (http://www.teachingworks.org/work-of-teaching /high-leverage-practices) to review two of Deborah Ball's 19 high-leverage practices related specifically to questioning—leading a group discussion and eliciting and interpreting individual students' thinking
	  ◊ *Create Success!* by Kadhir Rajagopal (http://www.ascd.org/publications/books/111022 /chapters/Culturally-Responsive-Instruction.aspx) to study Chapter 1, "Culturally Responsive Instruction," focusing on the section pertaining to questioning
	  ◊ The CEC's high-leverage practices to review HLP #7: Establish a Consistent, Organized, and Respectful Learning Environment (https://highleveragepractices.org/wp-content /uploads/2017/06/SEBshort.pdf and https://highleveragepractices.org/about-hlps/)
	• *Professional online community platforms.* Use edWeb (https://home.edweb.net/) or PBworks (http://www.pbworks.com/) to create an online PLC for weekly e-book study discussion.
	• *Social media.* Follow Teaching Works on Twitter (https://twitter.com/) and Facebook (https:// www.facebook.com/). Engage in weekly Twitter chats using #culturallyresponsivequestioning, #questioningforclassroomdiscussion, and #socialemotionallearning.
	• *Online videoconferencing and robotic platform for video streaming and capture.* Use Skype (https://www.skype.com) with Call Recorder (http://www.ecamm.com/mac/callrecorder/) and Swivl (https://cloud.swivl.com/) to observe and electronically capture models and demonstrations of teachers using effective, culturally sensitive questioning during literacy instruction.
	• *YouTube.* Teachers and other school professionals select video models showcasing how to use "I wonder . . ." questions during literacy instruction and view clips such as "Before, During and After Questions: Promoting Reading Comprehension and Critical Thinking," posted by The Balanced Literacy Diet (https://www.youtube.com/watch?v=Sd1FlXxpVIw) on YouTube. In all, 55 video models pertaining to effective comprehension questioning during literacy instruction are available through the Balanced Literacy Diet channel on YouTube (https://www.youtube.com/watch?v=psakxRT9hdA&list=PL5178787DB725559D). These videos could be reviewed for models and demonstrations showcasing effective, culturally relevant questioning.

How will participants demonstrate understanding of the topic of study and the models and demonstrations observed?	• Create low-stakes chapter quizzes for e-book study using Google Docs (https://www.google .com/docs/about/) or SurveyMonkey (https://www.surveymonkey.com/). • Design and deliver one or two interactive presentations on culturally responsive questioning and two of Deborah Ball's 19 high-leverage practices related specifically to questioning—leading a group discussion and eliciting and interpreting individual students' thinking—with peers/colleagues using Pear Deck (https://www.peardeck.com/), Nearpod (https://nearpod.com/), or Classkick (https://classkick.com/). • Earn digital badges/microcredentials for effective questioning, culturally responsive questioning, two of Deborah Ball's 19 high-leverage practices related specifically to questioning—leading a group discussion and eliciting and interpreting individual students' thinking—and one of the CEC's high-leverage practices (i.e., HLP #7: Establish a Consistent, Organized, and Respectful Learning Environment)—via ASCD or Digital Promise (http:// digitalpromise.org/initiative/educator-micro-credentials/).

Figure 4.3

Expanded Instructional Design Plan That Includes Technology-Enabled Group Coaching–Questioning Example

Guiding Questions	Sample Instructional Design Planning for Technology-Enabled Study, Observation, 1:1, Real-Time, In-Ear Coaching, and Group Coaching of Specific Content or Pedagogy
How will participants demonstrate transfer of the topic of study and the models and demonstrations observed?	• Engage in 10 to 15 one-on-one, real-time eCoaching sessions, demonstrating effective questioning, culturally responsive questioning, and high-leverage social, emotional, and behavioral practices. • Provide evidence of positive K–12 student impact in each session.
*How will participants **support one another in solving problems of practice that result when transferring** content or pedagogy that has been studied, observed, and coached previously?*	• Participate in technology-enabled group coaching sessions, once or twice a month, exploring and solving problems of practice associated with effective questioning, culturally responsive questioning, and high-leverage social, emotional, and behavioral practices. • Provide evidence of positive K–12 student impact following each technology-enabled group coaching session.

for technology-enabled group coaching to take root. Instructional leadership is second nature for many of today's experienced teachers, eCoaches, administrators, and other school professionals. Transformational and shared leadership, by contrast, are not. As such, teachers, eCoaches, administrators, and other school professionals need to intentionally cultivate shared and transformational leadership knowledge, skills, and dispositions, not only in themselves but also in others. One way to do so is by tapping in to reputable online resources. For example, the Center for Creative Leadership's Education Sector (https://www.ccl.org/leadership-solutions/industries-sectors/education/) offers a wealth of on-campus and online leadership development opportunities, including "lead-it-yourself solutions" that can be customized to meet each group's unique needs at an affordable rate. As Vanblaere and Devos (2016) emphasize, "It is important that this [transformational leadership] originates at the top and consequently permeates all levels of the school" (p. 35). Only then can new norms, such as deprivatization and collective responsibility, be embraced authentically and achieved fully.

Coach-Supported Group Coaching

As is the case with leadership, learning to work effectively with one's peers in a group requires new norms. Drawing on team-supported coaching literature, we agree with Aguilar (2016): "Community agreements build culture" (p. 96). The community agreements that support the culture needed for technology-enabled group coaching to thrive are many and varied, including procedural and behavioral norms that blend personal and collective needs so that group goals can be achieved (Aguilar, 2016). Procedural norms reflect the processes or manner in which group members carry out their charge. By contrast, behavioral norms indicate the ways in which group members agree to interact with one another socially, emotionally, and behaviorally. Examples of procedural and behavioral norms include agreements about e-mailing meeting agendas in advance, adhering to the problem-solving framework, listening to one another respectfully, and resolving conflict in healthy ways. The eCoach or expert facilitator plays an important role in coaching group members, not only as they establish new norms for working with one another to solve problems of practice, but also as they carry them out on a day-to-day basis. In this way, the group coach works to cultivate genuine, rather than contrived, collegiality among members (Wang, Hall, & Rahimi, 2015), which is vital to achieving improved outcomes.

Results-Oriented Climate

During technology-enabled coaching, if group members are not careful, they can quickly become mired in problems of practice. When this happens, negativity abounds, frustration ensues, and dysfunction reigns. To avoid this slippery, unproductive slope, eCoaches, teachers, administrators, and other school professionals must continually shift the group's focus to achieving positive results for students. This results-driven focus should be informed by the evidence or data that members collect on relevant teacher and student performance, rather than mere opinion. Cultivating a results-driven climate requires new norms, too. Chief among them are habits of mind and professional practice characterized by ongoing commitments to inquiry and improvement. Establishing these new norms requires members to leverage social capital, establish joint goals, adopt a shared vision, value assessment, and strive for group cohesiveness—all in the spirit of achieving collective efficacy and enhancing students' learning (Birenbaum, Kimron, & Shilton, 2011).

Contemplating the Benefits and Cautions Associated with Technology-Enabled Group Coaching

As was the case with the previous three components of the eCoaching continuum, there are benefits and drawbacks associated with technology-enabled group coaching. In what follows, we briefly describe each. We hope this information assists school professionals in maximizing the benefits and minimizing the liabilities encountered during technology-enabled group coaching.

Benefits

Unlike face-to-face group coaching, the technology-enabled option allows group members (e.g., teachers, eCoaches, other school professionals, or administrators across or within grade level or disciplines) to be located across the hall, district, state, region, country, or globe. This unparalleled flexibility eliminates traditional barriers, such as time and distance (Blitz, 2013). Because video clips illustrating problems of practice can be archived electronically, scheduling conflicts may also be reduced. Moreover, electronic connections offer teachers increased levels of support and decreased feelings of frustration and isolation (Curry, 2008). Perhaps, most important, Blitz (2013) posits that self-reflection of teaching and learning in online PLCs trumps that which occurs in traditional face-to-face interactions. Researchers have pinpointed additional benefits associated with online or face-to-face group coaching, including the following:

- Revitalizes school professionals by sparking excitement and energy (Marzano, 2011)
- Generates new ideas from peers for solving problems of practice (Marzano, 2011)
- Enhances coaching efficiency through peer learning and support (Fettig & Artman-Meeker, 2016)
- Contributes to individual, team, and school improvements (Brown & Grant, 2010)
- Helps teachers take risks, make adjustments, and put into practice content or pedagogy (including social, emotional, and behavioral domains) more effectively with the support of their peer group (McLaughlin & Talbert, 2006)
- Builds teachers' analytical skills (Murray, Ma, & Mazur, 2009)
- Cultivates teachers' social networks and social capital (Stelter et al., 2011)
- Enhances teachers' ability to handle challenging career situations and promotes general well-being (Stelter et al., 2011)

Cautions

Some group members' motivation may decline when collaborating online (Blitz, 2013). Connectivity can also be interrupted from time to time, so technology support and troubleshooting require ongoing attention and consideration. Special care must be taken, too, to secure private web-based environments when analyzing problems of practice or viewing live or archived videos of classroom instruction. Cost may warrant further consideration in that free options often pose space limitations, while pricier alternatives may exceed typical budgets. Ongoing training must be provided to group members not only on the use of web-based technology but also on the CFG or instructional rounds protocol. Finally, group members need to guard against the perils of contrived collegiality (Wang et al., 2015) and faulty decision making, such as that resulting from groupthink (Janis, 1982).

Translating the eCoach's Role into Action During Technology-Enabled Group Coaching

As emphasized in previous chapters, we reiterate in this one that the eCoach plays a vital and unique role in each of the four components of the eCoaching continuum. Here we offer a list of roles and responsibilities eCoaches could shoulder in facilitating technology-enabled group coaching to foster learning transfer and enhance K–12 student outcomes. To do so successfully, eCoaches need administrator and colleague support, including dedicated release time, clearly delineated job roles and responsibilities, and ongoing training and job-embedded professional development.

- Take a leadership role in helping administrators, teachers, and other school professionals understand the unique and compelling reasons for undertaking technology-enabled group coaching.
- Schedule training for technology-enabled group coaching, such as that needed for CFGs and instructional rounds.
- Secure protocols for technology-enabled group coaching, such as those used in CFGs and instructional rounds.
- Assist teachers and other school professionals in identifying and prioritizing problems of practice.
- Ensure that problems of practice selected for technology-enabled group coaching align with the content and pedagogy (including social, emotional, and behavioral domains) studied, observed, and coached (1:1 in real time).
- Facilitate the three-part organizational framework for carrying out technology-enabled group coaching.
- Offer guidance on determining availability of technology-enabled options, equipment, software, apps, and so forth that support technology-enabled group coaching.
- Coordinate evaluation of technology-related options, equipment, software, and apps and consider goodness of fit, using guiding questions.

- Build on the instructional design plan for technology-enabled group coaching and modify as needed.
- Schedule and facilitate technology-enabled group coaching sessions with teachers and other school professionals.
- Capture technology-enabled group coaching electronically, so that others can access the data, including digital visualizations and recordings of the coaching, as needed, for reflection and improvement.
- Co-create norms for technology-enabled group coaching.
- Partner with school librarians, technology support specialists, and legal counsel to review training in relevant policies, such as FERPA's video and audio stipulations.
- Locate, adapt, or generate data collection protocols and templates for focused technology-enabled group coaching.
- Develop digital badges/microcredentials for technology-enabled group coaching.
- Create modules for training on new and existing technologies and approaches that support technology-enabled group coaching.
- Monitor the progress of technology-enabled group coaching and evaluate professional learning.

Moreover, just as teachers and other school professionals use technology to engage in group coaching to facilitate learning transfer, so, too, do eCoaches. For instance, returning to the example provided in Chapters 1–3, after viewing the "Coaching Conversations" module in Coursera (https://www.coursera.org/specializations/coaching-skills-manager), electronically archiving debriefing observations that included coaching conversations with teachers and other school professionals and viewing them to self-assess learning transfer, and participating in 1:1, real-time, in-ear coaching, eCoaches can engage in technology-enabled group coaching, sharing and solving problems of practice experienced through the eCoaching continuum.

Revisiting Important Ideas

In this chapter, we've described in detail how to carry out technology-enabled group coaching to further refine teachers' transfer of content and pedagogy, including social, emotional, and behavioral domains. We've also emphasized why doing so is important, as well as known benefits and cautions. Before moving on to Chapter 5, let's take a minute to review the important ideas we've shared:

- Clarify and communicate to key stakeholders the unique, varied, and compelling purposes for carrying out technology-enabled group coaching—online or hybrid.

- Ensure alignment among technology-enabled study, observation, 1:1 coaching, and group coaching.
- Tailor the technology-enabled group coaching sessions to teachers and other school professionals' unique learning needs about the content or pedagogy, including social, emotional, and behavioral domains.
- Make technology-enabled group coaching work, in part by adopting a three-part organizational framework comprising focused activities before, during, and after the online or hybrid group coaching sessions.
- Collect performance data and use commercially produced or homegrown protocols and templates as a guide to focus learning transfer and gain deeper meaning from technology-enabled group coaching sessions.
- Consider online or blended/hybrid variations for carrying out technology-enabled group coaching.
- Consider equipment, software, apps, and so forth in accord with budgets and professional learning needs.
- Determine the best technology fit, in part based on answers to the guiding questions provided.
- Build on the blueprint, also referred to as the instructional plan, developed in Chapters 1–3, by adding technology-enabled group coaching that supports the transfer of content or pedagogy (including social, emotional, and behavioral domains) that has been studied, observed, and coached 1:1 previously.
- Create and sustain norms that support technology-enabled group coaching, including demonstrating leadership, providing coach-supported group coaching, and embracing a positive, engaged, results-oriented climate.
- Contemplate the benefits and cautions carefully, and make decisions about how to proceed with technology-enabled group coaching.
- Ensure that the eCoach's roles and responsibilities regarding technology-enabled group coaching are clearly articulated and supported by administrators, teachers, and other school professionals.

No doubt, this chapter is filled with important information. To help prevent teachers and other school professionals from becoming overwhelmed by the information we've shared, we offer an At-a-Glance Checklist. As noted in preceding chapters, using the checklist will empower teachers and other school professionals to move forward with technology-enabled group coaching effectively and efficiently. Realizing the power of technology-enabled group coaching requires that you understand just 12 simple things!

AT-A-GLANCE CHECKLIST

Preparing for Successful Technology-Enabled Group Coaching

- ☐ The purpose for technology-enabled group coaching is clear, unique, and compelling.
- ☐ The content or pedagogy (including social, emotional, and behavioral domains) selected for technology-enabled group coaching aligns with that which was selected for technology-enabled study, observation, and 1:1 coaching.
- ☐ The protocol (e.g., critical friends, instructional rounds) for technology-enabled group coaching is selected and necessary training provided.
- ☐ An expert or peer eCoach is identified to facilitate technology-enabled group coaching.
- ☐ The three-part organizational framework (before, during, and after) is developed and used, in part to make technology-enabled group coaching work.
- ☐ Problems of practice are identified based on the content or pedagogy selected for technology-enabled study, observation, 1:1 coaching, and group coaching.
- ☐ Performance data are collected and templates or protocols are used during technology-enabled group coaching to promote transfer and deepen learning.
- ☐ Technology-enabled options, equipment, software, apps, and so forth are identified based on goodness of fit.
- ☐ The instructional design plan is expanded to guide technology-enabled study + observations + 1:1 coaching + group coaching and can be modified as needed.
- ☐ Norms for technology-enabled group coaching are established and supported.
- ☐ Benefits and cautions associated with technology-enabled group coaching are considered, and choices are made accordingly.
- ☐ eCoaches' roles and responsibilities, specific to technology-enabled group coaching, are clearly articulated and supported.

5

Carrying Out the Technology-Enabled Coaching Continuum

Assembling Learning Teams, Sharing Responsibilities, and Aiming for Impact

Marcia Rock

In collaborative cultures, failure and uncertainty are not protected but shared and discussed to gain support. —Andy Hargreaves (n.d.)

How can technology be used to support a learning team approach when carrying out the four components of the technology-enabled coaching continuum?

Understanding the Purpose of a Technology-Enabled Learning Team Approach

The mere mention of working in a team evokes a variety of emotional reactions, ranging from eager anticipation to all-consuming dread and everything in between. Why? Although teaching is often considered an isolated and lonely endeavor (Sagor, 2000), most education professionals have had more than a few experiences working in teams, ranging from energizing and impactful experiences to those that are soul sucking and useless. Consequently, the varied emotional responses associated with teaming are expected and understandable.

Most individuals, including teachers, administrators, and other school professionals, learned initially about teaming through their life experiences as family members. Like professional teams, some families are healthy and high performing. Others, not so much. These family experiences often play a pivotal role in shaping how one interacts as a team member (Johnson & Johnson, 2016). The important point is that when undertaking any group-focused form of professional learning, including a technology-enabled approach to the coaching continuum, team composition and development must be intentional and dynamics must be monitored.

Given that challenges often permeate team-based work, why should teachers, administrators, and other school professionals consider the approach? And why should they use technology to support it? Think back to the Introduction. There, I explained that the technology-enabled coaching continuum could be carried out in a variety of ways—a notion I referred to as adoption through flexible use. Essentially, this means that both individuals and teams can use the eCoaching continuum to maximize professional development. An eCoach can work individually with a teacher or other school professional using the technology-enabled coaching continuum as the basis for professional learning. Or an eCoach can work with teams of frontline practitioners using the technology-enabled coaching continuum as the basis for professional learning. And that's not all. The technology-enabled continuum is also ideal for self-coaching.

When teachers, other school professionals, administrators, and eCoaches carry out the technology-enabled coaching continuum using a team-based approach, the learning team model is especially well suited. Chappuis, Chappuis, and Stiggins (2009) identified four essential features of a learning team model—"job-embedded, sustained over time, centered on active learning, and focused on student outcomes" (p. 57)—all of which are nested within and across the four components of the eCoaching continuum. When combined, they offer a powerful, much-needed alternative to hit-or-miss, one-shot professional development.

Generally, the purpose of taking a learning team approach when carrying out the technology-enabled coaching continuum is for teachers, other school professionals, administrators, and eCoaches to join in strengthening one another's professional learning. As noted in Chapter 4, and Borko (2004) pointed out more than a decade ago, teachers' knowledge and practice improve when working together in professional learning communities (PLCs). Learning teams are PLCs. Kruse and Louis (1997) found, too, that teaming could be used successfully for cultivating professional community and bolstering school improvement. In embracing a learning team approach, Fulton and Britton (2011) asserted that the traditional aim in professional learning, which is typically centered on developing good teachers, shifts to an expanded one focused on cultivating great teaching and improved learning. The roots of social learning, long established as vital to "meaning making," run deep in education (see Vygotsky, 1962).

The role of technology in supporting team-focused professional learning is twofold. First, technology supports learning team members in carrying out the four components of the eCoaching continuum (i.e., study, observation, 1:1 coaching, and group or peer coaching)—singly and collectively. In each of the preceding chapters, I, along with contributors, explained how to do this, as well as why doing so is important. Second, technology helps learning team members connect and communicate regularly, monitor and evaluate the effectiveness of their professional learning and its impact on K–12 students over time, and electronically archive their activities.

In the remainder of this chapter, I describe how to assemble learning teams, how to monitor and evaluate their effectiveness, how to select digital options that support not only team learning but also the delivery of the technology-enabled coaching continuum, and how the eCoach can support the learning team. That said, when members of the learning team pull together is when the approach is most effective. Because many frontline practitioners are familiar with PLCs, they will likely find this undertaking easier than expected because much of the information that follows builds on their prior knowledge and experience.

Setting the Stage for Technology-Enabled Learning Teams

When teachers, administrators, eCoaches, and other school professionals work together in learning teams to carry out the technology-enabled coaching continuum, their success hinges on a variety of factors, including developing a deeper understanding of teaming, and reviewing and selecting the digital tools that support teaming. I'll begin by focusing on what it takes to put together high-performing learning teams. Then I'll focus on the digital options that support learning team members as they interact and carry out the technology-enabled coaching continuum. Approaching these tasks systematically, but not rigidly, helps learning team members ensure success from the start.

Essential Features of a Team

What are the essential features of a team? In other words, what makes a team a team? Drawing on relevant, seminal literature in organizational psychology, Kozlowski and Bell (2008) defined teams as "two or more individuals who (a) exist to perform organizationally relevant tasks, (b) share one or more common goals, (c) interact socially, (d) exhibit task interdependencies (i.e., work flow, goals, outcomes), (e) maintain and manage boundaries, and (f) are embedded in an organizational context that sets boundaries, constrains the team, and influences exchanges with other units in the broader entity" (p. 334). How do the components of this definition apply to frontline practitioners who want to take a learning team approach when carrying out the technology-enabled coaching continuum? Keep reading for applied examples:

- *Include two or more individuals.* eCoaching continuum learning teams comprise the eCoach, teachers, other school professionals, or administrators.
- *Perform organizationally relevant tasks.* eCoaching continuum learning team members engage in meaningful, job-embedded professional development by connecting and carrying out the four components of the eCoaching continuum with a common mission of improving teaching and learning.
- *Share common goals.* Learning team members adopt the eCoaching continuum approach to job-embedded professional development, not only to enhance teacher performance but also to improve educational and life outcomes for students with and without disabilities. In doing so, teaching and learning centered on the "whole" child is embraced by all.
- *Interact socially.* eCoaching continuum learning team members focus on building and sustaining relationships through informal and formal interactions, including team building, described later in this chapter. But a word of caution is in order here. Most teachers, other school professionals, administrators, and eCoaches agree that all should guard against the perils of mandated fun, also known as "fundatory" activities, and focus instead on engaging in authentic, meaningful enterprises that help learning team members work well together in better meeting the educational needs of the whole child.
- *Exhibit task interdependencies.* Learning team members develop procedures and guidelines for sharing expertise, resources, information, and decision making when carrying out each component of the eCoaching continuum. Doing so helps everyone remain on the same page, while also preventing and minimizing conflict within the team. For instance, learning team members might decide together to complete and follow the instructional plan provided in Chapter 1 when identifying the content targeted for study, observation, 1:1 coaching, and group or peer coaching. Alternatively, they might determine that jigsawing the sections of the instructional plan and coming together afterward for shared discussion and review would be a more efficient and effective option.
- *Maintain and manage boundaries.* eCoaching continuum learning team members work closely when connecting and carrying out the four components of the continuum. Because complexities abound in this work, learning team members join in establishing and maintaining healthy boundaries. For instance, investing time initially in identifying learning team members' roles and responsibilities

goes a long way toward establishing respectful boundaries and minimizing dysfunctional team behaviors, such as "freeloading" or "overstepping boundaries."

- *Embed in an organizational context.* eCoaching continuum learning team members undertake meaningful, job-embedded professional development topics guided by the greater organizational context of the school and the district. This means they consider the unique learning needs of their K–12 students and strive to meet them strategically, collaboratively, and systematically. For example, learning team members who jointly identified questioning for classroom discussion as a target for professional learning would also take time to figure out current district, school, and classroom barriers that preclude the practice, such as insufficient teacher knowledge, poor classroom transfer, and lack of culturally sensitive questioning, as well as K–12 student issues, such as inadequate prior knowledge, that might contribute to the current need. Then they can tailor the technology-enabled coaching continuum so that obstacles operating at multiple levels can be addressed positively and substantively, resulting in improved student learning.

Potential Learning Team Members and Configurations

Who should be included in the learning teams? As mentioned previously, those who are carrying out the technology-enabled coaching continuum (i.e., teachers, administrators, other school professionals, and eCoaches, internal or external) should be included. Common configurations include teams at the international, national, regional, state, district, school, grade, teacher, content-area, and tiered-support levels (see Figure 5.1).

Team leadership. What about team leadership? Morgeson, DeRue, and Karam (2010) pointed out that team leadership can be external, internal, or a combination of the two. If an internal approach is taken, then one or more of the learning team members serves as the team leader(s). By contrast, external leaders are not team members. A combined approach includes both. Learning team members must determine which leadership approach best meets their needs, budget, and resources, and then proceed accordingly. Regardless of whether team leadership is internal, external, or combined, the leader's aims remain constant—enhanced learning team functioning and improved effectiveness (Morgeson et al., 2010).

Team structure. How much structure do learning team members need to enhance their performance when carrying out the technology-enabled coaching continuum? Is more structure better than less, or vice versa? Bresman and Zellmer-Bruhn (2013) concluded that "multiple levels of structure, and their interactions, should be taken into consideration when assessing structural effects on team learning" (p. 1120). In other words, there are times when too much structure impedes

Figure 5.1

Learning Team Configurations–Configurations and Examples

Team Configuration	Example
International, national, regional, or state level	Teachers, administrators, other school professionals, and eCoaches with shared professional learning needs come together from across the globe, the nation, the region, or the state. This approach works well when the professional development topic needs to be tailored to meet the unique needs of a specific group of K–12 students with low-incidence disabilities. For example, if teachers of students with severe intellectual disabilities and autism are interested in improving effective questioning for discussion in inclusive classrooms, this configuration would work well because there may be only one teacher who serves them in a given school.
District-level	When members of the eCoaching continuum learning team are drawn from across the school district, the configuration represents districtwide commitments that target a shared academic or behavioral goal for improvement. For example, teachers, administrators, other school professionals, and eCoaches employed in different school buildings within the same school district may come together to form a learning team and use the technology-enabled coaching continuum to improve their use of culturally sensitive questioning during classroom instruction in high-needs schools.
School-level	Teachers, administrators, other school professionals, and eCoaches employed in the same school building assemble as learning teams and use the technology-enabled coaching continuum to improve their use of effective questioning during classroom instruction with an emphasis on ensuring equity in responding.
Grade-level	Teachers, administrators, other school professionals, and eCoaches who focus on 3rd grade student learning outcomes come together in a learning team, and use the technology-enabled coaching continuum to establish age-appropriate norms and craft frames for high-quality focus questions during classroom instruction.
Teacher-level	An individual teacher or a few teachers who share a common professional learning interest work(s) with an eCoach. In this way, the dyad, triad, or small group forms a learning team. Individual teachers form teams based on shared interests or needs related to a professional development topic. For example, based on school assessment data confirming a need to facilitate deeper learning, a small group of teachers profess interest in improving critical questioning tactics using varied approaches (i.e., teacher guided, student driven, structured small group) during classroom instruction. They form a learning team to do so, using the technology-enabled coaching continuum as the basis for professional learning.
Content-area level	Content-area teachers assemble learning teams based on specific professional learning needs. For instance, using the technology-enabled coaching continuum, team members want to learn how to create their own designs for effective questioning during classroom discussion in 10th grade biology.
Tiered-support level	Teachers, administrators, other school professionals, and eCoaches organize learning teams that focus professional learning on topics reflecting a tiered or multitiered systems of support (MTSS) approach to K–12 student support. Although Tiers 1, 2, and 3 vary in intensity, effective questioning for classroom discussion could remain the focus for improvement by emphasizing how to effectively differentiate delivery of effective classwide questioning (i.e., Tier 1), small group questioning (i.e., Tier 2), and individual student questioning (i.e., Tier 3).

Note: All topics relate to effective questioning, drawing on the work of Walsh and Sattes (2015).

learning team members' professional development. Conversely, there are circumstances in which too little structure also thwarts team members' learning. That means team members must continuously monitor and assess the structural context and how it impacts learning team members' performance as well as K–12 student outcomes.

Characteristics of high-performing teams. What do high-performing teams have in common? Hackman and Wageman (2005) identified three dimensions associated with high-performing teams: productivity, social processes, and positive learning. Although the relative importance of each dimension varies over time, high-performing teams keep them working harmoniously.

- *Productivity*. Distinguished by timely, effective decision making that meets or exceeds achievement of shared goals.
- *Social processes*. Distinguished by engaging in interdependent interactions, detecting and correcting issues, and noticing and taking advantage of opportunities.
- *Positive learning*. Distinguished by group dynamics that result in more positive than negative professional and personal development and well-being.

If learning team members aspire to high performance, then consideration of Hackman and Wageman's (2005) three dimensions is a must. One way to do so is through team coaching. Because the eCoach is a member of the learning team, he often assumes this responsibility. Hackman and Wageman (2005) found that team coaching improves team effectiveness under four conditions:

- Team members have the knowledge, skill, will, and ability needed for success and are not constrained by organizational demands.
- The team is well designed and supported by the organizational structure.
- The coach focuses feedback on important task-related performance and does not waste time or effort on matters not under the team's direct control.
- The coach provides team members with feedback when the time is right— motivational feedback at the beginning, strategy-specific feedback at midpoint, and knowledge- and skill-related feedback at the end.

Conditions for success. What conditions are needed for learning teams to flourish rather than flounder? Researchers identified six conditions necessary for maximizing team effectiveness and achieving shared success (see Hackman, 2002; Hackman & Edmondson, 2008; Hackman & O'Connor, 2004; Wageman, Nunes, Burruss, & Hackman, 2008). Three of the conditions are considered essential:

- *"Real team."* Characterized by clear boundaries, interdependence, and moderately stable membership.

- *Right people*. Characterized by members with the necessary knowledge, skills, abilities, and attitudes.
- *Compelling direction*. Characterized by a clear purpose that includes challenge and consequence.

The other three are enabling conditions:

- *Sound structure*. Characterized by tasks, composition, and norms of conduct that facilitate and support teamwork.
- *Supportive context*. Characterized by a social system that provides resources and support for carrying out collective work.
- *Expert coaching*. Characterized by a capable individual who helps members navigate "hot spots," interact in prosocial and effective ways, and improve performance over the course of the team life cycle.

How important is it for frontline school professionals to create these conditions within learning teams? Based on statistical analysis of more than 60 U.S. intelligence community teams, Hackman and O'Connor (2004) found that 74 percent of the variance was attributed to these conditions. Simply put, they matter—nearly 75 percent of the time.

How can learning team members determine whether these much-needed conditions are at play? Fortunately, the Team Diagnostic Survey provides an assessment and summary report centered on them (Wageman & Hackman, 2005). Learning team members can electronically access the survey and a wealth of other reputable resources pertaining to team dynamics at http://team-diagnostics.com/. The survey requires less than 20 minutes to complete.

Making a Technology-Enabled Team-Based Approach Work

After setting the stage for successful team learning (also referred to as frontloading), practitioners must dedicate time and effort to determining how they will make it work on a day-to-day basis. They must consider how team stages and cycles influence taskwork and teamwork, who does what and when, how members interact effectively, and how members evaluate the impact and effectiveness of their professional learning.

The Role of Team Stages and Cycles

Most teachers, administrators, and other school professionals have heard of Tuckman's infamous and self-explanatory stages of team development—forming, storming, norming, performing, and adjourning (Tuckman, 1965; Tuckman &

Jensen, 1977). Learning team members must think about these five stages through which they will likely progress as they carry out the technology-enabled coaching continuum. At the same time, the eCoach must consider how to provide feedback to the learning team as they progress through these stages. But that's not all.

In terms of structuring members' taskwork and teamwork, teaching cycles are a good fit for carrying out the technology-enabled coaching continuum in learning teams. Ball and Cohen (1999) defined teaching cycles as "centered in the critical activities of the profession, that is, in and about the practices of teaching and learning" (p. 13). Using teaching cycles comprising three phases—preparation, observation, and analysis—learning team members work together to plan, observe, and critique lessons and units of study. Each teaching cycle lasts approximately four to six weeks. Within each teaching cycle, learning team members not only plan and deliver the instructional unit, but they also identify how they embed the technology-enabled coaching continuum to bolster their professional learning while they carry out the instructional unit. The key to success, however, is that learning team members resist the temptation to view each teaching cycle or unit separately. Instead, they should take a bigger picture view of curriculum, focusing on how teaching cycles or units support one another to form a cohesive whole (Di Michele Lalor, 2016).

For example, 4th grade teachers may join with the eCoach to form a learning team and design a mathematics unit on fractions. Based on existing assessment data, they decide that questioning needs improvement to foster their students' ability to think critically about what they are learning in math; specifically, how fractions connect to the real world (i.e., where they show up in students' daily lives) and why it is important to learn them. They decide to focus on embedding three formats—teacher-directed discussion, small group–directed discussion, and student-directed discussion—into the instructional unit on fractions. To do so, they rely on the four components of the technology-enabled coaching continuum (i.e., study, observation, 1:1 coaching, group or peer coaching). In this way, the teaching cycle and the technology-enabled coaching continuum intersect and form the basis for impact, not only on teacher learning but also on their 4th grade students' understanding of fractions and other essential math competencies addressed in future teaching cycles or units, as illustrated in Figure 5.2.

Harmonizing Taskwork and Teamwork

Marks, Mathieu, and Zaccaro (2001) pinpointed important distinctions between taskwork and teamwork. Taskwork entails what teams are doing. Teamwork involves how they go about doing so with one another. When carrying out the technology-enabled coaching continuum using a learning team format, the

FIGURE 5.2 FRACTIONS UNIT–4TH GRADE MATHEMATICS INSTRUCTION

Professional Learning Topic-Questioning for Classroom Discussion

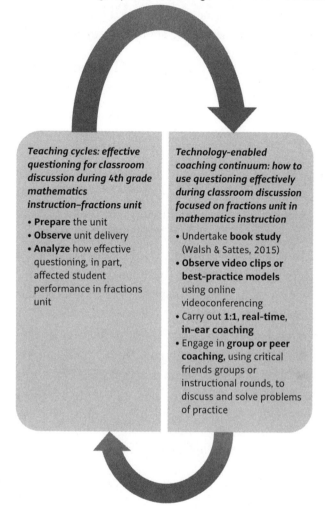

Teaching cycles: effective questioning for classroom discussion during 4th grade mathematics instruction–fractions unit

- **Prepare** the unit
- **Observe** unit delivery
- **Analyze** how effective questioning, in part, affected student performance in fractions unit

Technology-enabled coaching continuum: how to use questioning effectively during classroom discussion focused on fractions unit in mathematics instruction

- Undertake **book study** (Walsh & Sattes, 2015)
- **Observe video clips or best-practice models** using online videoconferencing
- Carry out **1:1, real-time, in-ear coaching**
- Engage in **group or peer coaching,** using critical friends groups or instructional rounds, to discuss and solve problems of practice

taskwork includes the four components described previously in Chapters 1–4. The teamwork encompasses how the team carries out the components.

Why is it important for learning team members to distinguish between taskwork and teamwork? McEwan, Ruissen, Eys, Zumbo, and Beauchamp (2017) reported that researchers have found teamwork to positively correlate with important aspects of team effectiveness, such as performance, cohesion, efficacy, and satisfaction. Generally, seminal researchers (i.e., Lewin, 1935) classify teamwork into two categories—locomotion (i.e., behaviors that regulate a team's performance) and maintenance (i.e., behaviors that keep a team together over time). Achieving harmony between the two should remain a top priority for learning team members. Worried about adding too much to an already-full plate (i.e., the technology-enabled coaching continuum)? The before, during, and after framework described in Figure 5.3 aligns well with what was described previously in Chapters 1–4 as ways for making each component of the continuum work.

Putting It All Together: How Learning Team Members Interact and Function Effectively

The professional literature in education and organizational psychology is replete with studies of teams. Translating those findings into real-world practice can be challenging. In the sections that follow, I describe what researchers have associated with effective teaming and what frontline practitioners have been able to carry out consistently and successfully.

Identify team member responsibilities. Taking time for learning team members to discuss who does what and when is important—especially when it comes to taskwork and teamwork. Using Figure 5.3 as a guide is a useful way to approach this task. The figure can be modified in a Google Doc to include columns for time frames, actions, and persons responsible. Then it can be shared with all for ongoing accountability as needed.

Embrace shared leadership. Shared, also referred to as distributed, leadership is the ideal when carrying out a job-embedded, team-based approach to professional learning. Within learning teams, shared leadership can be achieved in

Figure 5.3

Teamwork–Locomotion and Maintenance Behaviors

Examples of Locomotion Behaviors	Examples of Maintenance Behaviors
Before (i.e., prior to carrying out the technology-enabled coaching continuum for professional learning): Members identify a shared mission, set goals, and generate action plans for goal attainment.	*Before, during,* and *after* (i.e., prior to, while, and after) carrying out the technology-enabled coaching continuum for professional learning): Members attend to interpersonal group dynamics, including conflict management, conflict resolution, and social support. When group dynamic issues go unaddressed, teams cannot function effectively.
During (i.e., while carrying out the technology-enabled coaching continuum for professional learning): Members communicate, coordinate, and cooperate as they carry out action plans for achieving goals.	
After (i.e., after carrying out the technology-enabled coaching continuum for professional learning): Members reflect on team performance, goal attainment, strategy, and so forth. Based on that reflection, they adjust and modify their approach for the next round of professional learning.	

Source: McEwan et al. (2017).

various ways. For instance, shared leadership happens when learning team members rotate the responsibility for serving as the team facilitator. Pieters and Voogt (2016) reported that although team facilitators' roles vary and are influenced by context, they generally carry out three important leadership responsibilities: providing logistical assistance with learning team activities (e.g., when and how the four components of the eCoaching continuum will be embedded in the teaching cycle), scaffolding professional learning, and monitoring effectiveness. They described the role of the facilitator as dynamic, flexible, hands-on, and just in time (Pieters & Voogt, 2016). Effective facilitators also develop trust, foster collaboration, and provide opportunities for continuous feedback and reflection with a focus on promoting professional learning and impact. Using focus group discussions with team members and semi-structured interviews with facilitators, Becuwe, Tondeur, Pareja, Roblin, Thys, and Castelein (2016) investigated the role and importance of facilitators in team-based professional development and found that the importance of the facilitator was influenced, in part, by team characteristics and phase (e.g., beginning, middle, end).

Generate expectations for team member interaction. Working with others effectively requires clear communication, psychological safety, and conflict management. Learning team members must dedicate time to figuring out how to establish these expectations in positive, healthy ways:

- *Communication.* Clear and open communication is a hallmark of effective teams (Miles & Mangold, 2002). What kinds of communication tactics are needed? Establishing ground rules for engaging in active listening, soliciting input from all members, taking turns participating in discussions, using nonverbal communication to indicate interest and engagement, requesting clarification, asking questions, respectfully challenging one another's views, providing feedback, offering genuine encouragement, and sharing information with all team members. When communication is haphazard, unclear, or fragmented, mistrust and distrust often result, adversely impacting desired outcomes for participants and their K–12 students.

- *Psychological safety.* How important is psychological safety in learning teams? Bresman and Zellmer-Bruhn (2013) found that "psychological safety mediates the positive relationship between team structure and team learning" (p. 1120). How do learning team members achieve psychological safety among members? Essentially, they do so by creating structure that is supportive but not stifling. What kind of structure? Clear roles and responsibilities, clear leadership, and established priorities and objectives. Teams with less structure are unpredictable, creating anxiety, uncertainty, frustration, and lack of trust among members.

- *Conflict resolution*. Based on the work of Masters and Albright (2002), Friend and Cook (2017) assert that conflict among team members generally falls into three categories: interests, rights, and power. When differences of opinion erupt around learning team goals, this is an example of interest-related conflict. Power-related disputes often stem from perceived differences in status. For instance, a teacher may disagree with an administrator but remain silent, opting instead to engage in passive-aggressive resistance to avoid direct confrontation and potential claims of insubordination. Regardless of the source, effective teams have processes and procedures in place that allow members to resolve inevitable conflicts in healthy ways. One easy-to-use method for resolving conflict is the S-B-I technique (Center for Creative Leadership, n.d.). Here is an example:

  Situation (S). During our regularly scheduled learning team sessions . . .

  Behavior (B). When we spend time complaining about how our students never come prepared and just don't seem to care . . .

  Impact (I). It takes valuable time and attention away from focusing on how our teaching impacts our K–12 students' learning, which frustrates me. Also, I wonder how this prevents us from taking ownership of what we can do differently in the classroom to maximize their learning.

Facilitate interdependence using the instructional design plan as a guide. Facilitating interdependence begins with the instructional design plan described in Chapters 1–4. How so? Learning team members need to use it as the basis for deciding how to carry out the four components of the technology-enabled coaching continuum within the context of learning teams and teaching cycles. They need to be sure when doing so that a calendar with time frames is developed. Also, they need to allow the theory of change (see Chapter 1) to help them prioritize and establish goals for professional learning and impact. As team members develop the overall plan for using learning teams and teaching cycles as the framework for carrying out the technology-enabled coaching continuum, they also need to include the teacher and K–12 student performance data they will collect as evidence of the collective responsibility they share in the work of improving teaching and learning. Combined, these activities help learning team members establish and maintain healthy interdependence. Based on the results of a comparative case study, Meirink, Imants, Meijer, and Verloop (2010) described four levels of collegial interactions among team members, varying from lower to higher levels of interdependence: storytelling and scanning, aiding and assisting, exchanging instructional materials and ideas, and joint instructional problem solving and planning. Teams that embraced the latter reported higher levels of professional learning.

Evaluating Impact and Effectiveness

As described in Chapters 1–4, frontline practitioners need to evaluate the impact and effectiveness of each component of the technology-enabled coaching continuum. The same holds true when carrying out each component within the job-embedded framework of learning teams and teaching cycles. In this case, team members evaluate impact and effectiveness in part through the shared experiences and interactions that result in team growth and impact (Cheng & Ko, 2009). Here are important dimensions for learning team members to consider when evaluating impact and effectiveness (see Chapter 6 for more detail):

- What are the team goals that guide teachers' professional learning? In what ways did goal attainment build teachers' capacity (e.g., increased content knowledge, improved pedagogy, enhanced comradery, renewed commitment)? How does the team know whether these goals were achieved—individually and collectively?
- What are the team goals that guide K–12 students' learning—academically, socially, behaviorally, and emotionally? In what ways did goal attainment improve students' performance holistically, rather than narrowly? How does the team know whether these goals were achieved?
- How does a learning team approach for carrying out the technology-enabled coaching continuum when embedded within teaching cycles impact school effectiveness? What are the important indicators? How does the team know whether this was achieved?

Considering Options for Carrying Out a Technology-Enabled Learning Team Approach

The list of technology tools available for learning team members' consideration when carrying out the technology-enabled coaching continuum continues to grow at a breakneck pace. The newest, shiniest technology options are not always the best. Instead, learning team members should favor those that support effective, efficient, and seamless professional learning. Learning team members need to keep an eye out for the digital tools that offer them quick, easy, and intuitive ways to organize, plan, prioritize, observe, and interact as they carry out the technology-enabled coaching continuum while delivering an instructional unit (i.e., embedded within the teaching cycle).

Remember, however, that digital tools are just that. Tools. It is up to the people—in this case, learning team members—to use them well. When carrying out the technology-enabled coaching continuum, learning team members can make good use of technology for communicating, meeting, scheduling, planning, collaborating, documenting, sharing files, managing activities, monitoring progress, evaluating effectiveness, archiving professional learning, and team building. That said, learning team members should not use technology to avoid face-to-face interaction. In the sections that follow, I offer brief descriptions and some examples of several technology tools.

Communication Tools

Team members use technology to ease and increase communication among learning team members as well as among experts. If all team members are working remotely from different schools within the district or from different schools outside the district, then electronic communication is vital. By contrast, if learning team members are all on-site, then a blended approach to communication (i.e., some face-to-face, some electronic) works best. If some team members are on-site and others are working remotely, then all members should be vigilant in ensuring no one is left out on important communication. E-mail, videoconferencing, and instant messaging (chat, text) are just a few of the options. Some are available free of charge, while others require paid subscriptions. Of the latter, many offer free trials or demos prior to purchasing a subscription. Most include ways to securely archive and share knowledge, screens, messages, files, data, and so forth among learning team members. Some also offer integrated voice, data, and video.

- Gmail (e-mail)—https://www.google.com/gmail/
- Outlook (e-mail)—https://outlook.live.com/owa/
- Yammer—https://www.yammer.com/
- Chatter—https://www.salesforce.com/products/chatter/overview/
- Jive—https://www.jivesoftware.com/

Online Meeting and Observation Tools (Video and Audio)

Members of the learning team meet, observe, and coach online and on-site when carrying out the four components of the eCoaching continuum embedded in the teaching cycle. When selecting the technology tools for doing so, consider cost, compatibility, quality, bells and whistles (e.g., remote control of camera, zoom capability), dependability, number of participants, district firewalls, and so forth. Here are some popular options that have worked for others:

- Skype—https://www.skype.com/en/
- Google Hangouts—https://hangouts.google.com/
- GoToMeeting—https://www.gotomeeting.com/

- Jive—https://jive.com/speek/
- Join.Me—https://www.join.me/
- BlueJeans—https://www.bluejeans.com/
- Zoom—https://zoom.us/

Scheduling Tools

When carrying out each component of the eCoaching continuum embedded within the teaching cycle, learning team members organize meetings and coaching sessions, and schedule dates and times for study sessions, observations, or group coaching. The list in this section suggests online scheduling tools that offer a variety of options, including voting or deciding on meeting times, scheduling meetings or observations, and confirming meetings or observations. When selecting one of these tools, learning team members should consider compatibility with mobile technology, cost, compatibility with e-mail, features, options for public and private sharing, platform (PC, Mac) availability, account requirements, and customization features.

- Doodle—http://doodle.com/
- Teamup—http://www.teamup.com/ (designed specifically for groups)
- Calendly—https://calendly.com/
- ScheduleOnce—http://www.scheduleonce.com/
- TimeandDate—https://www.timeanddate.com/
- Meet-O-Matic—https://www.meetomatic.com/calendar.php
- NeedToMeet—http://www.needtomeet.com/
- Rallly—http://rallly.co/
- Google Calendar—https://www.google.com/calendar

Timeline Templates

Digital timeline templates are especially useful for planning the scope and sequence (i.e., an overview) of how learning team members will embed the four components of the eCoaching continuum in the teaching cycle. Taking time to create a digital timeline allows learning team members to be intentional about how they will embed the four components of the eCoaching continuum during the six-week teaching cycle.

- Ganttopia (for use with PowerPoint)—www.ganttopia.com/ (provides templates for creating Gantt chart timelines)
- Lucidchart—https://www.lucidchart.com/pages/timeline-maker
- Timeglider—https://timeglider.com/
- Preceden—https://www.preceden.com/

Collaboration and Management Tools

Although the platforms listed in this section have been designed for improved management of business and marketing projects, learning team members can use them successfully when working together to carry out the eCoaching continuum within the teaching cycle. Rather than using messy e-mail chains, these platforms allow learning team members to organize how the four components of the eCoaching continuum are embedded within the teaching cycle by delineating the necessary teamwork and taskwork activities that support each component and the people associated with each.

- Basecamp—https://basecamp.com/
- Redbooth—https://redbooth.com/
- Slack—https://slack.com/
- ActiveCollab—https://activecollab.com/
- Huddle—https://www.huddle.com/
- Goplan—https://goplanapp.com/
- Blackboard Collaborate—http://www.blackboard.com/online-collaborative-learning/blackboard-collaborate.aspx
- Lighthouse—https://lighthouseapp.com/
- HiveDesk—https://www.hivedesk.com/

Document Tools

When carrying out each component of the eCoaching continuum embedded within the teaching cycle, learning team members create units and lesson plans, take book study notes, generate observation summaries, complete templates suggested in Chapters 1–4, annotate coaching videos, draft group or peer coaching records, and so forth. The ability to create and edit documents collaboratively online in real time is a real time-saver. Following are some options for consideration:

- Google Docs—https://docs.google.com/
- Office Online—https://www.office.com/
- Zoho—https://www.zoho.com/ (allows learning team members to create custom apps)
- Conceptboard—https://conceptboard.com/ (includes online whiteboards)
- Scribblar—https://scribblar.com/ (offers chat, audio, and virtual whiteboards)

File-Sharing Tools

Because learning team members also need to share the documents and files they create, the following options may come in handy:

- Google Drive—https://www.google.com/drive/
- Dropbox—https://www.dropbox.com/

- Box—https://www.box.com/home
- Hightail—https://www.hightail.com/
- MediaFire—https://www.mediafire.com/
- OneDrive—https://onedrive.live.com/about/en-us/
- SugarSync—https://www.sugarsync.com/en/

Professional Development Management Tools

Similar to the collaboration and project management tools identified previously, these tools help learning team members identify teamwork and taskwork, delineate member assignments and responsibilities, arrange scheduling, and so forth. In short, these tools help learning team members organize, streamline, and sync their activities. Why bother? Doing so helps learning team members keep track of the big picture and the supporting details needed to carry out each component of the eCoaching continuum embedded within the teaching cycle, and it also helps them to seamlessly integrate the details—all in one online platform. Here are several options:

- Microsoft Project—https://products.office.com/en-us/project/project-and-portfolio-management-software
- Teamwork—https://www.teamwork.com/ (video tour available at https://www.youtube.com/watch?v=oGf_OxcN6zE)
- Asana—https://asana.com/
- Podio—https://podio.com/site/en
- Trello—https://trello.com/
- ProofHub—https://www.proofhub.com/
- Wrike—https://www.wrike.com/
- LiquidPlanner—https://www.liquidplanner.com/
- WorkflowMax—https://www.workflowmax.com/
- Mavenlink—https://www.mavenlink.com/
- Zoho Projects—https://www.zoho.com/projects/

Team-Building Tools

Learning team members can also make good use of digital tools designed for building trust, increasing communication, solving problems, working collaboratively, resolving conflict, and achieving goals—all of which are especially important when carrying out the eCoaching continuum embedded within teaching cycles. One of the key considerations for deciding among the tools is whether learning team members are located on-site or offsite. Another is budget. If some participate remotely, and there are funds available, then digital options may be appealing. Alternatively, a blended format (i.e., some online, some face-to-face) could be considered. Both types of team-building resources are provided in the list that follows.

Two are carried out online, one is a boxed set that could be played online via web conferencing if some members are located remotely, and one requires on-site participation.

- *WestEd (face-to-face [i.e., boxed set or online via web conferencing])*. Learning team members can access information about "Leading Professional Learning: Building Capacity for Sustained Practice, A Simulation Game for Educators," developed by Katherine Stiles, Susan Mundry, and Carol Bershad, through WestEd's website at https://www.wested.org/resources/leading-professional-learning-simulation-game/. Described as engaging and noncompetitive, the game includes five specific learning outcomes that are achieved through participation in a simulation. The cost is $600 for up to 20 participants.
- *Prelude (online)*. Learning team members can check out this game online, engage in a complimentary demonstration, sign up for team members to play, and download white papers at www.playprelude.com. Click on the Education tab to view options that focus on building team members' "soft skills." Also, check out the YouTube video tour (https://www.youtube.com/watch?v=-ztsCsL92wA).
- *VirtuWall (online)*. If learning team members are interested in collaborating more effectively to achieve common goals, then VirtuWall might be for them. Learning team members can access information and request a demonstration online at http://www.globalteambuilding.com/virtuwall/. This option is costly, at approximately $4,250 per group. If funds are not available, the eCoach, administrators, teachers, and other school professionals could write a grant to secure the monies needed. Other options, such as Space Rescue, are available for as low as $6.00 per person.
- *Breakout Games (on-site)*. Breakout Games is a franchised business, located in cities across the United States, serving corporate teams, schools, and nonprofits. Learning team members can go online (https://breakoutgames.com/team-building/) for more information about various team-building activities, including cost.

Determining Which Technology Options Are the Best Fit for a Learning Team Approach

Technology options and online vendors abound, but criteria for selecting the digital tools that support a learning team approach are largely absent. Here I offer guidelines for learning team members to consider when reviewing and selecting technology that supports their work. Although similar to those offered previously in Chapters 1–4, the questions and considerations included here are designed uniquely for learning teams as they carry out the eCoaching continuum within the context of teaching cycles.

Blended or Online Options

As described previously, learning teams may comprise members who are engaged in carrying out the eCoaching continuum on-site and online. Consequently, it is important for them to consider questions such as these: How much of the work can be done face-to-face? How much of the work needs to be done online?

Budget

In each of the previous chapters, the importance of considering the initial and ongoing budget when selecting technology for each component included in the eCoaching continuum was pointed out. When teachers, administrators, other school professionals, and eCoaches carry out the eCoaching continuum using a learning team approach, they also need to think about the funds that are available initially and over time. Determining the start-up budget is the first step. Are monies available for purchasing new technology? If so, how much? The second step involves taking into account whether funds will be available over time. These funds are needed to secure upgrades, technology support, and so forth.

Team Members' Needs and Purposes

Rather than scooping up all the latest and greatest technologies, learning team members should carefully consider how the digital tools support and lend value to the teaming aspects associated with professional learning. In other words, avoiding fatigue and frustration is a must. Consider questions such as these: Do learning team members actually need the technology? What technology tools are currently on hand that learning team members could leverage to get the job done? How will new and existing digital tools enable them to carry out the work of embedding the eCoaching continuum into teaching cycles more effectively and efficiently? When would face-to-face, no-tech, or low-tech options be better? How accessible is the technology across devices (e.g., laptop computers, desktop computers, electronic tablets, smartphones)? Are Android and iOS options available?

Team Members' Familiarity

Learning team members must be mindful of their prior knowledge and their energy levels when it comes to selecting tech tools. In short, too much additional training + too much digital fatigue = a recipe for disaster. Consider questions such as these: How familiar are team members with the technology? How much training is required? How many different platforms are used? How much digital fatigue is already evident? How much buy-in is needed? How are short-term feelings of frustration and anxiety, often associated with learning new technologies, mitigated by longer-term benefits?

Compatibility

Does the technology support the taskwork and teamwork required of learning team members as they carry out the technology-enabled coaching continuum when it is embedded in teaching cycles? If so, how compatible are the technology tools? What steps or actions are needed to ensure greater compatibility?

Technology Support

When they are in good working order, technology tools can help learning team members work more effectively and efficiently. When that's not the case, frustration, anxiety, tension, and inefficiency run amok. Because digital woes are inevitable, it is essential that learning team members consider what supports (e.g., expertise, accessibility, responsiveness) are available, at what cost, through school districts and vendors.

Security, Confidentiality, and Privacy

As mentioned in previous chapters, learning team members must also consider how security, confidentiality, and privacy of teachers and K–12 students will be protected. As learning team members carry out the technology-enabled coaching continuum embedded in teaching cycles, they share teacher and student performance data that require ironclad protection. Consequently, contacting technology support specialists and legal counsel for guidance and advice is a must.

Creating Norms That Support a Technology-Enabled Learning Team Approach

Establishing and Maintaining an Overall Coaching Culture

In the preceding chapters, ways in which new norms could be created that support each component of the eCoaching continuum were described. In this chapter, I focus on how frontline practitioners play a vital role in shaping the *overall* climate and culture needed when carrying out the eCoaching continuum under the umbrella of learning teams and teaching cycles.

An Established Culture

The definition of a coaching culture must be established. Otherwise, how will teachers, administrators, other school professionals, and eCoaches know when it exists? Based on an extensive review of the professional literature pertaining to coaching cultures, Gormley and van Nieuwerburgh (2014) offered the following definition: "Coaching cultures exist when groups of people embrace coaching as a way of making holistic improvements to individuals within their organizations through formal and informal coaching interactions" (p. 92). Drawing on their extensive review, Gormley and van Nieuwerburgh (2014) also identified common themes evident within established coaching cultures. Focusing on these themes, teachers, administrators, other school professionals, and eCoaches can use the rating scale presented in Figure 5.4 when assessing coaching climate. Then they can use the findings to set guiding goals for gradually improving the coaching culture. Engaging in monitoring checks periodically supports frontline practitioners in maintaining an overall climate supportive of coaching.

Commitment

As Lindbom (2007) asserted, a "culture of coaching requires commitment, consistency, and dedication from leadership" (p. 102). This means that if learning teams and teaching cycles are to be used effectively as the job-embedded framework for carrying out the technology-enabled coaching continuum, administrators and school leaders must publicize it as a priority and work with others in creating not only the infrastructure, but also the day-to-day routines that support it. Clutterbuck and Megginson (2005) identified four indicators leaders can use when taking stock of their commitment to creating and maintaining a coaching culture:

- *Nascent.* Commitment to creating and maintaining a coaching culture is characterized as little to none. Coaching activities are carried out sporadically and haphazardly.
- *Tactical.* The value of coaching is recognized; however, what it means and how it can be carried out effectively require further development.
- *Strategic.* Investments are made in training and resources that support coaching. Top administrators "walk the talk" and demonstrate good coaching practices.
- *Embedded.* Frontline practitioners at all levels engage in coaching, which is used as the primary vehicle for dealing with difficult issues and achieving overall improvement.

Change

Taking a team approach requires change. And change is difficult. Making the shift from a passive, workshop-based approach to an active, job-embedded, team-oriented model requires a different mindset and a different set of professional behaviors. Understandably then, before making the transition, teachers,

Figure 5.4

Climate Rating Scale—Evidence of Thematic Indicators

Technology-Enabled Coaching Continuum Climate Rating Scale—Evidence of Thematic Indicators			
Coaching Climate Theme	**Strength** ✔ **Consistently Demonstrated**	**Emerging** ✔ **Inconsistently Demonstrated**	**Need** ✔ **Not Demonstrated**
The technology-enabled coaching continuum is the primary way organizations, including schools, develop personnel.			
Evidence for Rating:			
The technology-enabled coaching continuum is embedded within existing frameworks for professional learning, feedback, and evaluation.			
Evidence for Rating:			
The technology-enabled coaching continuum is aimed at maximizing the potential of personnel—individually and collectively.			
Evidence for Rating:			
The technology-enabled coaching continuum is focused on improving the performance of all.			
Evidence for Rating:			
The technology-enabled coaching continuum is used to communicate a clear commitment to growth.			
Evidence for Rating:			
The technology-enabled coaching continuum is carried out with the recognition that creating a supportive, growth-oriented culture takes time.			
Evidence for Rating:			
The technology-enabled coaching continuum is undertaken with shared understanding and agreement that it leads to positive changes for key stakeholders, including teachers, administrators, other school professionals, K–12 students, parents/guardians, and community members.			
Evidence for Rating:			

administrators, other school professionals, and eCoaches must join in establishing new norms that support team-based learning (Chappuis et al., 2009). Consider the following examples:

- Maintain the focus of professional learning on improving K–12 students' educational outcomes.
- Be sure everyone has a voice and an opportunity to be heard.
- Focus on prioritizing, accomplishing, and harmonizing teamwork and taskwork.
- Please come to the meetings prepared and with a positive, "can do" attitude.
- Be self-directed and team oriented not only by taking responsibility for your professional learning and growth but also by encouraging the same among team members.

Contemplating the Benefits and Cautions Associated with a Technology-Enabled Team-Based Approach

As with any approach to professional learning, benefits and drawbacks are associated with this one. Thoughtfully considering the benefits and drawbacks helps frontline practitioners make informed decisions about how to best approach professional learning.

Benefits

One undeniable benefit associated with using learning teams and teaching cycles when carrying out the technology-enabled coaching continuum is the deeper, longer-lasting learning associated with it (Chappuis et al., 2009). It is this deeper, longer-lasting, growth-oriented, job-embedded approach to professional learning that has been associated with improving teachers' capacity while also better serving K–12 students (Gregory, 2010). Enough said? Or do you still remain to be convinced? Malone and Gallagher (2010) also described a number of benefits associated with teaming, including considering diverse perspectives, sharing ideas and information, joint problem solving and decision making, and achieving improved processes and results. Vangrieken, Dochy, and Raes (2016) found that when learning teams evidenced greater unity, cohesion (i.e., social and task), and interdependence, they achieved greater effectiveness. Finally, Meirink et al. (2010) reported that when characterized as temporary, voluntary, and task oriented, team-based professional learning can provide teachers, administrators, other school professionals, and eCoaches with essential feedback, moral support, shared experiences, and improved learning.

Cautions

When approaching professional learning through learning teams and teaching cycles, a number of pitfalls can derail members' efforts, adversely impacting the process and outcomes. For example, lack of commitment and time are frequently identified as barriers that impede team effectiveness. Chappuis and colleagues (2009) cautioned that frontline practitioners need to commit to investing more time and effort when participating in team learning than is typically required when attending one-shot professional development offerings, such as after-school workshops. Relatedly, they noted, too, that learning teams require teachers, other school professionals, and administrators to work and learn together, not only during learning team meetings but also between them. Insufficient meeting time is another commonly identified constraint (Malone & Gallagher, 2010). When it comes to team membership, voluntary participation is preferable to involuntary. As Chappuis and colleagues (2009) reported, involuntary participation can sometimes work against team learning. Also, when the roles and responsibilities of learning team members are not identified and communicated to all, confusion and frustration often result, contributing to premature disengagement (Chappuis et al., 2009). Finally, although team-based learning is a collective effort and group development is important, some attention must be paid to individual members' needs (Malone & Gallagher, 2010). For instance, Gregory (2010) reported that participants who held negative expectations at the outset did not improve in professional knowledge and skill through a team-based approach.

Translating the eCoach's Role into Action

eCoaches play a vital and unique role when working with learning team members as they engage in teaching cycles to carry out the four components of the technology-enabled coaching continuum. When doing so, eCoaches shoulder several roles and responsibilities. To be successful, however, eCoaches need administrator and colleague support, including dedicated release time, clearly delineated job roles and responsibilities, and ongoing training and professional development.

- Take a leadership role in helping administrators, teachers, and other school professionals understand the unique and compelling reasons for using learning teams as the framework for carrying out the technology-enabled coaching continuum in practical, powerful, and impactful ways.
- Facilitate the development of effective learning teams by helping frontline practitioners develop a knowledge and practice base in essential team features, potential team members, various team configurations, team leadership,

team structure, characteristics of high-performing teams, and conditions for success.

- Offer guidance on how to make a learning team approach work by embedding the four components of the technology-enabled coaching continuum into four- to six-week teaching cycles.
- Facilitate the three-part organizational framework for carrying out technology-enabled group coaching within teaching cycles.
- Lend guidance on determining availability of technology-enabled options, equipment, software, apps, and so forth that support technology-enabled learning teams and teaching cycles when carrying out the technology-enabled coaching continuum.
- Coordinate the evaluation of technology-related options, equipment, software, and apps, and consider goodness of fit, using guiding considerations and questions.
- Schedule and facilitate learning team sessions with members.
- Capture learning team sessions electronically, so that others can access them, as needed, for reflection and improvement.
- Co-create norms for establishing an overall climate that supports ongoing professional learning through the technology-enabled coaching continuum, learning teams, and teaching cycles.
- Partner with school librarians, technology support specialists, and legal counsel to review training in relevant privacy and confidentiality policies, such as FERPA, when sharing teacher and student performance data online or on-site.
- Develop digital badges/microcredentials for using learning teams and teaching cycles as the framework for carrying out the technology-enabled coaching continuum.
- Create modules for training on new and existing technologies and approaches that support learning teams and teaching cycles as the framework for carrying out the technology-enabled coaching continuum.
- Monitor and evaluate how using learning teams and teaching cycles to carry out the technology-enabled coaching continuum influences professional learning and has a positive impact on K–12 students' educational performance.

Revisiting Important Ideas

In this chapter, I've described how frontline practitioners use learning teams and teaching cycles effectively when carrying out the technology-enabled coaching continuum for improved professional learning, collaborative engagement, and positive educational impact. I've also explained why doing so is important, as well as known benefits and cautions. Before moving on to Chapter 6, here's a review of the important ideas I've shared:

- Clarify and communicate to key stakeholders the unique, varied, and compelling purposes for using learning teams and teaching cycles as the framework when carrying out the technology-enabled coaching continuum—online or hybrid.
- Set the stage for using learning teams and teaching cycles as the framework for carrying out the technology-enabled coaching continuum by developing stakeholders' knowledge and practice in team dynamics, composition, configurations, structure, leadership, development, and so forth.
- Make learning teams work as a framework for carrying out the technology-enabled coaching continuum, in part, by using teaching cycles and adopting a three-part organizational framework comprising focused activities before, during, and after the online or hybrid team session.
- Consider online or blended/hybrid variations for using learning teams and teaching cycles when carrying out the technology-enabled coaching continuum.
- Consider equipment, software, apps, and so forth in accord with budgets and professional learning needs.
- Determine the best technology fit, in part based on answers to the guiding questions and considerations provided.
- Create and sustain norms that support technology-enabled group coaching, including demonstrating leadership, providing coach-supported group coaching, and embracing a results-oriented climate.
- Weigh the benefits and cautions carefully and make decisions accordingly about how to proceed when using learning teams and teaching cycles as the framework for carrying out the technology-enabled coaching continuum.
- Ensure that the eCoach's roles and responsibilities are clearly articulated and supported by administrators, teachers, and other school professionals.

As was the case with preceding chapters, this chapter offers practical, important, "how-to" information. To avoid overwhelming frontline practitioners, I offer an At-a-Glance Checklist. As noted in Chapters 1–4, using the checklist empowers teachers and other school professionals when translating content into real-world practice. Realizing the power of using team learning and teaching cycles when carrying out the technology-enabled coaching continuum requires that you understand just nine simple things!

AT-A-GLANCE CHECKLIST

Preparing for a Successful Technology-Enabled Team-Based Approach

☐ The purpose for taking a learning team approach when carrying out the technology-enabled coaching continuum is clear, unique, and compelling.

☐ Teachers, administrators, eCoaches, and other school professionals invest time and labor in setting the stage for success in assembling learning teams.

☐ The three-part organizational framework (before, during, and after) is developed and used, in part, to make carrying out the technology-enabled coaching continuum work within the learning team and teaching cycle framework.

☐ Technology-enabled options, equipment, software, apps, and so forth that support learning team members in carrying out the technology-enabled coaching continuum within teaching cycles are identified based on goodness of fit.

☐ Norms for using learning teams, teaching cycles, and the technology-enabled coaching continuum for professional learning and positive impact are established and supported.

☐ Benefits and cautions associated with a learning team approach are considered and choices are made accordingly.

☐ eCoaches possess the knowledge, skills, and abilities needed to be effective in supporting learning teams as they use teaching cycles when carrying out the technology-enabled coaching continuum approach to professional learning.

☐ eCoaches' roles and responsibilities are clearly articulated and supported.

☐ Learning team engagement and impact are monitored and evaluated.

6

Carrying Out the Technology-Enabled Coaching Continuum
Assessing Results and Evaluating Impact

Marcia Rock, Paula Crawford, and Morgan V. Blanton

> *A brain scan cannot interpret itself and neither can a data dashboard in education.* —Andy Hargreaves (n.d.)

How can technology support formative and summative assessment of teacher and K–12 student learning when carrying out the four components of the technology-enabled coaching continuum?

Understanding the Purpose of Using Technology to Assess Results and Evaluate Impact

As mentioned in the Introduction, billions of dollars are spent annually on professional development (Thurlings & den Brok, 2017), not only in the United States but also worldwide. Yet there is scant evidence that professional development yields a positive impact on teachers or their K–12 students (Desimone, 2009; Harris & Sass, 2011; Yoon et al., 2007). In Chapters 1–4, the four components included in the technology-enabled coaching continuum—that is, study, observation, 1:1 coaching, and group or peer coaching—were described. Taken together, the components offer a job-embedded approach to professional development based on key ingredients required for effectiveness. Though the four components are described in separate chapters, they are designed to work in tandem. *When carried out in a coordinated, intentional, interactive manner, the components maximize the opportunity for positive impact, not only on teachers and other school professionals but also on the students with whom they work.* Though teachers and other school professionals can carry out the four components included in the eCoaching continuum on an individual basis, they can and should carry them out through learning teams and teaching cycles, as described in Chapter 5. In this chapter, we describe two important reasons for using technology to assess results and demonstrate positive impact when evaluating professional learning. We also explain how to make the approach work, how to determine which technology options are the best fit, and how to establish supportive cultural norms. Finally, we explain the benefits and cautions that warrant consideration as well as ways of defining and translating the eCoach's role into action.

Given the ongoing focus on accountability (Goe, Biggers, & Croft, 2012), carrying out a job-embedded approach to professional development, such as the eCoaching continuum, is no longer enough. As such, it is important that teachers and other school professionals monitor and assess the results of job-embedded professional learning in intentional ways (Hochberg & Desimone, 2010; King, 2014). Currently, states such as Wisconsin, New Jersey, Missouri, Texas, and many others have adopted various professional development frameworks aimed at enhancing accountability. In those states, teachers and other school professionals employ the frameworks when planning, implementing, and evaluating their professional learning. Using technology to support existing state or district frameworks, or to develop their own well-designed plan for professional learning grounded in the eCoaching continuum, allows teachers and other school professionals to demonstrate results and determine the positive impact of job-embedded professional learning—quantitatively (e.g., ratio of higher- to lower-order questions posed during literacy instruction) and qualitatively (e.g., video clips illustrating engagement and responses of students to higher- and lower-order questions posed during literacy instruction). Central to understanding why teachers and other school professionals should use technology when assessing results and determining impact are two central premises: doing so supports multiple levels of evaluation *and* cultivates collective teacher efficacy (CTE)—both of which have been linked to positive impacts and outcomes.

Using Technology to Engage in Multiple Levels of Evaluation

The days of focusing solely on teachers' satisfaction as the primary measure of the effectiveness of professional development have passed (King, 2014). Today, when evaluating the impact of job-embedded professional development, such as the eCoaching continuum, the focus has shifted to a more well-rounded approach that includes investigating improvements in students' learning (Earley & Porritt, 2014; McDonald, 2012). Embracing a more holistic view when evaluating professional learning, such as that which has occurred through the eCoaching continuum, requires teachers and school professionals to think not only about how they will capture evidence of impact on multiple levels, using a planned, rather than a reactive approach (Earley & Porritt, 2014), but also how they will leverage technology to help them do so.

Taking a planned approach is not new and has been reflected in the frameworks available for evaluating the impact of professional development. Composed of four basic levels, earlier models (e.g., Kirkpatrick, 1959/1994; Stake, 1967) were fairly simple and straightforward, focusing primarily on evaluating the training impact on the teacher. As accountability demands mounted and understanding of the complexities associated with evaluating the impact of professional development became more sophisticated, so too did the models. More recent frameworks have expanded to include more than 12 levels targeting three areas of potential impact: organizational change, teacher change, and student change (Bubb & Earley, 2010; Guskey, 2002; King, 2014).

Today's expanded frameworks for evaluating the impact of professional learning align well with job-embedded approaches, such as the eCoaching continuum. Yet adopting a multilevel approach to evaluating the impact of the eCoaching continuum means that teachers and other school professionals proactively and reactively consider many varied data sources (e.g., district, building, classroom, teacher, student), which can quickly become unwieldy and resource intensive, leading to frustration, fatigue, and premature abandonment. Using technology in selective and intentional ways to support evaluation activities is one way to make the process more meaningful, relevant, and feasible. Doing so requires teachers and other school professionals to carefully consider what technologies they use to capture, store, and analyze the most important data within and across multiple levels as they plan their tactics for evaluating professional learning. See Figure 6.1 for a sample multilevel evaluation plan.

Using Technology to Cultivate Collective Teacher Efficacy

Goddard, Hoy, and Hoy (2000) defined collective teacher efficacy as "the perceptions of teachers in a school that the efforts of the faculty as a whole will have a positive effect on students" (p. 480). Teachers and other school professionals often tell us that CTE sounds like a "warm and fuzzy" value statement and are surprised that researchers have found CTE matters. In fact, CTE matters so much that it affects student learning more than socioeconomic status, past school achievement, home environment, and family involvement (Donohoo, 2017; Donohoo & Velasco, 2016; Hattie, 2016; Tschannen-Moran & Barr, 2004).

Given the importance of CTE, how can teachers and other school professionals use technology when evaluating the impact of the eCoaching continuum to foster it? In short, technology allows teachers and other school professionals to capture,

FIGURE 6.1 TECHNOLOGY-ENABLED EVALUATION WITHIN AND ACROSS MULTIPLE LEVELS

Organizational Change	Teacher Change	K–12 Student Change
Guiding Questions *What data confirm what building- or district-level changes have occurred? Why are these changes meaningful? What other data sources do we need and why?* **Measures** Student achievement data, attendance data, office discipline referral data, parent/family engagement data, community engagement data **Technologies** Data dashboards—student achievement, attendance, office discipline referrals, parent, family, and community engagement metrics DistrictTools.org—community, parent, and family survey summaries and graphic displays	**Guiding Questions** *What data confirm what teachers or other school professionals have learned? Why does this learning matter? What other data sources do we need and why?* **Measures** Teacher knowledge-based assessments Teacher performance-based assessments **Technologies** Quizlet results Audio recordings of classroom instruction Video archives of classroom instruction TeachFX visualizations of teacher talk (including questioning) during classroom instruction	**Guiding Questions** *What data confirm what K–12 students have learned? Why does this learning matter? What other data sources do we need and why?* **Measures** Student knowledge-based assessments Student performance-based assessments, including engagement **Technologies** Digitally archived student work samples Audio recordings—students' responses to Q & A TeachFX visualizations of student talk (including responses to questioning) during classroom instruction Video recordings—students' academic, behavioral, and social-emotional engagement

store, analyze, and interpret performance data formatively and summatively. We have found that formative data provided through "just in time," technology-enabled feedback provide teachers and other school professionals with the information they need to make adjustments, during instruction, and to experience firsthand the ensuing improvements in student responding and engagement. When these opportunities occur regularly, they become empowering, fueling teachers' and other school professionals' belief that they can have a positive impact on learning. Summatively, using technology when sharing, reviewing, and using evaluation data to inform longer-term decision making cultivates teachers' and other school professionals' sense of collective efficacy when data confirm they are changing learning or behavioral outcomes for students in a specific grade, a particular school building, or across a district.

Determining the Focus for Technology-Enabled Impact Evaluation

Successful impact evaluation commences at the beginning of professional learning, rather than at the end. We agree with Tomlinson (2018) that evaluation begins after teachers and other school professionals determine *what* is most important to measure. Recall that, in previous chapters, how to select the focus for each of the four components included in the eCoaching continuum when planning and carrying out each, singly or collectively, was explained. Because teachers and other school professionals have had a voice in determining the foci for professional learning for each component as well as the supporting data (e.g., see Figure 6.2), it is important that they draw on both while planning how to evaluate impact. Doing so ensures alignment between the foci of technology-enabled professional learning and evaluation. Two planning approaches we have found valuable for deciding what matters most when determining impact include developing a road map and formulating a multilevel evaluation plan.

Developing a Road Map

The underlying assumption of all professional learning and development is that change occurs. However, given the lack of evidence supporting this long-standing assumption (Desimone, 2009; Harris & Sass, 2011; Yoon et al., 2007), our view, which is consistent with Guskey's (2002) and many others', is that a more intentional approach is warranted. Logic models and theory-of-change methodologies

FIGURE 6.2 ECOACHING CONTINUUM DATA PLAN

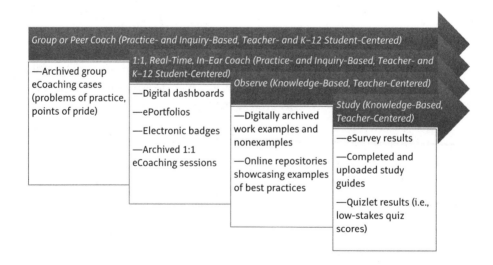

Group or Peer Coach (Practice- and Inquiry-Based, Teacher- and K–12 Student-Centered)

1:1, Real-Time, In-Ear Coach (Practice- and Inquiry-Based, Teacher- and K–12 Student-Centered)

Observe (Knowledge-Based, Teacher-Centered)

Study (Knowledge-Based, Teacher-Centered)

—Archived group eCoaching cases (problems of practice, points of pride)

—Digital dashboards

—ePortfolios

—Electronic badges

—Archived 1:1 eCoaching sessions

—Digitally archived work examples and nonexamples

—Online repositories showcasing examples of best practices

—eSurvey results

—Completed and uploaded study guides

—Quizlet results (i.e., low-stakes quiz scores)

are examples of intentional approaches (see Chapter 1). Both serve as road maps for evaluating the impact of professional learning. In short, developing a theory of change allows teachers and other school professionals to determine what organizational, teacher, and student changes they want to achieve, as well as why they matter, and to backward map how engaging purposefully in each component of the eCoaching continuum supports their efforts to do so. In this way, developing a theory of change affords teachers and other school professionals a series of deliberate opportunities for thinking through the necessary technology resources and activities, including how they are assessing and evaluating impact, within and across each eCoaching continuum component. Drawing on the logic model/theory-of-change plan as well as the instructional plan described in earlier chapters (see Figures 1.6, 2.6, 3.2, and 4.3) helps teachers and other school professionals ensure alignment between the professional learning activities included in each of the four components of the technology-enabled continuum and the intermittent monitoring and overall evaluation of impact (see Figure 6.1). An obvious advantage to developing a theory of change is that it allows teachers and other school professionals to determine what educational changes are most important to their students, classrooms, schools, and communities, as well as how they will know that professional learning through the eCoaching continuum has contributed to those desired changes.

Formulating a Multilevel Evaluation Plan

Designing a multilevel evaluation plan for professional learning allows teachers and other school professionals to decide *what* data they will collect; *how* they will collect, archive, analyze, and interpret data; and *why* it matters. Though it might be tempting to forego this process, we encourage all to resist the temptation. Engaging in the eCoaching continuum without a multilevel evaluation plan is analogous to taking on a personal health and wellness program without determining how one will measure success and why doing so matters. Because change is difficult, the absence of *meaningful* progress measures or indicators most often leads to fear that the new approach is not working, which results in frustration, discouragement, and premature abandonment (Guskey, 2002). Conversely, when progress is monitored and measured intermittently along the way, changes and modifications can be made as needed and successes can be celebrated, resulting in encouragement and renewed commitment.

As mentioned previously, when formulating a multilevel evaluation plan, teachers and other school professionals draw on content included in the theory of change and the instructional plan, described in Chapters 1–4. Doing so assists them not only in breaking down content included in the theory of change in *meaningful and manageable* ways but also in identifying how they will monitor impact, while carrying out the four components of the technology-enabled coaching continuum. This aspect of multilevel evaluation planning entails putting together the eCoaching Continuum Data Plan (see Figure 6.2). The multilevel evaluation plan includes multiple elements to capture organizational, teacher, and student changes (see Figure 6.1).

Making Technology-Enabled Evaluation Work

Developing a road map and formulating an evaluation plan are vital to establishing and maintaining a *clear and compelling focus* for determining the impact of professional learning through the eCoaching continuum. In our experience, however, if a technology-enabled approach to evaluation is to work, then eCoaches, teachers, and other school professionals need to employ additional tactics. We have found four tactics particularly useful—tackle it as a team; employ interactive, cyclic processes; use goal setting, monitoring, and attainment logs; and think through how technology helps rather than hinders.

Tackle It as a Team

Evaluating impact on multiple levels, using a team approach, allows teachers and other school professionals to do so within a professional learning community (PLC) or personalized learning network. This is important because teachers and other school professionals evaluate the impact of professional learning through the eCoaching continuum in the same context in which it is carried out—through job-embedded learning teams, as described in Chapter 5. At the same time, working in teams poses unique and at times seemingly insurmountable challenges. Why, then, should teachers and other school professionals bother? Simply put, Marsh, Bertrand, and Huguet (2015) reported "that coaches and professional learning communities played important roles in mediating teachers' responses to data and were often associated with instances in which teachers used data to alter their instructional delivery (as opposed to surface-level changes in materials and topics)" (p. 1). Moreover, using technology to evaluate professional learning through a team approach, such as PLCs, also helps teachers and other school professionals access, share, store, analyze, interpret, and use multilevel data in more effective, efficient, and meaningful ways. Finally, because most change efforts are at times hard, slow, and difficult, taking a team approach allows teachers and other school professionals to support one another in staying the course (Guskey, 2002).

Employ Iterative, Cyclic Processes

Transforming static, event-based professional learning and evaluation into a dynamic, ongoing process-informed approach requires teachers and other school professionals to develop new habits of mind and practice (Guskey, 2002). One way of developing the latter is to employ *meaningful* evaluation processes and procedures. The data team procedure (see Earl & Katz, 2006), which is iterative and cyclic rather than linear (Schildkamp & Poortman, 2015), allows teachers and other school professionals to intertwine impact evaluation with teaching cycles (described in Chapter 5). Earl and Katz's (2006) popular data team procedure includes eight steps, illustrated in the Figure 6.3.

Alternatively, eCoaches, teachers, and other school professionals may opt to use the Plan-Do-Study-Act (PDSA) cycle of improvement (Langley et al., 1996) when evaluating the impact of professional learning. PDSA cycles are grounded in improvement science. Borrowing from health care and organizational psychology, teachers and other school professionals use improvement science principles and fundamentals, such as PDSA cycles, to improve educational practice and reduce achievement gaps. The PDSA cycle is illustrated in Figure 6.4.

FIGURE 6.3 DATA TEAM PROCEDURE

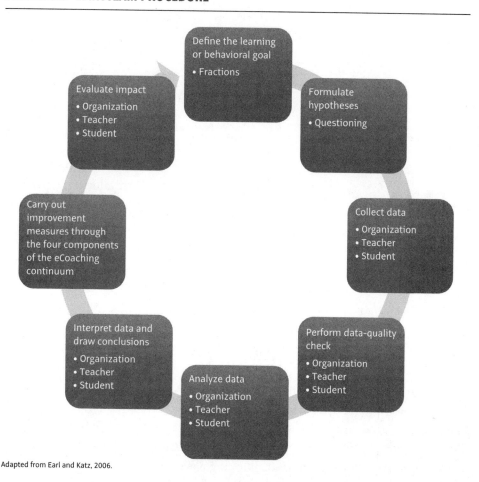

Adapted from Earl and Katz, 2006.

FIGURE 6.4 **TECHNOLOGY-ENABLED IMPACT EVALUATION USING THE PLAN-STUDY-DO-ACT CYCLE**

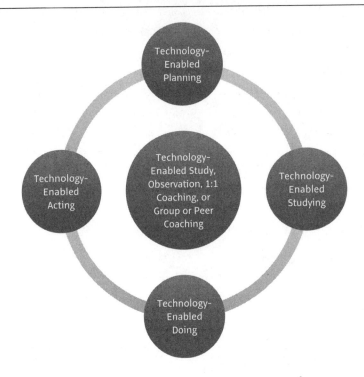

Use Goal Setting, Monitoring, and Attainment Logs

In today's fast-paced world, there is little time for dedicated professional learning. As such, the approach to professional learning and evaluation described throughout this book is job embedded. Yet when teachers and other school professionals juggle the pressure of heightened accountability (King, 2014) with the many competing demands of day-to-day teaching and learning in the classroom, it's easy to lose sight of the focus and data priorities to which team members previously agreed. In short, embedded efforts can become forgotten or overlooked and fall by the wayside entirely. Goal setting, monitoring, and attainment logs help eCoaches, teachers, and other school professionals not only carry out but also track the impact of professional learning within and across levels. The logs include prompts (see Appendix) that make them easy to use. We have found the logs help eCoaches, teachers, and other school professionals keep a pulse on teacher and student learning while carrying out the eCoaching continuum. Data from the logs are also used as needed to assist team members in evaluating effects on the organization (i.e., district, school, classroom), teachers, and students. Using electronic versions of the logs makes them easily accessible to all for regular review, comment, and updating.

Think Through How Technology Helps Rather Than Hinders

As is the case when using technology to carry out each component of the eCoaching continuum, taking time to consider how and why teachers and other school professionals use technology when evaluating impact is worth the investment. Adopting additional technology simply because it is shiny and new often impedes evaluation efforts. Instead, the aim is for *meaningful* evaluation of professional learning and impact to remain in the forefront and for technology to take a supportive role—easing data collection, archival, analysis, interpretation, and sharing, and facilitating informed assessment and decision making. As such, initial questions for consideration include the following:

- What technologies are available and in use currently?
- What technologies are working well?
- What technologies are causing more fatigue and frustration than benefit?
- What technologies could improve communication, data sharing, and informed decision making?

Because technology is advancing at a breakneck pace and there are many factors to consider, in the next section we offer specific questions and considerations as a guide for making in-depth decisions about technology.

Considering Options for Carrying Out Technology-Enabled Evaluation

In addition to considering the technology options that support each of the four components of the eCoaching continuum, as well as the learning team approach for carrying it out, teachers and other school professionals must weigh the technology options that will maximize their evaluation efforts. In this section, we briefly describe several platform and product choices. As noted in previous chapters, consulting school or district technology specialists is always wise. Doing so ensures that selections do not exceed the capacity of the district's technical infrastructure and confirms compatibility with previously selected technology options.

Professional Learning Communities (PLCs)

As described in Chapter 1, professional learning communities (PLCs), referred to variously as personalized learning networks (PLNs), are self-generated and unique to the individual professional. Each professional uses technology to find ways of connecting and learning with other professionals (Trust, Krutka, & Carpenter, 2016). Most often PLN, technologies include blogs and social media platforms such as Twitter

(Ross, Maninger, LaPrairie, & Sullivan, 2015). When used to support technology-enabled evaluation, each learning team member decides which technologies she will use, in part to determine the impact of her professional learning through the eCoaching continuum. If school professionals opt for a learning team approach, then team members collect, share, interpret, and analyze PLN data to determine impact. In this way, individual or collective engagement and impact can be determined, according to the theory of change and the multilevel evaluation plan.

Learning Management Systems (LMSs)

LMS technologies are typically used when designing and delivering online courses. When used to support technology-enabled impact evaluation, the LMS functions as a hub (Eaton, 2017), not only for uploading multiple data sources (e.g., teacher video/audio, student work samples, peer observations, attendance, online surveys) but also for interacting with one another via discussion boards, videoconferencing, and so forth to make decisions about how to change instruction to better meet students' academic, social, emotional, and behavioral needs. In this way, the LMS also serves as an online repository for documenting growth within and across organizations, teachers, and students.

Digital Learning Dashboards

The National Education Technology Plan (U.S. Department of Education, 2017) defines digital learning dashboards as web- or network-based technology platforms that "integrate information from assessments, learning tools, educator observations, and other sources to provide compelling, comprehensive visual representations of student progress in real time" (p. 64). Various K–12 student performance data can be uploaded, integrated, and displayed visually. Teacher and family dashboards are also available. The challenges lie in deciding which data are the most important to collect, how to analyze and interpret multiple data sources in meaningful ways, with whom to share the data, and how to coordinate multiple dashboards across multiple levels. School district leaders and professionals who are considering digital dashboards can access planning tools and checklists online, such as Future Ready's Interactive Planning Dashboard (https://futureready.org/dashboard/), prior to purchasing additional technology.

Intelligent Adaptive Learning Platforms (e.g., Smart Sparrow)

In the same way teachers use eLearning platforms to support their K–12 students' learning, they can use this technology to design personalized professional learning experiences throughout each component of the eCoaching continuum. Data uploaded to eLearning platforms can also be used to support impact evaluation either by individual teachers or by learning team members. School professionals can view videos and check out demos of Smart Sparrow online (https://www.smartsparrow.com/).

ePortfolios

ePortfolios are not just for preservice teachers. Early-, middle-, or late-career teachers or learning team members can use ePortfolios as the platform of choice, not only to tell the digital story of their professional learning (Boulton, 2014) but also to evaluate the impact across multiple levels (i.e., organizations, teachers, students). Jun, Anthony, Achrazoglou, and Coghill-Behrends (2007) ascertained that the "interconnectivity of artifacts across pages in an electronic portfolio can promote a deeper understanding of the relationship between standards and performance, promoting a sense of professional efficacy" (p. 45). When used for technology-enabled evaluation purposes, individual teachers or learning team members must develop clear, concise rubrics that include descriptive indicators and competency criteria. Finally, ePortfolios can be linked to and used in conjunction with PLCs, an approach referred to as PLC- or PLN-based ePortfolios (Shepherd & Skrabut, 2011).

Microcredentials or Digital Badges

According to Berry, Airhart, and Byrd (2016), "[M]icrocredentials offer a new way for teachers to document their learning using work samples, videos, and other artifacts and have the potential to transform professional development" (p. 34). Though currently in the early stages of development, microcredentials are self-directed competency based, personalized, on demand, shareable, and bite sized (Berry et al., 2016). For example, teachers and other school professionals could earn microcredentials or badges for culturally responsive questioning. The microcredentials or badges are then shared within the PLN, ePortfolio, LMS, or digital dashboard as another type of data or evidence illustrating learning and impact. Digital Promise (http://digitalpromise.org/initiative/educator-micro-credentials/) and the Friday Institute (https://place.fi.ncsu.edu/course/view.php?id=15) offer additional resources and information on microcredentialing and digital badges.

Google Apps for Education

Molnar and colleagues (2014) concluded that many school districts are opting for Google Apps for Education, referred to as G Suite Enterprise for Education (https://edu.google.com/K–12-solutions/g-suite/?modal_active=none), which offers cloud-based tools, analytics, and communication for customized classwide use. In this way, G Suite is similar to ePortfolios. When used for evaluation purposes, G Suite works with other systems (e.g., PLN, LMS, or digital dashboard) to provide multiple sources and types of data or evidence for documenting engagement and impact.

REVIEWING PLATFORMS AND PRODUCTS:
FIVE TIPS FOR SAVVY TECHNOLOGY CONSUMERS

When considering technology options for evaluating the eCoaching continuum, teachers and other school professionals need to be savvy consumers. Being a savvy consumer means doing one's homework on available technology platforms and products. Though time constraints might seem onerous in the beginning, our experience is that the investment pays off in the long run by reducing frustration and increasing satisfaction. In that spirit, we offer five tips:

- *Visit reputable websites designed for professionals.* For example, EdSurge https://www.edsurge.com/product-reviews /school-operations/professional-development) has developed a Framework for Professional Development for use by educational personnel that includes filtered options for reviewing 67 professional development products available for school or district adoption, including ASCD's PD In Focus, as well as Edthena, IRIS Connect, and many other technology options mentioned in previous chapters. Similar products are also available for review and consideration for individual teacher adoption by selecting EdSurge's Professional Learning option (https://www.edsurge.com/ product-reviews). Individual teachers and learning team members who subscribe to EdSurge receive weekly updates, eliminating the need to visit the website periodically.

- *Talk with colleagues who have experience using the options you or your team members are considering.* Colleagues are a valuable source of information. Many have used technology platforms and products in current and previous positions. Consequently, they may be able to shed light on those being considered. Request a few minutes of their time to pose targeted questions and be sure to reciprocate in some way, by offering to buy them coffee or by sharing your experiences or expertise in another area. Following up with a handwritten or electronic thank-you note is always appreciated, too. Finally, finding ways to connect during district or school meetings, state-level meetings, and professional conferences eases scheduling difficulties, making time to chat easier for all.

- *Check in with school or district technology specialists.* As mentioned earlier, prior to purchasing technology platforms or products, consulting school or district technology specialists is a must. Doing so ensures not only that the technological infrastructure is intact, but also that other products and platforms are compatible. Also, because school or district technology specialists often network with one another, they might be able to connect teachers and other school professionals with individuals within or outside the district who are currently using or have previously used the platform or products.

- *Question platform or product review sales personnel.* The platform or product vendor has sales personnel available for discussion. In addition to asking technical questions, teachers and other school professionals should inquire about the availability of free trial periods, no-cost demonstrations, and tiered-pricing options commensurate with customized needs. Like school or district technology specialists, sales personnel know of others nearby (i.e., in the same school, district, region, or state) who have experience with a given platform or product. It never hurts to ask if they know of anyone in the area and whether they would be willing to make connections.

- *Peruse social media.* Twitter, Facebook, blogs, and vendors' websites can be a treasure trove of information for solicited and unsolicited product and platform reviews. Satisfied and disgruntled users post comments that are often useful. Take a few minutes to gather a representative sample and consider them along with information obtained through other review sources.

Determining Which Technology Options Are the Best Fit for Evaluating Impact

We offer in this section questions and considerations for use by individual teachers or learning team members when weighing technology products and platforms within and across three categories: functionality, cost, and support (see also the box with tips for reviewing platforms and products). Similar questions and considerations were provided in previous chapters. Those we specify here are unique to evaluating the multilevel engagement and impact achieved through the eCoaching professional learning continuum.

Platform and Product Functionality

- What are the options for immediacy?
  - ◊ What are the real-time capabilities for data capture and sharing?
- What are the capabilities for multiple data levels?
  - ◊ What are the capabilities for multilevel (e.g., district, building, classroom, student, eCoach) data collection, archival, sharing, and analysis?
- How are data accessible?
  - ◊ What are the capabilities that support multiple stakeholders' access, individually and collectively? Who controls data? Who uploads and shares data?
  - ◊ How accessible are data across levels (e.g., organization, teachers, students, families/guardians)?
  - ◊ What capabilities protect the privacy and confidentiality of data without thwarting accessibility?
- How are data stored?
  - ◊ What are the long- and short-term storage options for immediately accessing and archiving data? Are there time limits or additional costs?
- What are the options for data sharing?
  - ◊ What capabilities promote ease of data sharing within and across individual teaching or learning team members across multiple levels (i.e., organization, teacher, students)?
  - ◊ What capabilities protect the privacy and confidentiality of data without thwarting data sharing?
- What are the options that support varied data types?
  - ◊ What are the capabilities for supporting differing types of data (e.g., text, video, numerical)?
- What are the options for data integration?
  - ◊ What are the capabilities for integrating varied data sources (e.g., student work samples, teacher video files, school/class attendance rates) across multiple levels (i.e., organization, teacher, students)?
- What data analytics are available?
  - ◊ What are the capabilities for analyzing and interpreting varied data sources (e.g., student work samples, teacher video files, school/class attendance rates) across multiple levels (i.e., organization, teacher, students)?
  - ◊ How compatible are the analytics with other cloud computing or software (e.g., SPSS, SASS, Qualtrics, Excel)?
- What are the data display options?
  - ◊ What are the capabilities for varied data displays (e.g., text, visual/graphic)?

- What are the customization options?
  - ◊ What are the capabilities for customization regarding data collection, archival, access, integration, sharing, analysis, and interpretation?
  - ◊ Are customization options available at different levels (e.g., organization, teacher, student)?
- What capabilities support data-informed decision making?
  - ◊ What capabilities support short- and long-term data-informed decision making? For instance, are push notifications available for immediate or short-term data-informed decision making (Jimerson & Wayman, 2015)? Alternatively, are trend analysis options available for long-term data-informed decision making?

Platform and Product Cost

- What costs are associated with purchasing the platform or product?
  - ◊ What are the initial costs? Are there add-on costs? Do tiered-cost options exist? Are trial options available? If so, for how long? How are often are upgrades provided and at what cost?

Platform and Product Support

- What are the training and technical assistance options?
  - ◊ What types of training (e.g., online manuals, webinars, in person) are provided and at what cost?
  - ◊ What types of technical assistance (e.g., chats, webinars, phone, videoconferencing, in person) are provided for how long and at what cost?

Creating Norms for Technology-Enabled Impact Evaluation

As pointed out earlier, using technology to evaluate the impact of job-embedded professional learning across multiple levels requires teachers, other school professionals, and administrators to do more than set aside a few minutes for completing satisfaction surveys. Instead, they must work, individually and collectively, toward establishing new norms that support more meaningful, authentic, and well-rounded assessment of impact, such as that which is achieved through technology-enabled multilevel evaluation. These new norms are characterized by a culture of inquiry (Danielson & McGreal, 2000); meaningful data use (Schildkamp & Poortman, 2015); and shared responsibility for collective, positive impact (Epps, 2011).

Cultivating a Culture of Inquiry

Almost two decades ago, Danielson and McGreal (2000) cautioned prophetically that a culture of inquiry does not develop by itself. Instead, they asserted, teachers and other school professionals must intentionally create and maintain it, in part by committing to using technology in support of ongoing professional learning with one another. That said, teachers willingly committing to a technology-enabled, job-embedded approach to evaluating professional learning, such as the one described in this and other chapters, is not enough. If advancements are to be made in organizational, teacher, and student learning, then a technology-enabled approach to evaluating impact must also be supported by activities that routinely invite authentic inquiry among individual teachers and team members. Examples of intentional activities include scheduling protected time and providing release time for learning team members, not only when carrying out the four components of the eCoaching continuum but also when monitoring and evaluating impact in *manageable and meaningful* ways across multiple levels (i.e., organization, teachers, students).

These and other inquiry-governed activities require that "open-door" teacher collaboration and regular freely flowing positive, solution-centered exchanges take the place of isolated classroom practices, conversations characterized by constant put-downs and other forms of negative talk (Danielson & McGreal, 2000). As such, school administrators, teachers, and other professionals must also promote risk taking and emphasize trust among learning team members by removing fear of retaliation and negative consequences (Danielson & McGreal, 2000). This can be achieved, in part, by promoting a shared understanding of how administrators will use technology and the performance data collected through it when evaluating the impact of the eCoaching continuum across multiple levels to inform each teacher's or other school professional's annual evaluation (Danielson, 2010). This means, as mentioned in Chapter 3, that teachers and other school professionals need to be assured that technologies for capturing performance data will not be used to catch teachers or other school professionals doing the wrong thing (i.e., "Big Brother" tactics), nor to cajole them into doing the right thing (i.e., nagging mother tactics). Only when technology and performance data are used in authentic, supportive ways to foster inquiry that fuels learning by team members can growth mindsets (Dweck, 2006) and healthy climates for continual learning (Danielson & McGreal, 2000) flourish rather than flounder.

Engaging in Meaningful Data Use

Productive professional norms and practices that support an inquiry-oriented approach to impact evaluation include meaningful data use. In fact, data-informed decision making by teachers and other school professionals has a positive effect on student achievement (Schildkamp & Poortman, 2015). As such, when individual teachers or learning team members decide *what* should be evaluated across multiple levels and *why* it is important, they must also consider not only the technology options described earlier in this chapter but also the factors that influence individual teacher and team data use. As illustrated in Figure 6.5, factors that influence data use are organized into three categories: data characteristics, school organization characteristics, and individual team characteristics (see Schildkamp & Poortman, 2015).

Based on our experiences, as well as findings from a recent study of individual teacher and data team use (see Schildkamp & Poortman, 2015), school professionals require initial and ongoing support in all facets and factors associated with meaningful data use. Meaningful data use requires intentionality to become part of the daily practice that informs the cycle of inquiry that supports job-embedded, technology-enabled impact evaluation. When norms fail to support meaningful data use, evaluation work reverts quickly to business as usual.

Sharing Responsibility for Collective, Positive Impact

Earlier in this chapter, we described how collective efficacy affects K–12 student performance (Donohoo, 2017; Donohoo & Velasco, 2016; Hattie, 2016; Tschannen-Moran & Barr, 2004). Collective efficacy requires an acceptance of shared responsibility. When teachers share beliefs about and responsibilities for learning that positively affect one another, their students, and their organization (i.e., school or district), they are more likely to achieve growth across multiple levels. Creating a

FIGURE 6.5 FACTORS THAT INFLUENCE DATA USE

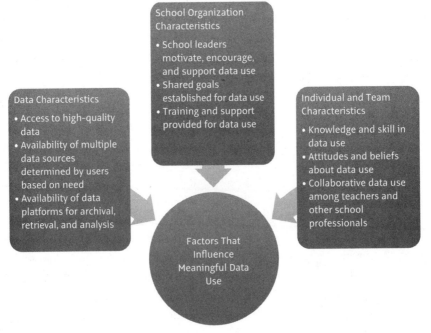

Adapted from Schildkamp and Poortman, 2015.

culture that cultivates a shared responsibility for collective impact requires consideration of five conditions (see Kania & Kramer, 2011):

- A common agenda
- Shared measurement systems
- Mutually reinforcing activities
- Continuous communication
- A backbone support organization

When teachers and other school professionals commit to using technology in ways that support these five conditions, they maximize their opportunity for collective impact. For instance, when individual teachers or learning team members use technology that supports shared measurement systems and shift from an overreliance on standardized test data to a more balanced approach that includes multiple measures of organizational, teacher, and student performance, they are more likely to evidence growth within and across all levels.

Contemplating the Benefits and Cautions Associated with a Technology-Enabled Approach to Evaluation

Earlier, we noted that accountability demands in education have increased markedly (King, 2014), and we explained how teachers and other school professionals use technology to evaluate the impact of their professional learning through the eCoaching continuum. Our view is that using technology in this manner helps teachers and other school professionals embrace accountability demands in job-embedded ways that are *meaningful and beneficial* to the day-to-day teaching and learning that takes place in classrooms. As is the case for any approach to evaluating the impact of professional learning, benefits and drawbacks are associated with this one.

Benefits

The obvious benefit of using technology when evaluating professional learning through the eCoaching continuum is the job-embedded context in which it is carried out. In short, classrooms become active, dynamic, lively, digital-age learning labs for all (Weitze, 2017). Also, technology-enabled data collection, archival, analysis, interpretation, and sharing enables timely, informed decision making by individual professionals and team members about what changes matter most in curriculum and instruction, teacher performance, and student learning. This is important because collecting, archiving, analyzing, interpreting, sharing, and using the most important hard and soft data, across multiple levels, leads to improved decision making and educational outcomes (DeWitt, 2015; Schildkamp & Poortman, 2015). Moreover, our emphasis on teachers facilitating instructional changes in their classrooms and in their colleagues' classrooms on the basis of multilevel data to build the school's capacity for success supports teacher leadership (ASCD *SmartBrief*, 2014; Harrison & Killion, 2007). Finally, evaluating the impact of professional learning in the job-embedded ways we described, across multiple levels, to improve school/district outcomes, teacher practice, and student learning, reflects a commitment to continuous improvement (Weitze, 2017).

Cautions

The power of technology-enabled, job-embedded impact evaluation is undeniable. Still, fatigue and frustration derail even the most willing and enthusiastic professionals. Data fatigue, platform fatigue, scheduling fatigue, and action fatigue often become overwhelming frustrations when *meaningful* priorities for professional learning and evaluation are not established and maintained. The outcome then becomes counterproductive, resulting in bitter, not better, teachers and learners (Frontier & Mielke, 2016). For instance, too much data of any kind, whether standardized or performance based, becomes mind-boggling and paralyzing. Teachers and other school professionals should decide early on which data are the most important to capture and for whom—the organization, teachers, or students (McTighe, 2018; Tomlinson, 2018). Platform fatigue and frustration erupt when teachers and other school professionals have to navigate too many clunky web-based systems, recall too many passwords, or receive too little value from the technology. Insufficient technical support and inadequate training on upgrades also contribute to fatigue and frustration factors. And scheduling issues often result in little to no common meeting time, which undoubtedly makes for weary eCoaches, teachers, and other school professionals. Finally, placing too much emphasis on action, during evaluation, and not investing enough time in planning, interpretation, and reflection (see Reed & Card, 2015) yields high levels of fatigue and frustration as well. Recognizing and generating solutions for dealing effectively with these potential pitfalls goes a long way toward helping eCoaches, teachers, and other school professionals successfully navigate the inevitable changes a technology-enabled approach to impact evaluation brings, so that they don't succumb to the growing pains associated with it.

Translating the eCoach's Role into Action

As mentioned earlier in this chapter, Marsh and colleagues (2015) reported "that coaches and professional learning communities played important roles in mediating teachers' responses to data and were often associated with instances in which teachers used data to alter their instructional delivery (as opposed to surface-level changes in materials and topics)" (p. 1). Thus, one of the central responsibilities eCoaches shoulder during technology-enabled impact evaluation includes helping teachers and other school professionals use data in *meaningful* ways to make changes that positively impact their practice, their students' learning, and their district/school outcomes. Here we offer specific ways eCoaches support individual teachers or learning team members as well as administrators in using technology to evaluate the impact of professional learning through the eCoaching continuum within and across multiple levels (i.e., organizations, teachers, students):

- Take a leadership role in helping administrators, teachers, and other school professionals understand the unique and compelling reasons for using technology to evaluate the technology-enabled coaching continuum in practical, powerful, and impactful ways across multiple levels.
- Work with individual teachers or learning team members to decide what matters most when evaluating impact as they develop a road map (i.e., theory of change) and formulate a multilevel evaluation plan.
- Support individual teacher's or learning team member's efforts to make a technology-enabled evaluation work when applying each of the four tactics—tackling it as a team; employing iterative, cyclic processes; using goal setting, monitoring, and attainment logs (see Appendix); and thinking through how technology helps rather than hinders.
- Facilitate integration of technology-enabled evaluation within learning teams and teaching cycles (see Chapter 5) to ensure an authentic, meaningful, job-embedded approach.
- Lend guidance on determining the availability of platforms and products that support technology-enabled evaluation.
- Assist with reviewing the platforms and products that support evaluation efforts, using the five tips for savvy technology consumers.
- Coordinate evaluation of platforms and products and consider goodness of fit in three categories (i.e., functionality, cost, support) using guiding considerations and questions.
- Provide guidance and support for individual teachers or learning team members on how to collect and use electronic data to support *meaningful* decision making that is embedded in day-to-day classroom instruction (Jimerson and Wayman, 2015).
- Co-create new norms, characterized by a culture of inquiry (Danielson & McGreal, 2000), meaningful data use (Schildkamp & Poortman, 2015), and shared responsibility for positive impact (Epps, 2011), to support technology-enabled evaluation.

- Facilitate discussion among individual teachers or learning team members in weighing the benefits and cautions associated with using technology for impact evaluation and guide them in generating strategies that maximize the former and minimize the latter.
- Develop digital badges/microcredentials for technology-enabled impact evaluation competencies.
- Create modules for training on new and existing technologies and approaches that support impact evaluation across multiple levels.
- Monitor and evaluate what's working and what's not and make adjustments as needed to more effectively support individual teachers or learning team members when carrying out technology-enabled impact evaluation.

Revisiting Important Ideas

In this chapter, we've described how frontline practitioners use technology to assess and evaluate the impact of their professional learning through the eCoaching continuum. We've also explained why doing so is important and pinpointed known benefits and cautions. Let's review the important ideas we've shared:

- Communicate the unique, varied, and compelling purposes for using technology to evaluate the impact of professional learning via the eCoaching continuum.
- Decide what matters most when evaluating impact by developing a road map and formulating a multilevel evaluation plan.
- When using technology, be sure to evaluate impact within and across three levels: organizations (i.e., districts, school buildings), teachers, and students.
- Apply four tactics to make technology-enabled evaluation work: tackle it as a team; employ iterative, cyclic processes; use goal setting, monitoring, and attainment logs; and think through how technology helps rather than hinders.
- Integrate technology-enabled impact evaluation with learning teams and teaching cycles to ensure an authentic, meaningful, job-embedded approach.
- Consider platforms and products that support evaluation needs, while remaining fiscally responsible.
- Use the five tips for savvy technology consumers to review platforms and products that support evaluation efforts.
- Determine the best-fit platforms and products, in part based on answers to the guiding questions and considerations in three categories: functionality, cost, and support.
- Support meaningful and manageable technology-enabled evaluation, in part by creating and sustaining new norms characterized by a culture of inquiry

(Danielson & McGreal, 2000), meaningful data use (Schildkamp & Poortman, 2015), and shared responsibility for collective, positive impact (Epps, 2011).

- Carefully weigh the benefits and cautions associated with using technology to evaluate the impact of the eCoaching continuum within and across multiple levels.

- Ensure that the eCoach's roles and responsibilities for supporting technology-enabled evaluation are clearly articulated and supported by administrators, teachers, and other school professionals.

As in preceding chapters, following are things that you must understand (in this case, for using technology to evaluate the impact of professional learning through the eCoaching continuum). To assist frontline practitioners in transferring chapter content into action, we also include an At-a-Glance Checklist.

AT-A-GLANCE CHECKLIST

Successful Technology-Enabled Impact Evaluation

☐ The purpose for taking a job-embedded approach to evaluating professional learning and impact via the eCoaching continuum is clear, unique, and compelling.

☐ Teachers, other school professionals, administrators, and eCoaches determine what matters most when evaluating impact by developing a road map and formulating a multilevel evaluation plan.

☐ Teachers, administrators, eCoaches, and other school professionals invest time and effort in setting the stage for successfully using technology to evaluate impact across three levels: organizations (i.e., districts, school buildings), teachers, and students.

☐ Teachers, other school professionals, administrators, and eCoaches apply four tactics to make technology-enabled evaluation work: tackling it as a team; employing iterative, cyclic processes; using goal setting, monitoring, and attainment logs; and thinking through how technology helps rather than hinders.

☐ Teachers and other school professionals integrate technology-enabled impact evaluation with learning teams and teaching cycles (see Chapter 5) to ensure an authentic, meaningful, job-embedded approach.

☐ Platforms and products that support individual teachers or learning team members when evaluating the impact of the eCoaching continuum are identified based on goodness of fit in three categories: functionality, cost, and support.

☐ Teachers, other school professionals, administrators, and eCoaches use the five tips for savvy technology consumers to review platforms and products that support evaluation efforts.

☐ Norms for using technology to evaluate professional learning and impact are established and supported.

☐ Benefits and cautions associated with technology-enabled impact evaluation are considered and decisions are made accordingly.

☐ eCoaches possess the knowledge, skills, and abilities needed to be effective in supporting individual teachers or learning team members as they use technology to evaluate the impact of the eCoaching continuum within and across multiple levels.

☐ eCoaches' roles and responsibilities in supporting multilevel, technology-enabled evaluation are clearly articulated and supported.

☐ Impact is evaluated formatively and summatively across multiple levels (i.e., organization, teachers, students) in meaningful and manageable ways.

Appendix

One-on-One, Real-Time, Technology-Enabled Coaching—Online

Guidelines for Getting Started and Connecting Online– Swivl Example

Getting ready to connect online means that the eCoach and the teacher need to follow a few simple steps:

1. Secure the necessary technology devices and components for 1:1, real-time, in-ear coaching.
2. Download the necessary software or apps.
3. Undertake several practice sessions.

Altogether, these three steps ensure a successful start. The sections that follow describe the recommended guidelines for getting started and connecting online.

Secure Equipment

Assembling various technology devices and components allows the teacher and the eCoach to connect and engage in 1:1, real-time, in-ear coaching online:

- Computer (desktop or laptop)
- Mobile device (tablet or smartphone)
- Wide-angle lens webcam (optional)
- Swivl (robotic platform for tablet or smartphone), optional
- Bluetooth earpiece

- External hard drive or cloud storage (required only if 1:1, real-time eCoaching sessions are electronically captured and archived)

Important note: Before installing any software programs, you must have administrative rights to install the software on the computer, mobile device, or robotic platform (e.g., Swivl) that you will be using. If you do not, please work with your school, district, or state technology support personnel.

Download the Videoconferencing Platform

The videoconferencing platform allows the eCoach to visit and observe the teacher's classroom remotely.

- The teacher and the eCoach download the agreed-upon online videoconferencing platform to the computer (laptop or desktop) or mobile device (tablet or smartphone) directly from the URL for the platform. Common videoconferencing platforms include the following:
  - ◊ Skype (free): https://www.skype.com/en/download-skype/skype-for-computer/
  - ◊ Google Hangouts (free): https://hangouts.google.com/
  - ◊ Zoom (paid subscription required): https://zoom.us/
- The eCoach and the teacher need to be sure they are running the most up-to-date versions of the videoconferencing platform. Running outdated or differing versions will often result in glitches, such as dropped calls.

Charge and Pair the Bluetooth Earpiece with the Computer or the Mobile Device

The Bluetooth earpiece allows the eCoach to provide discreet, immediate feedback to the teacher.

- Charge and pair the Bluetooth by following the directions included in the Bluetooth earpiece packaging.
- If a desktop or laptop computer is used that does not have Bluetooth capability, then you need to purchase and install a Bluetooth adapter. The adapter looks like a travel stick, memory stick, or jump drive and allows a Bluetooth earpiece to be paired with the laptop or desktop computer. To install the adapter properly, follow the instructions provided by the manufacturer.

Ensure the Camera or Webcam in the Computer or the Mobile Device Is in Good Working Order

The camera or webcam allows the eCoach and the teacher to see one another as well as the K–12 students. If desired, an external wide-angle webcam can be added to a desktop or laptop computer for enhanced viewing.

Set Up the Swivl (https://www.swivl.com/)

Swivl, which is optional, is a robotic platform that allows the mobile device to track the teacher during classroom instruction. Getting Swivl operational includes the following: connecting all cables/USBs, updating the firmware, pairing the Marker(s), and fully charging the battery. Then, using the instructions provided by Swivl, insert the mobile device into the Swivl platform and practice using the neck or wrist lanyard to ensure tracking functions properly. The teacher can also record and capture video electronically using Swivl.

Secure the Video Call Recorder

The video call recorder allows the eCoach to electronically capture and record the live eCoaching session(s). Some videoconferencing platforms, such as Skype, require you to purchase apps for Apple (i.e., Call Recorder) or PC (i.e., Pamela). Others, such as Google Hangouts and Zoom, offer internal options. Screen capture software, such as Camtasia, is another option that requires purchase. URLs are provided here:

- Call Recorder (Skype/Mac): http://www.ecamm.com/mac/callrecorder/
- Pamela (Skype/PC): http://www.pamela.biz/
- Camtasia: http://shop.techsmith.com/store/techsm/en_US/pd/productID. 289738300

Set Up the External Hard Drive or Cloud Storage

The purpose of the external hard drive or cloud storage is to archive the 1:1, real-time eCoaching sessions that are captured electronically for later viewing and reflection. Either option can be used; however, the eCoach needs to be certain the hard drive and the cloud storage are secure. This means that confidentiality is ensured to the greatest extent possible through password protections, encryption, and so forth. If a web-based option, such as YouTube, is used for electronic video storage, be sure the channel set up is private.

Practice Connecting Online in Real Time

Schedule a few brief sessions to ensure all the necessary components and equipment are working properly. As noted in the Troubleshooting Guidelines document, the trial sessions should be scheduled during routine breaks in instructional time so opportunities for teaching and learning are not interrupted. If possible, it is best to have school or district technology support personnel at the ready to provide just-in-time support during initial practice and 1:1, real-time eCoaching sessions. Also, have the "General Troubleshooting Guidelines" section of this Appendix on hand for good measure. Here is a list of recommended steps for connecting online in real time during the practice sessions:

1. Schedule a predetermined time to connect
2. Determine who will place the video call
3. Greet one another warmly
4. Troubleshoot audio, video, connectivity, and recording issues as needed
5. Keep a log of any tech issues encountered during practice sessions
6. Request that school or district technology support personnel be at the ready to lend real-time support
7. Sign off warmly and end the video call

Best wishes for success! Remember, practice with feedback makes permanent!

General Troubleshooting Guidelines for eCoaches and Teachers

During 1:1, real-time eCoaching sessions, eCoaches and teachers could encounter four hot spots when using the online BIE system. The four troublemakers are as follows:

- Internet connectivity
- Audio
- Video
- Recording (if you have opted to electronically capture and archive the eCoaching sessions)

Important note: After making adjustments to audio, video, or other settings (described in the sections that follow), hang up and call again (i.e., reconnect via the videoconferencing platform [such as Skype, Google Hangouts, Zoom]) if the connection does not occur immediately.

Internet Connectivity Issue: Cannot Connect Online, or Video Connection Drops (often referred to as dropped calls)

- *Check the status of the Internet provider* (e.g., school or district Wi-Fi; home Wi-Fi; or cellular connection, such as 3G, 4G, or 5G) to be sure the connection is secure and in good working order.
- *Check online connectivity on the computer or mobile device.* Using an iPhone as an example: Go to Settings. Then, check Wi-Fi or Cellular (depending on how you are choosing to access the Internet). Be sure your desired option is activated and

in good working order. Also, check the strength of your signal. Weak signals can cause problems, such as dropped calls.

- *Check online connectivity in the videoconferencing platform.* Using Skype as an example: Click on Skype in the menu options (i.e., top left-hand corner of screen). Then, select Preferences. Look for a new window to open. After it does so, select Advanced. Be sure the Enable Wi-Fi box is checked.

Audio Issue: Cannot Hear During the eCoaching Session

- *Use the instant messaging (IM) feature in the videoconferencing platform (e.g., Skype, Google Hangouts, Zoom) to troubleshoot audio with the teacher.* This should take only a minute or two. Offer encouragement and reassurance using emojis and texts while instant messaging. There are two places where audio settings need to be checked: in the control panel of the desktop or laptop computer and in the videoconferencing platform controls. Also, the Bluetooth setting needs to be checked on the computer or mobile device. Finally, the Bluetooth earpiece itself requires consideration (see next items).

- *Check the Bluetooth connection to the computer or mobile device.* Using an Apple MacBook Pro as an example: Open System Preferences, which is accessed by clicking on the Apple icon in the upper left-hand corner of the screen. Then, select Bluetooth from the available options. When the new window opens, be sure the Bluetooth option is turned on *and* be sure the Bluetooth is paired with the laptop. If the Bluetooth does not pair correctly with the laptop, it might require the teacher to go offline, shut down, and restart the laptop. This could take 5–10 minutes. If after doing so, re-pairing is successful, reconnect online to resume the 1:1, real-time eCoaching session. If not, simply reschedule. Using an iPhone as another example: Go to Settings. Be sure Bluetooth is on. Then, be sure the Bluetooth is paired with the iPhone. If not, as was the case with the laptop example, the teacher might need to turn off the iPhone and restart to successfully re-pair the Bluetooth.

- *Check the audio settings in the computer (desktop or laptop) or the mobile device (smartphone or tablet).* Using an Apple MacBook Pro as an example: Go to System Preferences. Then, go to Sound. Check Input and Output options to be sure the selections are correct. Teachers should select Bluetooth, and eCoaches should select Internal options, unless they are using a headset. If that's the case, then the headset option should be selected.

- *Check videoconference platform settings.* Using Skype as the example: Click on Skype in the menu options (i.e., top left-hand corner of the screen). Then, select Preferences. Look for a new window to open. After it does so, select Audio/Video. Check all options included therein (i.e., microphone, ringing, speakers, volume, camera) to be sure all settings are accurate. The teacher should select Bluetooth, and the eCoach should select Built-In options. Both teachers and eCoaches can and should ensure audio is in good working order by conducting a test call in Skype. To do so, enter "Skype test call" into the search option in Skype. Then, click on the Skype test call result.

Audio Troubleshooting Tip: Be sure the Bluetooth is paired properly with the computer (desktop or laptop) or the mobile device (smartphone or tablet). If it is *not* paired properly (see the second item in this list), Bluetooth will *not* appear as an option in the settings/control panels of the videoconferencing platform (e.g., Skype, Google Hangouts, Zoom), in the computer (desktop or laptop), or the mobile device (smartphone or tablet). Also, be certain that in the control panel/settings the mute box is *not* selected.

- *Check the Bluetooth earpiece.* Be sure that it has been fully charged. If not, simply reschedule the 1:1, real-time eCoaching session. If so, try turning the Bluetooth earpiece off and on three or four times. *Note:* If Bluetooth has been off the charger, the computer or mobile device may need to be shut down and restarted. Doing so often requires you to re-pair the Bluetooth with the device or the computer. The code is almost always 0000 to re-pair Bluetooth with the computer. *To be certain, however, check the instructions that came with the Bluetooth.* Again, be certain that in the computer's control panel the mute box is *not* selected. After carrying out these steps, try connecting again online to see whether the audio is working. You will also need to recheck the audio settings as described previously.

- *Check for possible physical obstacles or barriers.* Sometimes the teacher needs to move the Bluetooth earpiece to her other ear so that it is closer to the computer or mobile device. Or, if there are too many obstacles (i.e., desks, chairs, kids) between the teacher and the computer or mobile device, they may need to be repositioned to allow for a clearer audio connection. Finally, if the teacher has long hair covering the Bluetooth earpiece, he might need to tuck it behind an ear or secure it in a ponytail or bun. Doing so also allows for a clearer audio connection.

Video Issue: Cannot See During the eCoaching Session

- *Check the internal camera/webcam on the computer or mobile device to be sure it is in good working order.* For example, when using an Apple MacBook Pro, you cannot control the internal webcam via Settings or System Preferences unless you have an external app. A simple alternative for doing so is to use Photo Booth. To access Photo Booth, simply type "Photo Booth" into the spotlight search. Then select Photo Booth from the results to open it. This allows you to be sure the internal webcam is working properly.

- *Check videoconference platform settings.* Using Skype as the example: Click on Skype in the menu options (i.e., top left-hand corner of screen). Then, select Preferences. Look for a new window to open. After it does so, select Audio/ Video. Check the Camera option included therein. The teacher and the eCoach should select the camera they are using—either a built-in or an externally added webcam will work. Just be sure the proper option is selected. Then, during a 1:1, real-time eCoaching session, be sure the webcam option is selected in the Skype window.

- *As noted earlier, you can use an external webcam by installing one on a laptop or desktop computer.* Why bother? There are webcams with wide-angle lens capability that allow the eCoach to see more of the classroom. If an external webcam is used, additional troubleshooting steps are needed:
  ◊ Check the webcam to ensure that the green or blue light is illuminated. If not, try unplugging and replugging it into the USB port.
  ◊ If incoming video is blurry, ask the teacher to adjust the focus on the webcam.
  ◊ If you cannot see the students or the teacher, ask the teacher to reposition the webcam.
  ◊ If video does not work after checking all the settings in the control panel and in the videoconferencing platform (e.g., Skype, Google Hangouts, Zoom), ask the teacher to unplug and replug the webcam into the USB. Hang up and reconnect online.
  ◊ If the preceding steps fail, the hardware (i.e., the webcam) may need to be reinstalled. If so, reschedule the 1:1, real-time eCoaching session because it requires too much time.

Electronic Recording Issue: Cannot Electronically Capture the eCoaching Session

- *Be sure the recording app is downloaded properly and is compatible with the videoconferencing platform you have selected.* Some videoconferencing platforms, such as Zoom and Google Hangouts, have an internal recording option, so you do not need to download and pay for apps, such as Call Recorder for Mac or Pamela for PC in Skype. With that said, you need to be sure the settings are private when recording. For example, Google Hangouts can be automatically recorded and archived in YouTube; however, you need to be certain the channel is private so that the files are not available publicly.

- *Using Call Recorder on a MacBook Pro as an example:* You will see a new icon, labeled Recording, available for selection in Skype Preferences. Click on Recording to open the window. Be sure all the proper boxes are checked. For instance, if desired, be certain the box is checked that allows you to record calls automatically. If not, you will have to click on the red Call Recording button each time you carry out a live eCoaching session. Sadly, it is easy to overlook doing so and the opportunity to electronically capture and archive the session is lost.

- *Also, be sure you have selected where you wish the electronically archived sessions to be saved (i.e., movies folder, desktop, documents folder, or custom).* Selecting the custom option allows you to save the electronically captured 1:1, real-time eCoaching sessions to a secure external hard drive or to a secure cloud-based storage system.

- *Finally, selecting the picture-in-picture option* allows you to electronically capture the eCoach in a smaller, thumbnail window within the screen that records the teacher and the classroom.

Overall Troubleshooting Tips

- *Involve school or district technology support personnel initially during set up and if chronic tech issues emerge.* Also, if any of the previously mentioned troubleshooting tactics fail to quickly remedy the connectivity, audio, video, or recording problem(s), then school or district technology support personnel should be consulted for assistance.

- *Reschedule 1:1, real-time eCoaching sessions if one or more tech problems persist or take more than a few minutes to resolve.* Rescheduling the 1:1, real-time eCoaching session via e-mail at a later date prevents unnecessary interruptions in instruction. *Instructional time is valuable and should not be squandered on troubleshooting tech issues.*

- *Try to schedule a few trial sessions prior to the first 1:1, real-time eCoaching sessions.* Trial sessions help everyone become familiar with connecting online and using a Bluetooth. Trial sessions also allow K–12 students to become acquainted with online visitors, as opposed to on-site visitors. Trial sessions should be conducted during breaks in the instructional routine, such as during lunch, planning time, before school, or after school. Doing so ensures that teaching and learning are not disrupted.

- *Keep a log of technology issues.* This log will help school or district technology support personnel troubleshoot any ongoing or chronic issues. Also, there are occasions when equipment (e.g., Bluetooth earpiece, wide-angle lens webcam, Swivl, mobile device) is faulty and needs to be replaced.

- *Ensure that the eCoach and the teachers are using the latest versions of the interactive videoconferencing platform and the recording apps.* When old or different versions are used, problems erupt, such as repeated dropped calls.

- *Be mindful that various operating systems, types of technology devices, and equipment require slightly different troubleshooting tactics.* The tips provided here constitute general approaches and are the most common things to consider.
- *Maintain a positive attitude.* Technology is, indeed, a blessing and a curse. A little patience and positivity go a long way when encountering technology issues. Remind yourself that although the live eCoaching session may not have taken place as planned, you have saved valuable time, money, and resources that would have been spent in travel and such. Contact the teacher via e-mail or phone to reschedule the 1:1, real-time eCoaching session at the next available opportunity.

eCoaching Technology Issues Log

Instructor/Teacher: _____

eCoach: _____

Date: _____

	Audio	Video	Internet Connectivity or Online Video-conferencing	Recording	Other
What went wrong?					
What troubleshooting steps were taken and for how long?					
Was the issue remedied? If so, how and by whom? If not, what are the next steps?					

eCoaching Goal Setting Log

Instructor/Teacher: _____

eCoach: _____

Date: _____

eCoach Feedback Goals
What specific feedback goals are you targeting?
1.
2.
3.
Instructor/Teacher Content Goals
What specific content goals are you targeting for feedback?
1.
2.
3.
Instructor/Teacher Pedagogical Goals
What specific pedagogies or learning technologies are you targeting for feedback?
1.
2.
3.
Instructor/Teacher Climate Goals: Social, Emotional, Behavioral
What specific climate (social, emotional, behavioral) goals are you targeting for feedback?
1.
2.
3.
Instructor/Teacher Assessment Goals: Formative or Summative
What specific assessment goals are you targeting for feedback?
1.
2.
3.

Do your best!

eCoaching Goal Monitoring Log

Instructor/Teacher: _____

eCoach: _____

Date: _____

eCoach Feedback Performance Data:
Instructor/Teacher Content Performance Data:
Instructor/Teacher Pedagogical or Technological Performance Data:
Instructor/Teacher Climate (Social, Emotional, Behavioral) Performance Data:
Instructor/Teacher Assessment (Formative or Summative) Performance Data:

eCoaching Goal Attainment Log

Instructor/Teacher: _____

eCoach: _____

Date: _____

eCoach Feedback Attainment Data		
Ideal	**Acceptable**	**Not Yet Acceptable**

Instructor/Teacher Content Attainment Data		
Ideal	**Acceptable**	**Not Yet Acceptable**

Instructor/Teacher Pedagogical or Technological Attainment Data		
Ideal	**Acceptable**	**Not Yet Acceptable**

Instructor/Teacher Climate (Social, Emotional, Behavioral) Attainment Data		
Ideal	**Acceptable**	**Not Yet Acceptable**

Instructor/Teacher Assessment (Formative or Summative) Attainment Data		
Ideal	**Acceptable**	**Not Yet Acceptable**

eCoaching Goal Setting, Monitoring, and Attainment Debriefing Log

eCoach: _____

Instructor/Teacher: _____

Site/Date: _____

What went well today, specific to goals previously set and monitored?   *What evidence supports this?*   1.   2.   3.
What did not go well today, specific to goals previously set and monitored?   *What evidence supports this?*   1.   2.   3.
How will we move forward to improve teaching and K-12 students' learning, specific to goals previously set and monitored?   *What evidence supports this?*   1.   2.   3.

Notes:

BIBLIOGRAPHY

Abilock, R., & Abilock, D. (2016). I agree, but do I know? Privacy and student data. *Knowledge Quest, 44*(4), 10–21.

Aguilar, E. (2016). *The art of coaching teams: Building resilient communities that transform schools.* San Francisco: Jossey-Bass.

Allen, J. P., Pianta, R., Gregory, A., Mikami, A. Y., & Lun, J. (2011). An interaction-based approach to enhancing secondary school instruction and science achievement. *Science, 333*(6045), 1034–1037.

ASCD *SmartBrief.* (2014, October 9). Ed pulse poll. Retrieved from http://www2.smartbrief.com/servlet /ArchiveServlet?issueid=4D05F1A7-CBE4-490BAF42-9661FE79835E&lmid=archives

Ball, D. L., & Cohen, D. K. (1999). Developing practice, developing practitioners: Toward a practice-based theory of professional education. In G. Sykes & L. Darling-Hammond (Eds.), *Teaching as the learning profession: Handbook of policy and practice* (pp. 3–32). San Francisco: Jossey-Bass.

Bambino, D. (2002). Critical friends. *Educational Leadership, 59*(6), 25–27.

Bandura, A. (1977). *Social learning theory.* Englewood Cliffs, NJ: Prentice-Hall.

Bandura, A. (1997). *Self-efficacy: The exercise of control.* New York: Freeman/Times Books/Henry Holt & Co.

Becuwe, H., Tondeur, J., Pareja Roblin, N., Thys, J., & Castelein, E. (2016). Teacher design teams as a strategy for professional development: The role of the facilitator. *Educational Research and Evaluation, 22*(3–4), 141–154. doi:10.1080/13803611.2016.1247724

Bell, A., & Mladenovic, R. (2008). The benefits of peer observation of teaching for tutor development. *Higher Education: The International Journal of Higher Education and Educational Planning, 55*(6), 735–752.

Berry, B., Airhart, K. M., & Byrd, P. A. (2016). Microcredentials: Teacher learning transformed. *Phi Delta Kappan, 98*(3), 34–40.

Birenbaum, M., Kimron, H., & Shilton, H. (2011). Nested contexts that shape assessment for learning: School-based professional learning community and classroom culture. *Studies in Educational Evaluation, 37*, 35–48. doi:10.1016/j.stueduc.2011.04.001

Birman, B., Le Floch, K. C., Klekotka, A., Ludwig, M., Taylor, J., Walters, K., . . . Yoon, K. (2007). State and local implementation of the No Child Left Behind Act: Vol. 2. Teacher quality under NCLB: Interim report. Washington, DC: U.S. Department of Education; Office of Planning, Evaluation and Policy Development; Policy and Program Studies Service.

Birman, B. F., Desimone, L., Porter, A. C., & Garet, M. S. (2000). Designing professional development that works. *Educational Leadership, 57*(8), 28–33.

Blamey, K. L., Meyer, C. K., & Walpole, S. (2008). Middle and high school literacy coaches: A national survey. *Journal of Adolescent & Adult Literacy, 52*(4), 310–323.

Blitz, C. L. (2013). *Can online learning communities achieve the goals of traditional professional learning communities? What the literature says* (REL 2013–003). Washington, DC: U.S. Department of Education, Institute of Education Sciences, National Center for Education Evaluation and Regional Assistance, Regional Educational Laboratory Mid-Atlantic. Retrieved from http://ies.ed.gov/ncee/edlabs

Borko, H. (2004). Professional development and teacher learning: Mapping the terrain. *Educational Researcher, 33*(8), 3–15.

Borko, H., & Putnam, R. (1996). Learning to teach. In D. Berliner & R. Calfee (Eds.), *Handbook of educational psychology* (pp. 673–708). New York: Macmillan.

Boulton, H. (2014). ePortfolios beyond pre-service teacher education: A new dawn? *European Journal of Teacher Education, 37*, 374–389. doi:10.1080/02619768.2013.870994

Bowles, E. P., & Nelson, R. O. (1976). Training teachers as mediators: Efficacy of a workshop versus the bug-in-ear technique. *Journal of School Psychology, 14*(1), 15–25.

Bracken, D. W., & Rose, D. S. (2011). When does 360-degree feedback create behavior change? And how would we know when it does? *Journal of Business Psychology, 26*, 183–192.

Bransford, J., Brown, A., & Cocking, R. R. (Eds.). (2000). *How people learn: Brain, mind, experience, and school.* Washington, DC: National Academies Press.

Bresman, H., & Zellmer-Bruhn, M. (2013). The structural context of team learning: Effects of organizational and team structure on internal and external learning. *Organization Science 24*(4), 1120–1139. doi:10.1287/orsc.1120.0783

Brown, P. C., Roediger, H. L., III, & McDaniel, M. A. (2014). *Make it stick: The science of successful learning.* Cambridge, MA: Harvard University Press.

Brown, S. W., & Grant, A. M. (2010). From GROW to GROUP: Theoretical issues and a practical model for group coaching in organisations. *Coaching: An International Journal of Theory, Research and Practice, 3*(1), 30–45.

Bubb, S., & Earley, P. (2010). *Helping staff develop in schools.* London: Sage.

Carpenter, J. P. (2016). Teachers at the wheel. *Educational Leadership, 73*(8), 30–35.

Carpenter, J. P., & Krutka, D. G. (2014). How and why educators use Twitter: A survey of the field. *Journal of Research on Technology in Education, 46*(4), 414–434. doi:10.1080/15391523.2014.925701

Casey, A. M., & McWilliam, R. A. (2011). The impact of checklist-based training on teachers' use of the zone defense schedule. *Journal of Applied Behavior Analysis, 44*, 97–401. doi:10.1901/jaba.2011.44-397

Cassada, K., & Kassner, L. (2018). Seeing is believing: Peer video coaching as professional development done with me and for me. *Contemporary Issues in Technology and Teacher Education, 18*(2). Retrieved from http://www.citejournal.org/volume-18/issue-2-18/general/seeing-is-believing-peer-video-coaching-as-pd-done-with-me-and-for-me

Center for Creative Leadership. (n.d.). *How feedback and talent conversations strengthen organizations.* Retrieved from https://www.ccl.org/articles/leading-effectively-articles/hr-pipeline-a-quick-win-to-improve-your-talent-development-process/

Chappuis, S., Chappuis, J., & Stiggins, R. (2009). Supporting teacher learning teams. *Educational Leadership, 66*(5), 56–60.

Charteris, J., & Smardon, D. (2013). Second look—second think: A fresh look at video to support dialogic feedback in peer coaching, *Professional Development in Education, 39*(2), 168–185. doi:10.1080/19415257.2012.753931

Cheng, L. P., & Ko, H. D. (2009). Teacher-team development in a school-based professional development program. *The Mathematics Educator, 19*, 8–17.

Cherasaro, T. L., Brodersen, R. M., Reale, M. L., & Yanoski, D. C. (2015). *Teachers' responses to feedback from evaluators: What feedback characteristics matter?* (REL 2017–190). Washington, DC: U.S. Department of Education, Institute of Education Sciences, National Center for Education Evaluation and Regional Assistance, Regional Educational Laboratory Central. Retrieved from http://ies.ed.gov/ncee/edlabs

City, E., Elmore, R., Fiarman, S., & Teitel, L. (2009). *Instructional rounds in education: A network approach to improving teaching and learning.* Cambridge, MA: Harvard Education Press.

City, E. A. (2011). Learning from instructional rounds. *Educational Leadership, 69*(2), 36–41.

Clutterbuck, D., & Megginson, D. (2005). How to create a coaching culture. *People Management, 11*(8, 21), 44–45.

Coburn, C. E., & Woulfin, S. L. (2012). Reading coaches and the relationship between policy and practice. *Reading Research Quarterly, 47*(1), 5–30.

Coggshall, J. G., Rasmussen, C., Colton, A., Milton, J., & Jacques, C. (2012). Generating teaching effectiveness: The role of job-embedded professional learning in teacher evaluation. Research and Policy Brief. National Comprehensive Center for Teacher Quality. Retrieved from: http://files.eric.ed.gov/fulltext/ED532776.pdf

Collie, R. J., Shapka, J. D., & Perry, N. E. (2012). School climate and social-emotional learning: Predicting teacher stress, job satisfaction, and teaching efficacy. *Journal of Educational Psychology, 104*, 1189–1204. doi:10.1037/a0029356

Croft, A., Coggshall, J. G., Dolan, M., Powers, E., & Killion, W. J. (2010). *Job-embedded professional development: What it is, who is responsible, and how to get it done well.* Issue Brief. Washington, DC: National Comprehensive Center for Teacher Quality.

Curlette, W. L., & Granville, H. G. (2014). The four crucial Cs in critical friends groups. *Journal of Individual Psychology 70*(1), 21–30. doi:10.1353/jip.2014.0007

Curry, M. (2008). Critical friends groups: The possibilities and limitations embedded in teacher professional communities aimed at instructional improvement and school reform. *Teachers College Record, 110*(4), 733–774.

Daniels, A. C., & Bailey, J. S. (2014). *Performance management: Changing behavior that drives organizational effectiveness* (5th ed). Atlanta, GA: Performance Management Publications.

Danielson, C. (2010). Evaluations that help teachers learn. *Educational Leadership, 68*(4), 35–39.

Danielson, C., & McGreal, T. L. (2000). *Teacher evaluation to enhance professional learning.* Princeton, NJ: Educational Testing Service.

Darling-Hammond, L. (1993). Reframing the school reform agenda. *Phi Delta Kappan, 74*(10), 752–761.

Dash, S., de Kramer, R. M., O'Dwyer, L. M., Masters, J., & Russell, M. (2012). Impact of professional development on teacher quality and student achievement in fifth grade mathematics. *Journal of Research on Technology in Education, 45*(1), 1–26.

Dede, C. (2004). Distributed-learning communities as a model for educating teachers. In R. Ferdig, C. Crawford, R. Carlsen, N. Davis, J. Price, R. Weber, & D. Willis (Eds.), *Proceedings of SITE 2004—Society for Information Technology & Teacher Education International Conference* (pp. 3–12). Atlanta, GA: Association for the Advancement of Computing in Education (AACE). Retrieved from https://www.learntechlib.org/primary/p/14523/

Denton, C. A., & Hasbrouk, J. (2009). A description of instructional coaching and its relationship to consultation. *Journal of Educational and Psychological Consultation, 19*, 150–175. doi:10.1080/10474410802463296

Desimone, L. M. (2009). Improving impact studies of teachers' professional development: Toward better conceptualizations and measures. *Educational Researcher, 38*, 181–200. doi:10.3102/0013189X08331140

Desimone, L. M., Smith, T., & Frisvold, D. (2007). Is NCLB increasing teacher quality for students in poverty? In A. Gamoran (Ed.), *Standards-based and the poverty gap: Lessons from No Child Left Behind* (pp. 89–119). Washington, DC: Brookings Institution Press.

Desimone, L. M., Smith, T. M., Hayes, S., & Frisvold, D. (2005). Beyond accountability and average math scores: Relating multiple state education policy attributes to changes in student achievement in procedural knowledge, conceptual understanding and problem solving in mathematics. *Educational Measurement: Issues and Practice, 24*(4), 5–18.

deVilliers, R. (2013). 7 Principles of highly effective managerial feedback. *Theory and Practice in Managerial Development Interventions, 11*, 66–74.

DeWitt, P. (2015, September 4). Leaders: Do your teachers say this about your observations? *Education Week.* Retrieved from https://blogs.edweek.org/edweek/finding_common_ground/2015/09/leaders_do_your_teachers_say_this_about_your_observations.html

Diaz-Maggioli, G. (2004). *A passion for learning: Teacher-centered professional development.* Alexandria, VA: ASCD.

Dick, W., Carey, L., & Carey, J. (2005). *The systematic design of instruction* (6th ed.). New York: Allyn & Bacon.

Di Michele Lalor, A. (2016). *Ensuring high-quality curriculum: How to design, revise, or adopt curriculum aligned to student success.* Alexandria, VA: ASCD.

Donohoo, J. (2017). Collective teacher efficacy research: Implications for professional learning. *Journal of Professional Capital and Community, 2*(2), 101–116. doi:10.1108/JPCC-10-2016-0027

Donohoo, J., & Velasco, M. (2016). *The transformative power of collaborative inquiry: Realizing change in schools and classrooms.* Thousand Oaks, CA: Sage & Learning Forward.

Duckworth, A. (2016). *Grit: The power of passion and perseverance.* New York: Scribner/Simon & Schuster.

Duckworth, A., & Gross, J. J. (2014). Self-control and grit related but separable determinants of success. *Current Directions in Psychological Science, 23*, 319–325. doi:10.1177/0963721414541462.

DuFour, R. (2004). What is a "professional learning community"? *Educational Leadership, 61*, 6–11.

Dunne, F., & Honts, F. (1998, April 13–17). *"That group really makes me think!" Critical friends groups and the development of reflective practitioners.* Paper presented at the annual meeting of the American Educational Research Association, San Diego, CA (ERIC Document Reproduction Service No. ED 423 228).

Dweck, C. S. (2006). *Mindset: The new psychology of success.* New York: Random House.

Dweck, C. S. (2007). Boosting achievement with messages that motivate. *Education Canada, 47*(2), 6–10.

Earl, L. M., & Katz, S. (2006). *Leading schools in a data-rich world: Harnessing data for school improvement.* Thousand Oaks, CA: Corwin.

Earley, P., & Porritt, V. (2014). Evaluating the impact of professional development: The need for a student-focused approach. *Professional Development in Education, 40*(1), 112–129. doi:10.1080/19415257.2013.798741

Easton, L. B. (2009). Protocols for addressing issues and problems. Chapter 5 in *Protocols for Professional Learning.* Alexandria, VA: ASCD. Retrieved from http://www.ascd.org/publications/books/109037/chapters/Protocols-for-Addressing-Issues-and-Problems.aspx

Eaton, M. (2017). The flipped classroom. *The Clinical Teacher, 14*(4), 301–302. doi:10.1111/tct.12685

Educational Testing Service. (2011). *Teacher Leader Model Standards.* Retrieved from https://www.ets.org/s/education_topics/teaching_quality/pdf/teacher_leader_model_standards.pdf

Engin, M. (2013). Questioning to scaffold: An exploration of questions in pre-service teacher training feedback sessions, *European Journal of Teacher Education, 36*(1), 39–54. doi:10.1080/02619768.2012.678485

Epps, D. (2011). *Achieving "collective impact" with results-based accountability.* Retrieved from https://clearimpact.com/wp-content/uploads/2016/10/Achieving-Collective-Impact-Clear-Impact.pdf

Fettig, A., & Artman-Meeker, K. (2016). Group coaching on preschool teachers' implementation of Pyramid Model strategies: A program description. *Topics in Early Childhood Special Education, 36*(3), 147–158. doi:10.1177/0271121416650049

Firestone, W. A. (1996). Images of teaching and proposals for reform: A comparison of ideas from cognitive and organizational research. *Educational Administration Quarterly, 32*(2), 209–235. doi:10.1177/0013161X96032002003

Firestone, W. A., & Pennell, J. R. (1993). Teacher commitment, working conditions, and differential incentive policies. *Review of Educational Research, 63*, 489–525.

Fishbach, A., Eyal, T., & Finkelstein, S. R. (2010). How positive and negative feedback motivate goal pursuit. *Social and Personality Psychology Compass, 4*(8), 517–530.

Fixsen, D. L., Naoom, S. F., Blasé, K. A., Friedman, R. M., & Wallace, F. (2005). *Implementation research: A synthesis of the literature.* Tampa, FL: University of South Florida, Louis de la Parte Florida Mental Health Institute, National Implementation Research Network (FMHI Publication #231).

Flanigan, R. (2011). Professional learning networks taking off. *Education Week.* Retrieved from https://www.edweek.org/ew/articles/2011/10/26/09edtech-network.h31.html

Franzak, J. K. (2002). Developing a teacher identity: The impact of critical friends practice on the student teacher. *English Education, 34*(4), 258–280.

Friend, M. P., & Cook, L. (2017). *Interactions: Collaboration skills for school professionals* (8th ed.). Columbus, OH: Pearson Merrill.

Frontier, T., & Mielke, P. (2016). *Making teachers better, not bitter: Balancing evaluation, supervision, and reflection for professional growth*. Alexandria, VA: ASCD.

Fullan, M., & Knight, J. (2011). Coaches as system leaders. *Educational Leadership, 69*, 50–53.

Fulton, K., & Britton, T. (2011). *STEM teachers in professional learning communities: From good teachers to great teaching*. Washington, DC: National Commission on Teaching America's Future and WestEd. Retrieved from http://www.nctaf.org/documents/NCTAFreportSTEMTeachersinPLCsFromGood TeacherstoGreatTeaching.pdf

Fusco, T., O'Riordan, S., & Palmer, S. (2015). Authentic leaders are . . . conscious, competent, confident, and congruent: A grounded theory of group coaching authentic leadership development. *International Coaching Psychology Review, 10*(2), 131–148.

Gawande, A. (2011, May 26). Cowboys and pit crews. *The New Yorker*. Retrieved from https://www.newyorker.com /news/news-desk/cowboys-and-pit-crews

Giebelhaus, C. R., & Cruz, J. (1994). The mechanical third ear device: An alternative to traditional student teaching supervision strategies. *Journal of Teacher Education, 45*, 365–373.

Glickman, C. D., Gordon, S. P., & Ross-Gordon, J. M. (2014). *SuperVision and instructional leadership: A developmental approach* (9th ed.). Upper Saddle River, NJ: Pearson Education.

Goddard, R. D., Hoy, W. K., & Hoy, A. W. (2000). Collective teacher efficacy: Its meaning, measure, and impact on student achievement. *American Educational Research Journal, 37*(2), 479–507. doi:10.2307/1163531

Goe, L., Biggers, K., & Croft, A. (2012). *Linking teacher evaluation to professional development: Focusing on improving teaching and learning*. National Comprehensive Center for Teacher Quality (ERIC Reproduction Service, ED 532775).

Goodwin, A. L., Low, E. L., & Ng, P. T. (2015). Developing teacher leadership in Singapore: Multiple pathways for differentiated journeys. *The New Educator, 11*(2), 107–120. doi:10.1080/1547688X.2015.1026782

Gormley, H., & van Nieuwerburgh, C. (2014). Developing coaching cultures: A review of the literature. *Coaching: An International Journal of Theory, Research and Practice, 7*(1), 90–101.

Gosling, D. (2002). *Models of peer-observation of teaching*. Learning and Teaching Support Network, Generic Centre. Retrieved from www.heacademy.ac.uk/resources

Gregory, A. (2010). Teacher learning on problem-solving teams. *Teaching and Teacher Education, 26*, 608–615. doi:10.1016/j.tate.2009.09.007

Gregory, J. B., Levy, P. E., & Jeffers, M. (2008). Development of a model of the feedback process within executive coaching. *Consulting Psychology Journal: Practice and Research, 60*(1), 42–56. doi:http://dx.doi.org/10.1037 /1065-9293.60.1.42

Grimm, E. D., Kaufman, T., & Doty, D. (2014). Rethinking classroom observation. *Educational Leadership, 71*(8), 24–29.

Gulamhussein, A. (2013). *Teaching the teachers: Effective professional development in an era of high stakes accountability*. Alexandria, VA: Center for Public Education. Retrieved from www.centerforpubliceducation.org/system /files/Professional%20Development.pdf

Guskey, T. R. (2002). Professional development and teacher change. *Teachers and Teaching: Theory and Practice, 8*(3), 381–391.

Guskey, T. R., & Yoon, K. S. (2009). What works in professional development. *Phi Delta Kappan, 90*(7), 495–500.

Hackman, J. R. (2002). *Leading teams: Setting the stage for great performances*. Boston: Harvard Business School Press.

Hackman, J. R., & Edmondson, A. C. (2008). Groups as agents of change. In T. Cummings (Ed.), *Handbook of organizational development* (pp. 167–186). Thousand Oaks, CA: Sage.

Hackman, J. R., & O'Connor, M. (2004). *What makes for a great analytic team? Individual vs. team approaches to intelligence analysis*. Washington, DC: Intelligence Science Board, Office of the Director of Central Intelligence.

Hackman, J. R., & Wageman, R. (2005). A theory of team coaching. *The Academy of Management Review, 30*(2), 269–287.

Hamilton, E. R. (2013). His ideas are in my head: Peer-to-peer teacher observations as professional development. *Professional Development in Education, 39*(1), 42–64. doi:10.1080/19415257.2012.726202

Hargreaves, A. (2007). Sustainable leadership and development in education: Creating the future, conserving the past. *European Journal of Education Research, Development and Policy, 42*(2), 223–233. doi:10.1111 /j.1465-3435.2007.00294

Hargreaves, A. (n.d.). 100 Quotes to teach and lead by: Key quotes from the selected works of Andy Hargreaves. Retrieved from http://andyhargreaves.weebly.com/100-quotes-to-teach-and-lead-by-1-25.html

Harlen, W., & Doubler, S. J. (2004). Can teachers learn through enquiry on-line? Studying professional development in science delivered on-line and on-campus. *International Journal of Science Education, 26*(10), 1247–1267. doi:10.1080/0950069042000177253

Harris, D. N., & Sass, T. R. (2011). Teacher training, teacher quality and student achievement. *Journal of Public Economics, 95*(7), 798–812.

Harrison, C., & Killion, J. (2007). Ten roles for teacher leaders. *Educational Leadership, 65*(1), 74–77.

Hattie, J. (2016). *Hattie ranking: Backup of 138 effects related to student achievement*. Retrieved from https:// visible-learning.org/2016/04/hattie-ranking-backup-of-138-effects/

Hendry, G. D., & Oliver, G. R. (2012). Seeing is believing: The benefits of peer observation. *Journal of University Teaching & Learning Practice, 9*(1).

Herold, P., Ramirez, M., & Newkirk, J. (1971). A portable radio communication system for teacher education. *Educational Technology, 11*, 30–32.

Hochberg, E., & Desimone, L. (2010). Professional development in the accountability context: Building capacity to achieve standards. *Educational Psychologist, 45*(2), 89–106.

Hord, S. M. (1997). *Professional learning communities: Communities of continuous inquiry and improvement.* Austin, TX: Southwest Educational Development Laboratory.

Janis, I. L. (1982). *Groupthink: Psychological studies of policy decisions and fiascos* (2nd ed.). Boston: Houghton Mifflin.

Jimerson, J. B., & Wayman, J. C. (2015). Professional learning for using data: Examining teacher needs and supports. *Teachers College Record 117*(4), 1–36.

Johnson, D. H., & Johnson, F. P. (2016). *Joining together: Group theory and group skills* (11th ed.). Columbus, OH: Pearson Merrill

Joyce, B., & Showers, B. (1982). The coaching of teaching. *Educational Leadership, 40*(1), 4–10.

Joyce, B., & Showers, B. (2002). *Student achievement through staff development* (3rd. ed.). Alexandria, VA: Association for Supervision and Curriculum Development.

Jun, M-K., Anthony, R., Achrazoglou, J., & Coghill-Behrends, W. (2007). Using ePortfolio™ for the assessment and professional development of newly hired teachers. *TechTrends: Linking Research and Practice to Improve Learning, 51*(4), 45–50.

Kania, J., & Kramer, M. (2011, Winter). Collective impact. *Stanford Social Innovation Review, 9*(1), 36–41. Retrieved from https://ssir.org/articles/entry/collective_impact

King, C. L. (2014). *Quality measures partnership effectiveness continuum (PEC).* Waltham, MA: Education Development Center, Inc.

Kinicki, A. J., Prussia, G. E., Wu, B. J., & McKee-Ryan, F. M. (2004). A covariance structure analysis of employees' response to performance feedback. *Journal of Applied Psychology, 89*(6), 1057–1069.

Kirkpatrick, D. L. (1959/1994). *Evaluating training programs: The four levels.* San Francisco: Berrett-Koehler.

Kluger, A. N., & DeNisi, A. (1996). The effects of feedback interventions on performance: A historical review, a meta-analysis, and a preliminary feedback intervention theory. *Psychological Bulletin, 119*(2), 254–284.

Knight, J. (2007). *Instructional coaching: A partnership approach to improving instruction.* Thousand Oaks, CA: Corwin.

Knight, J. (2014). What you learn when you see yourself teach. *Educational Leadership, 71*(8), 18–23.

Knowles, M. S. (1980). *The modern practice of adult education: From pedagogy to andragogy.* Englewood Cliffs, NJ: Cambridge Adult Education.

Knowles, M. S. (1984). *Andragogy in action: Applying modern principles of adult learning.* San Francisco: Jossey-Bass.

Korner, I. N., & Brown, W. H. (1952). The mechanical third ear. *Journal of Consulting Psychology, 16*, 81–84.

Kozlowski, S. W., & Bell, B. S. (2008). Team learning, development and adaptation. In Valerie Sessa, & Manuel London (Eds.), *Work group learning: Understanding, improving & assessing how groups learn in organizations* (pp. 15–44). Mahwah, NJ: Lawrence Erlbaum Associates.

Kretlow, A. G., & Bartholomew, C. C. (2010). Using coaching to improve the fidelity of evidence-based practices: A review of studies. *Teacher Education and Special Education, 33*(4), 279–299.

Kruse, S. D., & Louis, K. S. (1997). Teacher teaming in middle schools: Dilemmas for a schoolwide community. *Educational Administration Quarterly, 33*(3), 261–289. doi:10.1177/0013161X97033003002

Kulhavy, R. W. (1977). Feedback in written instruction. *Review of Educational Research, 47*(1), 211–232. doi:10.3102/00346543047002211

L'Allier, S. K., & Elish-Piper, L. (2007). "Walking the walk" with teacher education candidates: Strategies for promoting active engagement with assigned readings. *Journal of Adolescent & Adult Literacy, 50*(5), 338–353.

L'Allier, S., Elish-Piper, L., & Bean, R. M. (2010). What matters for elementary literacy coaching? Guiding principles for instructional improvement and student achievement. *The Reading Teacher, 63*(7), 544–554. doi:10.1598/RT.63.7.2

Langley, G. J., Moen, R. D., Nolan, K. M., Nolan, T. W., Norman, C. L., & Provost, L. P. (1996). *The improvement guide: A practical approach to enhancing organizational performance.* San Francisco: Jossey-Bass.

Larson, J. R. (1984). The performance feedback process: A preliminary model. *Organizational Behavior and Human Performance, 33*, 42–76.

Lave, J., & Wenger, E. (1991). *Situated learning: Legitimate peripheral participation.* Cambridge, UK: Cambridge University Press.

Lawley, J., & Linder-Pelz, S. (2016). Evidence of competency: Exploring coach, coachee, and expert evaluations of coaching, *Coaching: An International Journal of Theory, Research and Practice, 9*(2), 110–128. doi:10.1080/17521882.2016.1186706

Lewin, K. (1935). *A dynamic theory of personality.* New York: McGraw-Hill.

Liang, J. (2015). Live video classroom observation: An effective approach to reducing reactivity in collecting observational information for teacher professional development. *Journal of Education for Teaching, 41*(3), 235–253. doi:10.1080/02607476.2015.1045314

Lindbom, D. (2007). A culture of coaching: The challenge of managing performance for long-term results. *Organisation Development Journal, 25*(2), 101–106.

Linderbaum, B. A., & Levy, P. E. (2010). The development and validation of the Feedback Orientation Scale (FOS). *Journal of Management, 36*, 1372–1405.

Loukas, A., & Murphy, J. L. (2007). Middle school student perceptions of school climate: Examining protective functions on subsequent adjustment problems. *Journal of School Psychology, 45*(3), 293–309. doi:10.1016/j.jsp.2006.10.001

Lowenhaupt, R., McKinney, S., & Reeves, T. (2014). Coaching in context: The role of relationships in the work of three literacy coaches. *Professional Development in Education, 40*(5), 740–757. doi:10.1080/19415257.2013.847475

Mahoney, J. L., Durlak, J. A., & Weissberg, R. P. (2018). An update on social emotional learning outcome research. *Phi Delta Kappan, 100*(4), 18–23. Retrieved from https://www.kappanonline.org/social-emotional-learning-outcome-research-mahoney-durlak-weissberg/

Malone, D. M., & Gallagher, P. A. (2010). Special education teachers' attitudes and perceptions of teamwork. *Remedial and Special Education, 31*(5), 330–342.

Markose, B. (2011). Influence of moderators in the relationship of supervisory feedback with goal orientation of salespeople: An empirical study. *International Journal of Business Insights & Transformation, 4*(2), 53–66.

Marks, M. A., Mathieu, J. E., & Zaccaro, S. J. (2001). A temporally based framework and taxonomy of team processes. *Academy of Management Review, 26*(3), 356–376.

Marsh, J. A., Bertrand, M., & Huguet, A. (2015). Using data to alter instructional practice: The mediating role of coaches and professional learning communities. *Teachers College Record, 117*(4), 1–40.

Marzano, R. (2011). What teachers gain from deliberate practice. *Educational Leadership, 68*(4), 82–84.

Masters, M. F., & Albright, R. R. (2002). *The complete guide to conflict resolution in the workplace.* New York: AMACOM.

Matsumura, L., Garnier, H. E., & Spybrook, J. (2013). Literacy coaching to improve student reading achievement: A multi-level mediation model. *Learning and Instruction, 25*, 35–48.

Mayer, R. E. (2001). *Multimedia learning.* New York: Cambridge University Press.

McDonald, P. L. (2012). *Adult learners and blended learning: A phenomenographic study of variation in adult learners' experiences of blended learning in higher education* (Doctoral dissertation or master's thesis). The George Washington University.

McEwan, D., Ruissen, G. R., Eys, M. A., Zumbo, B. D., & Beauchamp, M. R. (2017). The effectiveness of teamwork training on teamwork behaviors and team performance: A systematic review and meta-analysis of controlled interventions. *PLoS ONE 12*(1), 1–23: e0169604. doi:10.1371/journal.pone.0169604

McLaughlin, M. W., & Talbert, J. E. (2006). *Building school-based teacher learning communities: Professional strategies to improve student achievement.* New York: Teachers College Press.

McTighe, J. (2018). Three key questions on measuring learning. *Educational Leadership, 75*(5), 14–20.

Meirink, J. A., Imants, J., Meijer, P. C., & Verloop, N. (2010). Teacher learning and collaboration in innovative teams. *Cambridge Journal of Education, 40*(2), 161–181.

Mezirow, J. (1997). Transformative learning: Theory to practice. *New Directions for Adult and Continuing Education, 74,* 5–12. doi:10.1002/ace.7401

Mezirow, J. (2000). *Learning as transformation: Critical perspectives on a theory in progress.* San Francisco: The Jossey-Bass Higher and Adult Education Series.

Miles, S. J., & Mangold, G. (2002). The impact of team leader performance on team member satisfaction: The subordinate's perspective. *Team Performance Management: An International Journal, 8*(5/6), 113–121. doi:10.1108/13527590210442230

Molnar, A. (Ed.), Rice, J. K., Huerta, L., Shafer, S. R., Barbour, M. K., Miron, G., Gulosino, C., & Horvitz, B. (2014). *Virtual schools in the U.S. 2014: Politics, performance, policy, and research evidence.* Boulder, CO: National Education Policy Center. Retrieved from http://nepc.colorado.edu/publication/virtual-schools-annual-2014

Moon, J., & Michaels, S. (2016, March 2). Is today's video-based teacher PD missing the picture? *Education Week.* Retrieved from https://www.edweek.org/tm/articles/2016/03/02/is-todays-video-based-teacher-pd-missing-the.html

Morgeson, F. P., DeRue, D., & Karam, E. P. (2010). Leadership in teams: A functional approach to understanding leadership structures and processes. *Journal of Management, 36,* 5–39. doi:10.1177/0149206309347376

Murray, S., Ma, X., & Mazur, J. (2009). Effects of peer coaching on teachers' collaborative interactions and students' mathematics achievement. *Journal of Educational Research, 102*(3), 203–212.

National Research Council. (2007). *Enhancing professional development for teachers: Potential uses of information technology.* Report of a Workshop. Committee on Enhancing Professional Development for Teachers, National Academies Teacher Advisory Council. Center for Education, Division of Behavioral and Social Sciences and Education. Washington, DC: National Academies Press. Retrieved from http://www.nap.edu/catalog/11995.html

New Teacher Project's Greenhouse Report, The. (2012). *Greenhouse schools: How schools can build cultures where teachers and students thrive.* Retrieved from https://tntp.org/assets/documents/TNTP_Greenhouse_Schools_2012.pdf

Park, G., Schmidt, A. M., Scheu, C., & DeShon, R. P. (2007). A process model of goal orientation and feedback seeking. *Human Performance, 20*(2), 119–145.

Pattison, A. T., Sherwood, M., Lumsden, C. J., Gale, A., & Markides, M. (2012). Foundation observation of teaching project—A developmental model of peer observation of teaching. *Med Teach, 34*(2), 36–42. doi:10.3109/0142159X.2012.644827

Pieters, J. M., & Voogt, J. M. (2016). Teacher learning through teacher teams: What makes learning through teacher teams successful? *Educational Research and Evaluation, 22*(3–4), 115–120. doi:10.1080/13803611.2016.1247726

Polly, D., Mraz, M., & Algozzine, R. (2013). Implications for developing and researching elementary school mathematics coaches. *School Science and Mathematics, 113*(6), 297–307.

Preddy, L. (2016). The critical role of the school librarian in digital citizenship education. *Knowledge Quest, 44*(4), 4–5.

Reed, J. E., & Card, A. J. (2015). The problem with plan-do-study-act cycles. *BMJ Quality & Safety Published Online First, 0*, 1–6. doi:10.1136/bmjqs-2015-005076

Rock, M., Gregg, M., Gable, R., Zigmond, N., Blanks, B., Howard, P., & Bullock, L. (2012). Time after time online: An extended study of virtual coaching during distant clinical practice. *Journal of Technology and Teacher Education, 20*(3), 277–304.

Rock, M. L., Gregg, M. L., Thead, B. K., Acker, S. E., Gable, R. A., & Zigmond, N. P. (2009). Can you hear me now? Evaluation of an online wireless technology to provide real-time feedback to special education teachers in training. *Teacher Education and Special Education, 32*(1), 64–82.

Rock, M. L., Schoenfeld, N., Zigmond, N., Gable, R. A., Ploessl, D. M., & Salter, A. (2013). Can you Skype me now? Developing teachers' classroom management practices through virtual coaching. *Beyond Behavior, 22*(3), 15–23.

Rock, M. L., Schumacker, R., Gregg, M., Gable, R. A., Zigmond, N. P., & Howard, P. (2014). How are they now? Longer term effects of eCoaching through online bug-in-ear technology. *Teacher Education and Special Education, 37*(2), 159–179. doi:10.1177/0888406414525048

Rock, M. L., Zigmond, N. P., Gregg, M., & Gable, R. A. (2011). The power of virtual coaching. *Educational Leadership, 69*(2), 42–47.

Ross, C.R., Maninger, R.M., LaPrairie, K.N., & Sullivan, S. (2015). The use of twitter in the creation of educational professional learning opportunities. *Administrative Issues Journal: Connecting Education, Practice, and Research, 5*(1), 55–76, doi:10.5929/2015.5.1.7

Sagor, R. (2000). *Guiding school improvement with action research.* Alexandria, VA: ASCD.

Scheeler, M. C., McAfee, J. K., & Ruhl, K. L. (2004). Providing performance feedback to teachers: A review. *Teacher Education and Special Education, 27*, 396–407.

Scheeler, M. C., McKinnon, K., & Stout, J. (2012). Effects of immediate feedback delivered via webcam and bug-in-ear technology on pre-service teacher performance. *Teacher Education and Special Education, 35*, 78–90.

Schildkamp, K., & Poortman, C. L. (2015). Factors influencing the functioning of data teams. *Teachers College Record, 117*(4), 1–42.

Schön, D. A., 1983. *The reflective practitioner: how professionals think in action.* New York: Basic Books.

Scott, R. (2013). *A research design conference: How can digital resources increase collaboration and support teachers implementing standards?* [white paper from conference led by the Teaching Channel with funding from the National Science Foundation0]. Retrieved from https://dqam6mam97sh3.cloudfront.net/resources/.../TchTeams_Research_Basis.pdf

Shepherd, C. E., & Skrabut, S. (2011). Rethinking electronic portfolios to promote sustainability among teachers. *TechTrends: Linking Research and Practice to Improve Learning, 55*(5), 31–38.

Sherman, R., Dlott, M., Bamford, H., & McGivern, M. (2003). *Evaluating professional development resources: Selection and development criteria.* Retrieved from https://www.calpro-online.org/pubs/99.pdf

Shipley, W. W. (2009). *Examining teacher collaboration in a kindergarten building: A case study* (Doctoral dissertation). Retrieved from https://dsc.duq.edu/cgi/viewcontent.cgi?article=2204&context=etd

Siemens, G. (2004). *A learning theory for the digital age.* Retrieved from http://www.elearnspace.org/articles/connectivism.htm

Stake, R. E. (1967). The countenance of educational evaluation. *Teachers College Record, 68*, 523–540.

Steelman, L. A., Levy, P. E., & Snell, A. F. (2004). The feedback environment scale: Construct, definition, measurement, and validation. *Educational and Psychological Measurement, 64*(1), 165–184.

Stelter, R., Nielsen, G., & Wikman, J. M. (2011). Narrative-collaborative group coaching develops social capital—A randomised control trial and further implications of the social impact of the intervention. *Coaching: An International Journal of Theory, Research and Practice, 4*(2), 123–137. doi:10.1080/17521882.2011.598654

Stone, D., & Heen, S. (2014). *Thanks for the feedback: The science and art of receiving feedback well.* New York: Penguin Random House.

Sykes, G. (1996). Reform of and as professional development. *Phi Delta Kappan, 7*, 465–467.

Tekkumru-Kisa, M., & Stein, M. K. (2017). Designing, facilitating, and scaling-up video-based professional development: Supporting complex forms of teaching in science and mathematics. *International Journal of STEM Education, 4*(27), 1–9. doi:10.1186/s40594-017-0087-y

Thurlings, M., & den Brok, P. (2017). Learning outcomes of teacher professional development activities: a meta-study. *Educational Review, 69*(5), 554–576. doi:10.1080/00131911.2017.1281226

Tomlinson, C. A. (2018). One to grow on/help teachers become master learners. *Educational Leadership, 76*(3), 88–89.

Trust, T., Krutka, D. G., & Carpenter, J. P. (2016). "Together we are better": Professional learning networks for teachers. *Computers & Education, 102*, 15–34. doi:10.1016/j.compedu.2016.06.007

Tschannen-Moran, M., & Barr, M. (2004). Fostering student learning: The relationship of collective teacher efficacy and student achievement. *Leadership and Policy in Schools, 3*(3), 189–209.

Tuckman, B. W. (1965). Development sequence in small groups. *Psychological Bulletin, 63*(6), 384–399.

Tuckman, B. W., & Jensen, M. C. (1977). Stages of small-group development revisited. *Group & Organization Studies, 2*(4), 419–427.

U.S. Department of Education (2017). *Reimagining the role of technology in education: 2017 National education technology plan update.* Retrieved from: http://tech.ed.gov

Vanblaere, B., & Devos, G. (2016). Relating school leadership to perceived professional learning community characteristics: A multilevel analysis. *Teaching and Teacher Education, 57,* 26–38. doi:10.1016 /j.tate.2016.03.003

Van der Mars, H. (1988). The effects of audio-cueing on selected teaching behaviors of an experienced elementary physical education specialist. *Journal of Teaching in Physical Education, 8*(1), 64–72.

Vangrieken, K., Dochy, F., & Raes, E. (2016). Team learning in teacher teams: Team entitativity as a bridge between teams-in-theory and teams-in-practice. *European Journal of Psychology of Education, 31*(3), 275–298. doi:http://dx.doi.org/10.1007/s10212-015-0279-0

Visser, R. D., Evering, L. C., & Barrett, D. E. (2014). #TwitterforTeachers: The implications of Twitter as a self-directed professional development tool for K–12 teachers. *Journal of Research on Technology in Education, 46*(4), 396–413. doi:10.1080/15391523.2014.925694

Vygotsky, L. S. (1962). *Thought and language* (Eugenia Hanfmann & Gertrude Vakar, Ed. & Trans.). Cambridge, MA: MIT Press. (Original work published in Russian in 1934)

Vygotsky, L. S. (1978). *Mind in society: The development of higher psychological processes.* Cambridge, MA: Harvard University Press.

Wageman, J. R., & Hackman, R. (2005). A theory of team coaching. *Academy of Management Review, 30*(2), 269–287.

Wageman, R., Nunes, D., Burruss, J., & Hackman, J. R. (2008). *Senior leadership teams: What it takes to make them great.* Boston: Harvard Business School.

Walkowiak, T. A. (2016). Five essential practices for communication: The work of instructional coaches. *The Clearing House: A Journal of Educational Strategies, Issues and Ideas, 89*(1), 14–17. doi:10.1080 /00098655.2015.1121121

Walsh, J. A., & Sattes, B. D. (2015). *Questioning for classroom discussion: Purposeful speaking, engaged listening, deep thinking.* Alexandria, VA: ASCD.

Wang, H., Hall, N. C., & Rahimi, S. (2015). Self-efficacy and causal attributions in teachers: Effects on burnout, job satisfaction, illness, and quitting intentions. *Teaching and Teacher Education, 47,* 120–130. doi:10.1016/j.tate.2014.12.005

Wei, R. C., Darling-Hammond, L., Andree, A., Richardson, N., & Orphanos, S. (2009). *Professional learning in the learning profession: A status report on teacher development in the United States and abroad.* Oxford, OH: National Staff Development Council.

Weitze, C. L. (2017). How student game designers design learning into games. In K. E. H. Caldwell, S. Syeler, A. Ochsner, & C. Steinkuehler (Eds.), *GLS Conference Proceedings 2017* (pp. 191–201). Pittsburgh, PA: Carnegie Mellon University Press.

Woods, B. (2013). Building your own PLN. *TD Magazine, 67*(11), 70–73. Retrieved from: https://www.td.org /magazines/td-magazine/building-your-own-pln

Yoon, K. S., Duncan, T., Lee, S. W. Y., Scarloss, B., & Shapley, K. (2007). *Reviewing the evidence on how teacher professional development affects student achievement* (Issues & Answers Report, REL 2007, no. 033). Washington, DC: U.S. Department of Education, Institute of Education Sciences, National Center for Education Evaluation and Regional Assistance, Regional Educational Laboratory Southwest. Retrieved from http://ies.ed.gov/ncee/edlabs

Zhang, M., Lundeberg, M. A., Koehler, M. J., & Eberhardt, J. (2011). Understanding affordances and challenges of three types of video for teacher professional development. *Teaching and Teacher Education, 27*(2), 454–462.

Zuger, S. (2016). Digital citizenship "raising" smart kids. *Technology & Learning, 36*(9).

INDEX

ABOUT THE AUTHOR AND CONTRIBUTORS

Marcia Rock, PhD, is an associate professor at the University of North Carolina Greensboro (UNCG). Prior to joining the Spartan community, she was an associate professor at The University of Alabama (UA). Throughout her career, she has dedicated her research, teaching, and service endeavors to working with others in solving real-world problems of educational practice. She has authored or coauthored articles that have appeared in *Educational Leadership, Journal of Technology and Teacher Education, Contemporary Issues in Technology and Teacher Education, Teacher Education and Special Education, Journal of Staff Development, Phi Delta Kappan, Exceptionality, Intervention in School & Clinic, Teaching Exceptional Children, Focus on Exceptional Children, Preventing School Failure, Education & Treatment of Children, The Journal of Positive Behavior Interventions, Journal of Behavioral Education, Education and Training in Autism and Developmental Disabilities Journal,* and *Career Development and Transition for Exceptional Individuals.* Rock is a past president for the Teacher Education Division (TED) of the Council for Exceptional Children (CEC). She has secured more than $2 million in federal personnel and leadership development grants. For the past 10 years, she has worked closely with state department personnel in North Carolina and Alabama to incorporate real-time coaching through a continuum into state improvement and state personnel development grants. Also, she has received a number of research and teaching awards at UA and UNCG. With collaboration and support from family and colleagues, Rock has devoted more than a decade to pioneering the research and development of real-time feedback and coaching on a continuum, personally conducting more than 800 sessions.

Contributors

Morgan V. Blanton, EdD, is a clinical assistant professor in the Reich College of Education at Appalachian State University. She holds a Doctor of Education degree in curriculum and instruction, a Master of Education degree in reading education, and a Bachelor of Science degree in elementary education. She currently teaches reading methods courses and provides field experience support for preservice teachers. In addition to reading courses, her experience in higher education includes teaching undergraduate and graduate courses in curriculum and instruction, instructional technology, and teacher leadership. Blanton also has experience serving students and teachers in North Carolina's public schools in roles such as an elementary class-room teacher, K–5 reading specialist, secondary curriculum coordinator (6–12), and secondary MTSS coordinator (5–9). Additionally, Blanton has experience as a real-time ("bug-in-ear") eCoach for inservice and preservice teachers. Her research interests include eCoaching, teacher development, and home literacy.

Aftynne E. Cheek, PhD, is an assistant professor in the Department of Reading Education and Special Education at Appalachian State University. She teaches introductory and methods courses in special education at the undergraduate and graduate levels. Cheek has taught undergraduate courses in developmental disabilities, introduction to special education, curriculum design, and individualized assessment, and she has taught graduate courses in assessment, instruction, and advanced studies of students with severe disabilities. Before her academic career, Cheek taught in the North Carolina public school system, where she educated students who were diagnosed with moderate and severe intellectual disabilities, physical disabilities, multiple disabilities, autism, traumatic brain injury, mental illness, and emotional and behavioral disorders. Cheek has served in several leadership roles at the national, state, and local levels in various organizations in her field, including the Teacher Education Division for the Council for Exceptional Children (TED-CEC) and the North Carolina Division for Autism and Developmental Disabilities (NC-DADD). Her research involves teacher preparation, eCoaching, and literacy/comprehension instruction for students with severe intellectual disabilities.

Paula Crawford, EdD, has since 2012 served as the section chief of program improvement and professional development with the North Carolina Department of Public Instruction Exceptional Children Division and the project director of the North Carolina State Improvement Project. She leads a statewide and regionally based team implementing continuous improvement in evidence-based instructional practices for preservice and inservice K–12 classroom teachers. Crawford was awarded the University of Kansas 2018 Gordon R. Alley Partnership Award. Additionally, she served as an adjunct professor for several UNC-System and private colleges and universities. Crawford earned a Bachelor of Science degree from Concord College and both her Master's and Doctor of Education degrees from North Carolina State University in curriculum and instruction and adult and higher education, respectively.

Kara B. Holden, PhD, is a visiting professor in the School of Education's Department of Specialized Education Services at the University of North Carolina Greensboro and is the president of the North Carolina Council for Children with Behavioral Disorders. She is committed to strengthening teacher preparation, advancing classroom behavior management, and enhancing research practices in the field of education. Holden's focus of study is on general and special education teacher preparation, behavior management, and observation methodologies. Additionally, she serves as a consultant for parents, administrators, and teachers in North Carolina. Holden's past experience includes being a self-contained autism teacher (K–5) and a resource teacher (K–5) in North Carolina. She received two Bachelor of Science degrees from Syracuse University—one in special and regular education and inclusive education, the other in communication and rhetorical studies. Holden received her master's and Doctor of Philosophy degrees in special education from the University of North Carolina Greensboro.

Jennie Jones, PhD, is an assistant professor of elementary and special education at the University of North Georgia. She earned her Doctor of Philosophy degree in specialized educational services from the University of North Carolina at Greensboro as an Office of Special Education Programs (OSEP) funded scholar and has more than 10 years of experience as an elementary teacher working with students and families that speak English as a second or other language. She has earned certifications in reading, English Language Learning, and National Boards. Jones's research focuses on teacher preparation and development, literacy instruction, and coaching.

Melissa Sullivan-Walker, PhD, is an assistant professor of special education in the College of Education at Montana State University Billings. Her primary research interests include teacher preparation and interdisciplinary collaboration with a focus on homeless education. She works with the Montana Office of Public Instruction to provide professional development to inservice teachers in this area. Sullivan-Walker earned both her Bachelor of Science degree in education and her Master's degree in advanced inclusive processes from St. Bonaventure University, and her Doctor of Philosophy degree in special education from the University of North Carolina Greensboro.

Related ASCD Resources

At the time of publication, the following resources were available (ASCD stock numbers appear in parentheses):

Print Products

Instructional Coaching in Action: An Integrated Approach that Transforms Thinking, Practice, and Schools by Ellen B. Eisenberg, Bruce P. Eisenberg, Elliott A. Medrich, and Ivan Charner (#117028)

Peer Coaching to Enrich Professional Practice, School Culture, and Student Learning by Pam Robbins (#115014)

Educational Coaching: A Partnership for Problem Solving by Cathy A. Toll (#118027)

Learning from Coaching: How Do I Work With an Instructional Coach to Grow as a Teacher? *(ASCD Arias)* by Nina Morel (#SF114066)

The Coach Approach to School Leadership: Leading Teachers to Higher Levels of Effectiveness by Jessica Johnson, Shira Leibowitz, and Kathy Perret (#117025)

Differentiated Literacy Coaching: Scaffolding for Student and Teacher Success by Mary Catherine Moran (#107053)

Effective Literacy Coaching: Building Expertise and a Culture of Literacy: An ASCD Action Tool by Shari Frost, Roberta Buhle, and Camille Blachowicz (#109044)

For up-to-date information about ASCD resources, go to www.ascd.org. You can search the complete archives of *Educational Leadership* at www.ascd.org/el.

ASCD myTeachSource®

Download resources from a professional learning platform with hundreds of research-based best practices and tools for your classroom at http://myteachsource. ascd.org/.

For more information, send an e-mail to member@ascd.org; call 1-800-933-2723 or 703-578-9600; send a fax to 703-575-5400; or write to Information Services, ASCD, 1703 N. Beauregard St., Alexandria, VA 22311-1714 USA.

WHOLE CHILD
TENETS

THE WHOLE CHILD

The ASCD Whole Child approach is an effort to transition from a focus on narrowly defined academic achievement to one that promotes the long-term development and success of all children. Through this approach, ASCD supports educators, families, community members, and policymakers as they move from a vision about educating the whole child to sustainable, collaborative actions.

The eCoaching Continuum for Educators relates to the **engaged, supported,** and **challenged** tenets. *For more about the ASCD Whole Child approach, visit* **www.ascd.org/wholechild.**

1 **HEALTHY**
Each student enters school healthy and learns about and practices a healthy lifestyle.

2 **SAFE**
Each student learns in an environment that is physically and emotionally safe for students and adults.

3 **ENGAGED**
Each student is actively engaged in learning and is connected to the school and broader community.

4 **SUPPORTED**
Each student has access to personalized learning and is supported by qualified, caring adults.

5 **CHALLENGED**
Each student is challenged academically and prepared for success in college or further study and for employment and participation in a global environment.